"CHE" GUEVARA
ON REVOLUTION

BOOKS BY JAY MALLIN

Fortress Cuba
Caribbean Crisis
Terror in Viet Nam

"CHE" GUEVARA ON REVOLUTION

A Documentary Overview

Edited and with an Introduction by

JAY MALLIN

ф

UNIVERSITY OF MIAMI PRESS

Coral Gables, Florida

To
JAY AND LINDA

Just children on their way to school again?
Nay, it is ours to watch a greater thing.
These are the World's Rebuilders!

2/72

CONTENTS

ILLUSTRATIONS

FOREWORD

For any study of the Cuban revolution, the writings of Ernesto Guevara are of exceptional importance. Guevara played a number of roles in that revolution, and he alone of the top leaders was a prolific writer. Guevara's interests and official responsibilities were varied, and he wrote on diverse topics—plans for industrialization, processes of high finance, the evils of bureaucracy. Historical perspective will probably show, however, that his most significant work related to his continuing discussion and interpretation of Communist revolutionary theory, particularly in the field of guerrilla warfare.

Guevara viewed the Cuban revolution as but a part of a larger revolution that he was convinced would soon engulf all of Latin America. Much of his writings aimed at both stimulating and guiding struggle in other Latin American countries.

Guevara did not attempt to strike out on new theoretical paths. His evident objective was to adapt established Communist precepts to the Latin American scene—first in terms of demonstrating the Marxist-Leninist nature of the Castro revolution and second in terms of providing strategic, tactical, and operational guidelines for revolutionary drives elsewhere in Latin America. Nevertheless—and probably because he did not himself fully understand the tenets of the Communist theoreticians he sought to interpret—Guevara turned out to be an innovator in two very important particulars.

One, he viewed guerrilla war as a means to total victory in a revolutionary struggle. China's Mao Tse-tung and Viet Nam's Vo Nguyen Giap, the two master theorists on revolutionary war in Communist ranks, had emphasized the limitations of guerrilla war and had seen it as the prime form of struggle in only one of the three stages that would necessarily mark any successful "armed revolution." Guevara echoed the three stages concept, but in his mind the stages differed in a quantitative sense, that is, in consequence of increases in the size and strength of guer-rilla forces. Mao and Giap saw the difference as qualitative, with guerrilla forces evolving into regular armies and with guerrilla-type methods and operations giving way to—or at least becoming subordinate to—regular, or conventional, warfare. Mao and Giap, in contrast to Guevara, ruled out success of an armed revolution through guerrilla war alone, no matter how large guerrilla forces might become.

Two, Guevara broke with the basic dictum of other Communist theorists that a generally favorable situation had to exist before an armed revolution could be successfully initiated. He argued that it was not "always necessary to await the existence of all the conditions for revolution: the insurrectional focus can create them." This was in direct contrast to:

> —Lenin: "If a revolutionary party has not the majority among the vanguard classes and in the country generally, there can be no question of insurrection. . . . To throw the vanguard alone into the decisive battle, before the whole class, before the broad masses have taken up a position either of direct support of the vanguard or at least one of benevolent neutrality towards it, and one in which they cannot possibly support the enemy, would be not merely folly but a crime."
> —Stalin: ". . . it must be born in mind that the overthrow of the bourgeoisie can be successfully accomplished only when certain absolutely necessary conditions exist, in the absence of which there can be even no question of the proletariat taking power."
> —Mao: ". . . strategically, we should despise all our enemies, but tactically we should take them all seriously . . . in dealing with concrete problems and particular enemies we shall be committing the error of adventurism unless we take them seriously . . . it is impossible to win victory in a people's war without taking full account of the enemy tactically and without regard to concrete conditions. . . . In seeking victory, those who direct a war cannot overstep the limitations imposed by objective conditions. . . ."
> —Lin Piao: ". . . every revolution in a country stems from the demands of its own people. Only when the people in a country are awakened, mobilized, organized, and armed can they overthrow the reactionary rule of imperialism and its lackeys through struggle; their role cannot be replaced or taken over by any people from outside."

Guevara's departure from the standard in these two regards had the effect of magnifying the potential of guerrilla warfare as an instrument of revolution. Guerrillas could not only get a revolutionary war under way; they could, if they applied "correct" strategy and tactics, carry it through to total victory. Even more important, a small guerrilla band, or nucleus, could, even if injected into an area from the outside, generate itself the conditions and dynamics necessary for a successful revolution-ary struggle against an entrenched regime.

This thinking evidently lies at the root of the adventurism of the Castro government with respect to the training of Latin Americans in guerrilla warfare and the dispatch and support of guerrilla forces in a suc-cession of Latin American countries. And, as Jay Mallin points out in his introductory statement, it well explains how Guevara could have brought himself to the abortive guerrilla effort in Bolivia that ended in his death.

Had Guevara lived out his days as a highly placed bureaucrat in Castro's Cuban government, what he wrote of revolutionary warfare would probably have been of interest and importance only to those spe-cialists who seek to penetrate and explain the mysteries that surround the Castro takeover and the evolution of Cuba's domestic and foreign policies. It is true that for a brief period after the Castro triumph Guevara shone brightly from his Cuban setting and gave promise of a significant role in the shaping of worldwide radical thought. But as he settled into his post of *alto funcionario*, and proved somewhat bungling and over-voluble in the capacity, he lost his allure. Such romanticism as still attached to the Cuban revolution centered increasingly on Castro himself.

Guevara, like a number of others through history, found a new and larger life in a bizarre death. His summary execution following the col-lapse of the tragicomic guerrilla campaign he and elements of the Cuban military imposed on an unwilling Bolivian peasantry projected the Guevara figure into a new dimension. Guevara the man gave way to Guevara the myth—and a myth that the dissidents of the world quickly seized upon for both symbol and example.

As part of Guevara's transformation from Cuban conspirator to hero of the New Left, widespread and avid interest has developed with regard to his writings and teachings. In less than a month after his death some 15,000 copies of his *Guerrilla Warfare* were sold in Italy alone. Guevara's thought on war and revolution has consequently become something far more than a guide to the formation of Cuban foreign policy. It has be-come a force to be reckoned with wherever men have become dissatisfied with their lot and with the societies in which they live. And here it can be of great importance that Guevara did not share the concern of other Communists over a premature or indiscriminate use of violence, but instead greatly exaggerated the ease and surety with which it could bring revolutionary changes in existing power structures. It can be of great im-portance that his counsel ran the exact opposite of Lenin's "never play with insurrection" and Mao's "engage in no battle you are not sure of winning."

Given the unrest and searchings for new ways that mark the contemporary world as it passes through an era of great change, Guevara's theories can have widespread and traumatic impact. Guevara's own experiences, both as a manager and manipulator of insurrections from within the Cuban government and as a commander of guerrillas in Bolivia, demonstrated how small the chances are that application of his theories will lead in fact to the revolutionary overturns that he so ardently desired. But that appears of little moment to the angry and the impatient. For these, Guevara's concept that a handful of uninhibited men with guns, torches, and grenades can make a revolution where and as they choose obviously has great appeal. Would-be revolutionaries in a hurry to tear down existing orders have evidently long since wearied of the cautions of the older generation of Communists. Much more to their mood is a call to action such as Guevara sounds, no matter how rash and reckless the call might appear to others.

The documents included in this volume well show the nature and force of Guevara's ideas. They present the relevant and significant of Guevara's thoughts on various aspects of the incubation and undertaking of revolution under modern conditions. Jay Mallin, editor of the volume, has been a long-time student of the Cuban Revolution with particular emphasis on the role of Guevara. Among other things, Mallin had opportunity to observe firsthand Castro's guerrilla operations in Cuba over a two-year period. Mallin also had opportunity to study firsthand Guevara's operations in Bolivia and to gather significant documentary materials relative to those operations.

This documentary study is one of a series on Cuba that the Center for Advanced International Studies is carrying forward under a grant from The Ford Foundation.

Mose L. Harvey
Director
Center for Advanced International Studies
University of Miami

Coral Gables, Florida
January, 1969

PREFACE

This book is not an effort to offer everything Guevara wrote and said about revolution. It seeks instead to present a selection that best and most completely reflects the essence of his thinking. It is for this reason that certain documentary materials not written by Guevara himself—such as the statement by Ciro Roberto Bustos—are also included: they provide additional insights into Guevara's thinking.

In a number of cases the text given in the volume represent a translation into English by the editor and his associates in the Center for Advanced International Studies of the University of Miami. In other cases English translations published by the Cuban government were obtained, but these were carefully checked against the original versions, and corrections were made where necessary. Every document went through at least two hands so that the translations would be as accurate as possible.

A bibliography of Guevara's writings and speeches, as published in Cuban magazines, is included in the volume as a guide to researchers who may want to explore other aspects of the Guevara story. This bibliography is limited to the original Cuban sources. It does not include references to Guevara items as published in countries other than Cuba. It also does not include references to items as they appeared in Cuban newspapers, but only as they appeared in Cuban magazines and journals. Research for the bibliography was conducted by the editor in the extensive Cuban collection of the libraries of the University of Miami.

Suggestions of material to be included were provided by staff members of the Research Institute for Cuba and the Caribbean. Two of these persons assisted greatly in the work of research and translation: Dr. Roberto Hernández and Dr. Margarita M. Pelleyá. Dr. Pelleyá also assisted ably in preparing the manuscript for publication. Dr. Hernández wrote the comparison of the Guevara diary and Bustos account.

The manuscript was read by Dr. Jaime Suchlicki, Assistant Professor of History and a Research Associate in the Center for Advanced International Studies, and by Major Ralph N. Hoffman, Jr., Associate Professor of Government at the U.S. Air Force Academy, who is presently on research assignment in the Center for Advanced International Studies of the University of Miami. Both made valuable suggestions.

The Director of the Center for Advanced International Studies, Dr. Mose L. Harvey, and the Associate Director, Dr. Clyde C. Wooten, also provided helpful advice and assistance.

JAY MALLIN

Coral Gables, Florida
January, 1969

"CHE" GUEVARA
ON REVOLUTION

INTRODUCTION

WANDERER TURNED WARRIOR

Warrior, theoretician, economist, organizer, writer, doctor—these were among the trades of Ernesto Guevara de la Serna, a man who at one time was second only to Fidel Castro in importance in Communist Cuba.

The versatile Guevara played many roles in Cuba. He was a member of the *Granma* expedition. He was one of Castro's guerrilla captains. He used his enormous power and influence to help swing Cuba behind the Communist curtain. He ran the Cuban economy, he was a foreign policy maker, and he attempted to organize and direct a campaign of subversion throughout the Western Hemisphere.

Guevara disappeared from sight in March, 1965—and a year later, and then two years later, it was still not known where he had gone, or even whether he was alive or dead. His was one of the great disappearing acts of modern times.

Guevara's background, like that of other modern guerrilla leaders, had nothing of the military in it. Mao Tse-tung had been a minor government official, Vo Nguyen Giap a lawyer, and Guevara a doctor. Born June 14, 1928, and raised in Argentina, Guevara studied at the Medical School of the University of Buenos Aires. His parents had separated, and he spent most of his time with his leftist-minded mother who exercised a strong influence during his formative years.

But if Guevara leaned early toward Marxism, as a student he was still personally cautious. Years later, Alberto Granados, a childhood friend, would recall that when it was suggested that Guevara participate in student demonstrations, "I was amazed at the response of young Ernesto Guevara, who said: 'Nothing doing, Alberto. Take to the streets so the police go after you with clubs . . . nothing doing. I'll go out only if they give me a "rod." ' "[1]

Guevara was an asthmatic, but he did not permit this condition to interfere with a strenuous physical life. He was particularly fond of sports. Granados remembered:

> From early youth he was a daring rugby player; his audacity and utter lack of fear were famous. Some of today's athletes recall the young Guevara who played on the second team for the Atalaya athletic club. At times he left the playing to give himself a vaporizer treatment when he was troubled with asthma. An education that alternated between Baudelaire's poetry and sports forged him spiritually and made him physically fit. From then on he became involved with travel and action.[2]

Guevara took frequent trips into the countryside, traveling by bicycle or motorcycle, or sometimes just hiking. He would pitch a tent and camp out. Years later this fondness for the outdoors would serve him in good stead as a guerrilla.

Increasingly restive, Guevara broke off his studies in 1952 and set out with his friend Granados on a transcontinental journey. They rode a motorcycle to Chile, and when the machine gave out, continued on their way by hitchhiking. In Chile Guevara obtained a temporary job as a guard at the American-owned Braden Copper Company—one of history's little ironies.

Later the two young men traveled on to Peru where they went to work in a leprosarium located on the shores of the Amazon River. Recalled Granados: ". . . We worked in the laboratory and also did some psychotherapy, trying to provide diversion for the leper patients, playing basketball with them and taking them on excursions in the vicinity, visiting the Indians, participating in a monkey hunt, and generally helping to distract them from their problems."[3]

After a while, the time came to move on again, and the patients helped build a raft on which the wanderers could cross the Amazon. They set out, planning to come ashore at the Colombian town of Leticia, but being unskilled in the handling of the raft, they rode past and finally ran aground on a Brazilian island. They exchanged the raft for a boat, and with this they reached Leticia, from there making their way to the capital, Bogotá, and then on to Caracas, Venezuela. Guevara had promised his mother that he would return to Argentina to complete his studies, and he now decided to do this—but not before taking a side trip to Miami.

Traveling on his Argentine passport, and having obtained an American nonimmigrant visa, Guevara entered the United States on a Peruvian plane, probably on July 26, 1952. Guevara's visa was good for ten days, but he remained beyond this time and late in August was officially advised that he must leave the country. It may be that his experiences in Miami contributed to—or perhaps even initiated—his anti-Americanism, an attitude which became so pronounced in future years.[4]

Guevara was in the United States for at least a month. Not much is known about his visit beyond what Granados (who did not accompany him that far) has written:

> Che told us that he had a hard time in Miami, that he went a lot to the library, that at first he had only a cup of coffee and milk during the day, that he became friendly with the owner of a cafeteria who gave him some food—until one noon a Puerto Rican came in and began talking against the Truman administration. He was overheard by an FBI agent, and it was the same old story. Che had to make himself scarce.[5]

Guevara returned to Argentina, completed his studies and received his medical degree in March, 1953. At this time doctors were being inducted into the army by dictator Juan Perón, so once again Guevara set out on his travels.

He went first to Bolivia, which at the time was undergoing a historic revolution aimed at dispossessing the rich of their land and tin mines. Guevara went on to Peru, Ecuador, Panama, Costa Rica, and then Guatemala. Guatemala was controlled by Communists around President Jacobo Arbenz, and it was a haven for Latin American leftists. Guevara, who by this time called himself a Marxist, fitted right in. His closest companion was a Peruvian girl named Hilda Gadea, an exiled member of APRA, Peru's leftist revolutionary movement. Guevara sold encyclopedias, then obtained a minor job in the agrarian reform program.[6]

In 1954 a U.S.-backed invasion by Guatemalan exiles was launched over the Honduran border. Guevara actively supported Arbenz. Hilda Gadea later recalled about Guevara, probably with some embellishments:

> ... He was among the groups who defended the city when there were raids of blackouts. He asked to be sent to the front, but was never sent. Everybody knew he wanted to be in the front lines . . . Che encouraged the Guatemalans with him. He kept saying, "You must fight." . . . He transported weapons from one place to another until it was impossible for him to continue and he took refuge in the Argentine Embassy.[7]

Although Guevara was evidently never in combat—it is not clear whether he actually manned an anti-aircraft gun—this was his first experience with war conditions. The Guatemalan affair doubtless served to reenforce his anti-American sentiments.

After the Arbenz regime fell, Guevara remained in the Argentine Embassy for two months before he could leave for Mexico. There he rejoined Hilda. Hilda met two exiles from Cuba, the Castro brothers, Fidel and Raúl, and she introduced them to Guevara. The four became close friends. (Guevara married Hilda in May, 1955, but divorced her a few years later.) Of his meeting with Fidel, Guevara said:

> I talked with Fidel all night, and by dawn I had become the doctor of the future expedition. In reality, after my experiences all over Latin America and the coup de grâce in Guatemala, it didn't take much to arouse my interest in joining any revolution against a tyrant, but even so my impression of Fidel was that of an extraordinary man.[8]

The events that followed are now a part of history. On November 25, 1956, the yacht *Granma* sailed from Mexico with the Castro brothers, Guevara, and seventy-nine other revolutionaries aboard. They landed on the southeast coast of Cuba, where the forces of dictator Fulgencio Bastista quickly decimated the invaders, reducing them to fifteen in number. From this nucleus, however, a sizable guerrilla group eventually grew.[9]

The guerrillas had several factors working in their long-range favor. There existed a rising tide of popular discontent directed at the Batista regime. Island-wide clandestine apparatuses served to polarize resistance. These organizations collected funds, funneled men and material to the guerrillas, carried out propaganda campaigns (such as contacts with American correspondents), and effected frequent acts of sabotage and terrorism. The regime reacted to this with increasingly bitter acts of police repression—which further inflamed the general unrest.

The economy deteriorated. Tourism, a major source of dollar income, especially suffered. The government's foreign reserves diminished as the Batista regime purchased weapons from abroad. (The United States had cut off arms shipments.) Internal commerce decreased under the growing stress of domestic conflict.

The government's army, largely purged of professional officers as a result of Batista's two "sergeants' revolts" within two decades, did not efficiently counter the guerrilla menace. At first the threat was not fully recognized; officers were content to have a few rebels running around the hills because this helped increase military allotments. When once the Castro threat had grown to substantial proportions, the Cuban army was incapable of eliminating the guerrillas. The army had no notion of counter-insurgency tactics or techniques. The guerrillas made it a point to help and befriend the *campesinos;* the military alienated the rural folk with bombings, repressive techniques, and mass removals.

Moral rot permeated the government and the military, eventually paralyzing their effectiveness.

The guerrillas rode the wave of discontent, nurtured with funds and weapons from the resistance movements (plus weapons captured from an army frequently in retreat). Youths from the cities, fleeing the police or bent on liberating their country, provided a steady flow of recruits for the guerrillas. Castro and his men sniped away at the army's troops, gradually extending the areas under rebel control. Some of this territory was won in battle; most went by default: the army had no heart to contest it.

Guevara emerged as one of the most determined and courageous of the guerrilla officers. It was he that led one of the groups that marched out of the Sierra Maestra and established a new base of operations in Cuba's mid-section, and it was his capture of the city of Santa Clara in December, 1958, that precipitated the collapse of the regime of dictator Fulgencio Batista. (Guevara's own account of the guerrilla campaign follows this introduction.)[10]

Guevara's troops were among the first rebel forces into Havana after Batista fled. With Castro in power, Guevara was put in command of Havana's La Cabaña Fortress, a key military bastion. Later he was named to head an indoctrination program in the army. Guevara used these posts to prepare the way for Communist control, and with the Communization of the army, Cuba was well on the way to becoming a Communist state.

Guevara had Castro's ear. As one of the Cuban leader's most influential advisers, Guevara held a number of governmental positions. Perhaps because Castro did not have many able administrators among his young followers, Guevara, who had no economic background, was called upon to try to restore the crumbling economy, first as President of the National Bank and then as Minister of Industries, but was signally unsuccessful.[11]

Guevara held an additional position in the Castro government—a post without a title but one which gave him an importance on the international scene second only to that of Castro. He masterminded a campaign of subversion that aimed at the farthest corners of the hemisphere. Special camps were set up in Cuba, and chosen Latin Americans were brought to these for training in guerrilla warfare and other methods of subversion. At the peak of the program an estimated 1,500 Latin Americans traveled to Cuba each year for this preparation. The agents were then returned to their own countries to carry out their clandestine work. In addition, Cuba, as

best it could, funneled weapons, funds, and propaganda to the other
Latin American countries. The long-term object was to spark guerrilla
outbreaks on the Cuban model in one Latin American country after
another.

WARRIOR TURNED THEORIST

Guerrilla warfare, basically, is conflict between irregular forces and regular armies. Germans waged guerrilla war against the Romans; the French
waged guerrilla war against the British toward the end of the Hundred
Years' War; the Indians waged guerrilla war against the American settlers; the American settlers used it against the British; the Spaniards
and Russians against Napoleon; the Cubans against the Spaniards, the
Filipinos against the Americans, the Yugoslavs against the Nazis, and on
and on, innumerable instances throughout recorded history.

The Communist contribution has been to adopt and adapt guerrilla
warfare to communism's political purposes, utilizing it as a concept for
conquest, endowing it with ideological overtones, broadening it to fit into
the theory of revolutionary warfare. For undeveloped regions, guerrilla
warfare has come to be for Communists the prime mover of revolutionary
warfare, although revolutionary warfare also encompasses a wide variety
of tactics ranging from the ancient arts of diplomacy and espionage to
modern techniques of sabotage and propaganda, and ultimately must
include, according to most tacticians, the build-up and use of regular
armies capable of crushing in open battle the forces of the enemy.

Soviet Premier Nikita Khrushchev publicly, albeit reluctantly, committed Communists to the use and support of this type of warfare—he
used the euphemistic term "national liberation wars"—in a speech delivered on January 6, 1961. He stated:

> There will be wars of liberation as long as imperialism exists, as long
> as colonialism exists. There are revolutionary wars. Such wars are not
> only possible but inevitable, since the colonialist will not voluntarily
> grant the peoples independence. Therefore, the peoples can win their
> freedom and independence only through struggle, including armed
> struggle.... Can such wars occur in the future? They can. Can there
> be such uprisings? There can. These are precisely wars of popular
> rebellion. Can conditions in other countries come to where the
> people exhaust their patience and rise up with arms in hand? They
> can. What attitude do Marxists have toward such uprisings? The most
> favorable. These uprisings must be identified with wars among
> states, with local wars, because in these uprisings the people are

fighting to exercise their right to self-determination and for the social and independent national development; these are uprisings against rotten reactionary regimes and against colonialists. Communists fully and unreservedly support such just wars and march in the van of the peoples fighting wars of liberation.[12]

There is a belief that guerrilla warfare is primitive. This is erroneous. The basic techniques of guerrilla warfare are ancient—hit, run, hide, hit, run, hide, until you wear down your enemy—but these techniques are as applicable in the nuclear age as they were in ancient Rome. Since World War II there have been over a score of major guerrilla campaigns around the world, and in several of these, ill-trained, lightly-equipped guerrillas eventually achieved successes against modern armies employing planes, tanks, and other modern equipment.

Guerrilla warfare is a flexible, sophisticated type of struggle, adapting itself to the contemporary age, utilizing automatic weapons or old fire-arms. It is a directly human type of combat: the guerrilla sees in his gun-sight the soldier he is shooting at, or is in close proximity to the target of his mortar shells. He does not direct artillery barrages against distant points nor aim bombs to be dropped through 30,000 feet of clouds. The effective guerrilla needs to be the most dedicated of soldiers. He is ever in peril and usually in discomfort, he may be long separated from his family, he has little to go on except faith and hope. The guerrilla pits his shrewdness and his endurance and his cause against the regular soldier. Brigadier General Samuel G. Griffith has remarked:

> Guerrilla warfare is . . . suffused with, and reflects, man's admirable qualities as well as his less pleasant ones. While it is not always humane, it is human, which is more than can be said for the strategy of extinction.[13]

The leading Communist theoreticians of guerrilla warfare have been China's Mao Tse-tung, Viet Nam's Vo Nguyen Giap, and Cuba's Ernesto Guevara. All three have written extensively about guerrilla warfare; all three have experienced successful campaigns.[14]

General Griffith holds that Mao produced "the first systematic study of the subject"[15] of guerrilla warfare. It must not be understood by this that Mao was the first person to originate or set down thoughts on the processes of guerrilla warfare. Mao was himself influenced by the ancient Chinese military philosopher Sun Tzu. Whereas Sun counseled, "Uproar [in the] East, Strike [in the] West,"[16] Mao wrote, "In guerrilla warfare, select the tactic of seeming to come from the east and attacking from

the west . . ."[17] Other works had their influence on Mao and his associates
—even one on George Washington. Robert S. Elegant stated that the
"first textbook on large-scale partisan warfare" used by Chu Teh, Mao's
top lieutenant, was "a short work on the tactics employed by General
George Washington in the Revolutionary War."[18] Mao himself is not
well read. He uses no foreign language and thus has had advantage of
only such foreign works as have been available in Chinese translation.
For his formative years he concentrated principally on Lenin and Stalin,
particularly Stalin. He had, however, some knowledge of Clausewitz.
Mao's main contribution has lain, as Katzenbach and Hanrahan have
said:

> . . . in pulling together a group of previously unrelated and unstudied
> techniques—shaping these into a single operational pattern. He is the
> man who has written it down for others; the man who has presented
> the Communist revolutionary with the workable blueprint.[19]

Mao set it down—the limited things he had learned from others and
what he had learned from personal experience in China's drawn-out
struggles—and others proceeded from where he left off. One of these was
Vo Nguyen Giap, the North Vietnamese military leader in the wars
against the French and the American and South Vietnamese forces.

Giap, as a refugee from French Indochina, may have spent some time
in Yenan, Mao's stronghold in China, and had the opportunity to observe
at firsthand Chinese guerrilla operations. But whether or not this was so,
Mao's thinking strongly influenced Giap's writings and the tactics he
would one day himself employ. Mao, for example, was the first military
theorist to define the three stages of revolutionary warfare. Writing
within the context of the Sino-Japanese War, he set these forth:

> The first stage covers the period of the enemy's strategic offensive
> and our strategic defensive. The second stage will be the period of the
> enemy's strategic consolidation and our preparation for the counter-
> offensive. The third stage will be the period of our strategic counter-
> offensive and the enemy's strategic retreat.[20]

Giap, in his own writings, echoed Mao thus: "The long-term revolutionary war must include several different stages: stage of contention,
stage of equilibrium, and stage of counter-offensive."[21]

Both Mao and Giap viewed guerrilla war as of only limited potential.
Under conditions of enemy superiority, guerrilla methods were basic
from the standpoint of both weakening the enemy and building up one's
own capabilities. But guerrilla operations would have to give way at some

stage to more sophisticated operations if victory were to be attained. Thus Mao said of the "people's struggle" against the Japanese:

> Among the forms of warfare in the anti-Japanese war mobile warfare comes first and guerrilla warfare second. When we say that in the entire war mobile warfare is primary and guerrilla warfare supplementary, we mean that the outcome of the war depends mainly on regular warfare, especially in its mobile form, and that guerrilla warfare cannot shoulder the main responsibility in deciding the outcome.[22]

Giap spoke in similar terms of the strategy that led to Communist success against the French in Indochina, although he laid greater stress on a straight-line evolution from a guerrilla strategy to a regular strategy than did Mao.

> From the strategic point of view, guerrilla warfare, causing many difficulties and losses to the enemy, wears him out. To annihilate big enemy manpower and liberate land, guerrilla warfare has to move gradually to *mobile warfare*. As our Resistance War was a long revolutionary war, therefore guerrilla warfare not only could but had to move to mobile warfare. Through guerrilla activities, our troops were gradually formed, fighting first with small units then with bigger ones, moving from scatttered fighting to more concentrated fighting. Guerrilla warfare gradually developed to mobile warfare—a form of fighting in which principles of regular warfare gradually appear and increasingly develop but still bear a guerrilla character. Mobile warfare is the fighting way of concentrated troops of the regular army in which relatively big forces are regrouped and operate on a relatively vast battlefield, attacking the enemy where he is relatively exposed with a view of annihilating enemy manpower, advancing very deeply then withdrawing very swiftly, possessing to the extreme dynamism, initiative, mobility, and rapidity of decision in face of new situations. As the Resistance War went on, the strategic role of mobile warfare became more important with every passing day. Its task was to annihilate a bigger and bigger number of the enemy forces in order to develop our own, while the task of guerrilla warfare was to wear out and destroy the enemy's reserves.[23]

Both Mao and Giap emphasized the totality of modern warfare, the need for meshing political, economic, and ideological efforts. Mao referred to "revolutionary war waged by the whole nation,"[24] and Giap wrote of "combining military operations with political and economic action."[25] The writings of both men dwell on the use of propaganda, the ideological content of revolution, and the role of the peasantry.

The strategic thinking of both rested upon the concept of using the countryside to engulf the cities. Mao saw as one means to this end enlisting the sympathy and support of the peasants through exemplary conduct on the part of revolutionary forces, including direct assistance to local populations in a variety of ways. Giap stressed the usefulness of terror and violence to bring civilian masses into line: ". . . We firmly upheld local people's power, overthrew men of straw, eliminated traitors . . ."[26] He bluntly explained what this involved:

> . . . *The most correct path to be followed by the peoples to liberate themselves is revolutionary violence and revolutionary war.* This path conforms strictly to the ethics and the fundamentals of Marxism-Leninism on class struggle, on the state, and on revolution. Only by revolutionary violence can the masses defeat aggressive imperialism and its lackeys and overthrow the reactionary administration to take power.[27]

The Viet Cong have utilized terror so extensively in South Viet Nam that violence has become a major instrument of policy and power in that country. Probably never before have terror tactics been so widely used by a political faction bent on achieving control of a country.

The third man in the Communist guerrilla triumvirate was Ernesto "Che" Guevara. It is not clear how much, if at all, Mao and Giap influenced the Cuban guerrilla campaign itself. Guevara has asserted that the Cuban leaders did not then know the theories of those two men. In the prologue he wrote for a Cuban edition of Giap's *People's War, People's Army*, Guevara stated, "Cuba, without knowing these writings [by Giap] nor others on the same subject that had been written on the experiences of the Chinese revolution, set out on the path toward its liberation through similar methods . . ."[28]

A contrary statement reportedly made by Guevara was contained in an interview published in a Communist Chinese journal. According to this journal, Guevara confessed:

> We have always looked up to Comrade Mao Tse-tung. When we were engaged in guerrilla warfare we studied Comrade Mao Tse-tung's theory on guerrilla warfare. Mimeographed copies published at the front lines circulated widely among our cadres; they were called "food from China." We studied this little book carefully and learned many things. We discovered that there were many problems that Comrade Mao Tse-tung had already systematically and scientifically studied and answered. This was a very great help to us. . . .[29]

Whether this statement was more accurate than the former or was invented by the zealous Chinese cannot be ascertained.

Whether or not Guevara knew of Mao's and Giap's writings at the time of Castro's guerrilla campaign, it is clear that they had a considerable impact on his subsequent thinking and writing. Note the echoing of Mao's three-stages concept:

> Guerrilla warfare or war of liberation will, in general, have three stages: the first, a strategic defense, in which a small hunted force bites the enemy; it is not protected for a passive defense in a small circle, but its defense consists in limited attacks which it can carry out. After this, a state of equilibrium is reached in which the possibilities of action of the enemy and the guerrilla unit are stabilized; and later the final moment of overrunning the repressive army that will lead to the taking of the great cities, to the great decisive encounters, to the total annihilation of the enemy.[30]

Guevara's first book, *Guerrilla Warfare*, was less a theoretical work than a basic guidebook for guerrilla warfare. It contains detailed comments and instructions on tactics, techniques, weapons, training, propaganda, indoctrination, morale, and even "the role of the woman." The book was specifically written for use by future guerrillas in actual operations. As such, the Cuban government printed at least one small-sized edition which would fit handily into any guerrilla's pockets. A note at the end stated,

> *Compañero:* This book seeks to be a synthesis of the experiences of a people; if you believe anything should be added or changed, communicate it to the Department of Instruction of the MINFAR [Ministry of the Revolutionary Armed Forces].[31]

Guerrilla Warfare was nevertheless a foretaste of the views Guevara would later project. There was a warning of things to come in his statement that the guerrilla goes to battle "with the intention of destroying an unjust order, and, therefore, more or less surreptitiously with the intention of putting something in place of the old,"[32] i.e., establishing a Communist regime.

Two years later Guevara brought his ideas to full fruition. He published an article entitled "Guerrilla Warfare: A Method" in *Cuba Socialista*,[33] at that time the leading doctrinal publication of the Castro regime. In compact form, Guevara described how a guerrilla campaign can be started and carried out:

> Relatively small nuclei of people choose favorable places for guerrilla warfare, either to begin a counterattack, or to weather the storm, and thus they begin to act. The following must be clearly established: at first, the relative weakness of the guerrilla movement is such that

it must work only to settle in the terrain, establishing connections with the populace and reinforcing the places that will possibly become its base of support.[34]

Guevara agreed with Mao and Giap on basic tactics. But whereas they referred to the "three stages" as qualitatively different phases of a revolutionary war—the envolvement of guerrilla forces into regular armies and a changeover from guerrilla methods to more sophisticated methods of conventional warfare—Guevara thought in terms of a continuing guerrilla effort with the "stages" differing only in the sense of size and strength of guerrilla forces. Guevara used "guerrilla war" and "liberation war" and "revolutionary war" interchangeably. Mao and Giap viewed a "guerrilla war" as but one of the three stages of a "revolutionary war," or "war of liberation," although they allowed for the use of guerrilla methods and tactics in support of the conventional type of operations of the later stages.

Guevara echoed Mao in his listing of the conditions necessary for guerrilla survival: "Constant mobility, constant vigilance, constant distrust." He advocated the utilization of terror on the model of Giap. He saw terror not only as a means of intimidating civilians to support and help the guerrilla forces but also as a means of forcing increasingly harsh and indiscriminate countermeasures on the part of government forces. He explained this tactic on grounds that in Latin America there exists "a state of unstable balance between the oligarchic dictatorship and the popular pressure," and this balance "must be upset." Guevara said:

> The dictatorship constantly tries to operate without the showy use of force; forcing the dictatorship to appear undisguised—that is, in its true aspect of violent dictatorship of the reactionary classes, will contribute to its unmasking, which will intensify the struggle to such extremes that then there is no turning back. The manner in which the people's forces, dedicated to the task of making the dictatorship define itself—to hold back or to unleash the battle—carry out their function depends on the staunch beginning of a long-range armed action.

Guevara believed that a small nucleus of well-trained men could be formed in, or introduced into, any country, and that this nucleus, with the use of proper tactics, would with surety grow into a revolutionary movement and would step by step weaken and ultimately destroy opposing government forces. Guevara argued that it was "not always necessary to await the existence of all the conditions for revolution; the insurrectional focus can create them." An insurrection in the form of a guerrilla movement can lead to a general revolution—so thought Guevara. In this, he differed importantly with both Mao and Giap and indeed with Communist thinking generally. He here reflected a naive faith in a sort of magic or mystique about guerrilla warfare that Fidel Castro and he had built up over the years, and which indeed became the foundation for much of Cuba's foreign policies. The mystique may be expressed as faith that any guerrilla operation, no matter how small or weak at its inception, can generate the means to its own success, that is, to a Castrolike takeover of power.

Castro and his followers, in speeches and writings, carefully nurtured the legend of the guerrilla "victory" in Cuba. Quite evidently the Castroites came to believe this legend, as evidenced by the fact that since 1959 efforts have been made to launch similar guerrilla campaigns in more than a dozen Latin American countries. Every one of these attempts has failed. In concentrating on rural guerrilla activities (with the partial exception of Venezuela, where "urban guerrillas" were also highly active for a period), the Castroites chose to overlook the fact that in Cuba the guerrilla campaign was but a phase of a general popular movement against Batista. Popular resentment against the Batista regime found expression in steadily widening clandestine activities: terrorism, sabotage, strikes, propaganda, passive resistance. It also found expression in the supply of the guerrillas with men, funds, and weapons. If it was true that the guerrillas were a major element in the wearing-away of the Batista army, it was also true that Castro rode—but did not generate or direct—a groundswell of national unrest.

Guevara's ideas became the practical, as well as theoretical, guide for the Castro-Communist drive for power in Latin America. His article was a blueprint for revolution. Tactics might vary somewhat from country to country, but basic emphasis was on fostering guerrilla warfare: "guerrilla warfare is . . . the central axis of the study,"[35] he declared.

> . . . The war [said Guevara] would be continental. This means also that it will be prolonged; there will be many fronts, it will cost much blood, innumerable lives for a long time. . . . In fact, the birth of the American struggle has begun. Will its vortex be in Venezuela, Guatemala, Colombia, Peru, or Ecuador. . . ? Will these present skirmishes be only manifestations of an unrest that does not bear fruit? It does not matter, for the final result, that one movement or another may be momentarily defeated. What counts is the decision to struggle that ripens day by day; the awareness of the need for revolutionary change, the certainty of its possibility.

ADVENTURER, AGAIN

Ernesto Guevara, a wanderer as a youth, continued traveling after the Castro regime came to power. Now he was a high official of that government, and as such he conferred with foreign leaders and attended international conferences. On December 9, 1964, he flew from Havana to New York to address the United Nations.[36] In two speeches he covered a wide spectrum of topics dealing with Cuba's foreign relations—he was Guevara, the international revolutionist, now giving his views before the entire world. He denied charges of Cuban "interference in the internal affairs of other countries," but significantly added:

> . . . We sympathize with those people who strive for their freedom, and we must fulfill the obligation of our government and people to state clearly and categorically to the world that we morally support and feel as one with people everywhere who struggle to make a reality of the rights of full sovereignty proclaimed in the United Nations Charter.

Perhaps at this moment Guevara was already thinking of the international role he would attempt personally to play, first in Africa and then, finally, in Bolivia.

From New York Guevara flew to Algiers, and thus began a trek that would take him to countries in Africa, Europe, and Asia. For three months Guevara traveled, talking to leaders of nations, preaching revolution and communism wherever he went.

On March 14, 1965, he flew back to Havana, where he was met by Castro, President Osvaldo Dorticós, and other high officials. This was the last time Guevara was seen in public in Cuba.

Two days later the Havana radio reported that Guevara had spoken informally about his trip to employees of his Ministry of Industries. This was the last time the Castro press or radio referred to his physical presence in Cuba.

Weeks and then months went by, and there was no further word about him. He did not appear to be in disgrace. He was mentioned favorably by Castro in speeches, his pictures were prominently displayed during the annual July 26 celebration, and Cuban publications ran photographs of the Castro brothers with his wife and daughter at a May Day rally. (After divorcing Hilda Gadea, Guevara had married a Cuban girl named Aleida March.)

In a speech on June 16 Castro touched on the speculation regarding Guevara's absence. Castro said, "If the compañero does not appear at a public gathering it is because Compañero Guevara has some reasons for not appearing at a public gathering." And Castro jibed the United States: "Why don't they take a picture of him with the U-2? Let them look for him and photograph him."

Then on October 3 there was a new development in the mystery. Castro read a letter allegedly written by Guevara and received by Castro on April 1, 1965. Declaring that he felt he had "carried out the part of my duty which tied me to the Cuban revolution," Guevara announced that he was giving up his Cuban citizenship and resigning his military rank and governmental posts. He declared:

> Other lands of the world claim the assistance of my modest efforts. I can do what is denied to you [Castro] because of your responsibility at the head of Cuba. . . . I have always been in accord with the foreign policy of our Revolution, and I continue to be thus. . . . Wherever I am I will feel the responsibility of being a Cuban revolutionary, and as such I will act.

As time passed and there was not the slightest indication of Guevara's whereabouts, the feeling grew among many Cuba experts that Ernesto Guevara was dead. How could a well-known international figure remain hidden for so long? Even if he had gone behind the Iron Curtain, surely after two years some inkling of his presence there would have filtered out. It appeared increasingly logical that Guevara had died at a time and under circumstances unknown.

Suddenly, in April, 1967, the baffling affair took a new turn. The official Cuban daily *Granma* published a set of photographs—not too clear —allegedly showing a beardless Guevara in the jungles of an unidentified country. Gloated *Granma*, "Like the Phoenix, he arose from his ashes, battle-hardened, a guerrilla fighter." The newspaper also published a lengthy statement from Guevara written for the magazine *Tricontinental*, an offshoot of the Tricontinental Conference which had been held in Havana in January, 1966.[37]

The main point of Guevara's article was reiteration of the coming battle for the Western Hemisphere: ". . . The struggle in Our America will achieve . . . continental proportions. It will be the scene of many great battles fought for the liberation of humanity." Guevara foresaw growing U.S. involvement in this struggle—"Little by little . . . the U.S. military 'advisers' will be substituted by U.S. soldiers until . . . they will be forced to send increasingly greater numbers of regular troops to ensure . . . relative stability . . ." Guevara declared:

Our aspirations to victory may be summed up thus: total destruction of imperialism by eliminating its firmest bulwark: imperialist domination by the United States of America. . . . What a luminous near-future would be visible to us if two, three or many Viet Nams[38] flourished throughout the world with their share of death and their immense tragedies, their everyday heroism and their repeated blows against imperialism obliging it to disperse its forces under the attack and the increasing hatred of all the peoples of the earth![39]

Why had Guevara left Cuba? There has been speculation that he might have broken with Castro—a clash of strong personalities—but no evidence of this has ever appeared. Indeed, for nine years Guevara accepted Castro's leadership, and Guevara's power in Cuba was due to a major degree to his ability to influence Castro quietly without displacing him from the public spotlight that Castro loves. Some speculation has centered on the dispute within the Cuban government over the relative merits of moral versus material incentives for workers—Guevara advocated moral incentives as being appropriate in a "socialist" society.[40] But the Cuban government finally did adopt the theory of moral incentives, after toying with material rewards, and so Guevara was the victor in the dispute. This issue, at any rate, would hardly have seemed to merit his abandoning the island. The theory has also been expressed that criticism by Guevara of Russia and other Communist nations for not adequately assisting underdeveloped countries might have caused Moscow to pressure Castro into exiling Guevara. Attempts to pressure Castro, however, usually have a reverse effect, and in this case probably would only have served to tighten the bonds between the two men.

More likely Guevara's departure was the result of a personal decision. He had reached his peak in Cuba, with no place further to go: he could not aspire to a higher position. He may have felt that his capabilities were wasted playing a secondary role; perhaps he concluded that he had been relegated to a hopeless task in attempting to straighten out the Cuban economy. This all may have weighed in Guevara's decision. Surely another factor was the same restlessness that he had displayed throughout his life. Perhaps nine years in one country was all that he could take. Another consideration may have even more strongly influenced him. Guevara probably did believe, as Communists often proclaim, that the age of "imperialism" was ending, that new Communist societies would be created, that there were new worlds to conquer. He may well have felt that his official position in the Cuban government placed severe limitations on the personal role he could play and that it would be the better for him if he gave up that position and even disassociated himself from Cuba itself.

Only portions of Guevara's travels during 1965 and 1966 are as yet known. He was in Africa and he was in Europe, and finally he went to South America and to Bolivia. It has been through photographs and documents captured in Bolivia, as well as the statements of men who were with Guevara, that it has become possible to piece together a partial picture of his journeys during the period that he was missing.

Ciro Roberto Bustos, an Argentinean who joined the guerrillas in Bolivia and was subsequently captured, wrote a lengthy, detailed report for Bolivian intelligence officials. In it he recalled a conversation with Guevara in which Guevara explained that his theories of guerrilla warfare were best applicable in Africa and Latin America, but that Africa was preferable because of its greater distance from the United States and its nearness to Communist and sympathetic countries. And so, according to Bustos:

> During his extensive voyage through Africa and Asia before disappearing from Cuba, Guevara arranged for his voluntary incorporation in the struggle in the Congo; that is, he chose Africa. But the experience turned out to be negative, because, he said, the human element failed. There is no will to fight, the leaders are corrupt; in a word, there is nothing to do. After six months Guevara left Africa.

On December 2, 1965, a balding, slightly chubby man using the name Ramón Benítez Fernández obtained a Uruguayan passport (No. 130220) in Montevideo. On December 22, 1965, the same man obtained a second passport (No. 130748), also in Montevideo. This one was in the name of Adolfo Mena González. Although the names were different, the same handwriting signed both passports, and both had identical pictures of a bespectacled man. That man was "Che" Guevara.

For several months afterward, the story of Guevara is a blank. Possibly he was behind the Iron Curtain. Perhaps he was somewhere in Asia. At any rate, at some point he secretly returned to Cuba. According to the Bustos statement, when Guevara failed in his efforts in Africa, he sent one of his aides, "Ricardo" (Roberto Aspuru—first name not certain), to prepare the ground for the launching of a guerrilla operation in Bolivia. Bustos recalled:

> It seems that during a trip that Ricardo made to Cuba he said that Ramón would have to enter Bolivia then or never. Thus, in order to assure his entry into Bolivia . . . he [Ramón] decided to come. This happened in October of last year, I think.

By the time "Ricardo" made his report to Guevara, a special guerrilla team had been put together and given training at a camp somewhere in Cuba. The diary of one of Guevara's lieutenants, Eliseo Reyes Rodríguez (nom de guerre: "Rolando"), was later captured by the Bolivian army, and it contained this entry:

> September
> We met with Ramón [Guevara] at the S. Farm. We were extraordinarily moved when we recognized him. We continued our training until October 22, 1966, at which time we went on leave after having been visited by C. [Castro], who spent 3 days with us.[41]

Still in disguise, still traveling secretly, Guevara again left Cuba. Dates stamped in his passports indicate that he entered Spain through Madrid's Barajas Airport on October 9, 1966. On October 19 he left through the same airport. Curiously, both of his passports—now in the hands of the Bolivian military—bear identical entrance and exit imprints.

Guevara next appeared in Brazil, entering São Paulo on November 1, 1966. He left there on November 3, and was on his way to Bolivia.

Guevara apparently crossed the border and made his way to La Paz, where he stayed at the downtown Copacabana Hotel, right on the capital's main street. Like any other tourist, Guevara, a camera bug, took pictures of local scenes and buildings. Then he headed south to begin his operations. He was still in disguise and he wore a jaunty hat, and he had a driver to handle his jeep.

A farm had been purchased in an isolated area near the town of Camiri by Roberto Peredo Leigue, a leader in the Moscow-oriented wing of the Bolivian Communist movement. This would be Guevara's base camp, and it was here that he began to train the recruits that were brought in, some evidently by "Tania" (Laura Gutiérrez), an Argentine girl who may have become Guevara's mistress. Guevara adopted the nom de guerre "Ramón."

Why had Guevara chosen Bolivia to be his target? The conditions in that country must have seemed ideal to him. The country is one of the poorest and least developed in Latin America. There were the vast jungle areas in which guerrilla units could incubate, grow, and spread out, eventually moving into adjoining countries. The Bolivian army consists mainly of one-year recruits—and the army has never won a war, but has lost three. Turmoil is chronic: in 142 years of independence Bolivia has had 55 different administrations and more than 150 congresses.

So there was Bolivia, strategically located in the heartland of South

Before going up to the guerrilla camp, Guevara was in La Paz and travelled around the Bolivian countryside reconnoitering the grounds for his future guerrilla operations. With him is "Tuma," who served as his driver and body-guard—and later as his double

Gun in hand, Guevara posed here showing how a guerrilla gets ready for action in an ambush position

America, and if Guevara could establish a secure base of operations, the guerrilla movement could be extended into Brazil, Argentina, Peru, Chile, and Paraguay. Guevara had asserted: "The war will be continental..."[42]

On March 23 the guerrillas staged their first ambush. It was a success, and so were others that followed. As a result of the rebel attacks, the army casualty toll steadily mounted, with more than 40 soldiers dying in action in the next few months. (The Bolivian army consists of 18,000 to 20,000 men, but of these only some 1,200 can be considered regulars, and, until the guerrilla outbreak occurred, virtually none of the troops had had any counterinsurgency training.)

Guevara's guerrillas, at their peak, probably numbered no more than some fifty men. But included were at least sixteen Cubans, among them three *comandantes*[43] and six captains of the Cuban army. Three of the officers had been members of the Central Committee of the Cuban Communist Party. Guevara had established what was, according to his concepts, a high-powered guerrilla "nucleus."

Despite initial successes in the way of ambushes of military units, the rebel movement failed to gain any real momentum. Then the tide began to turn strongly against Guevara and his men. They were running short of food; the army had encircled their area with large numbers of troops: clandestine support being provided in the cities was uncovered and broken up. On September 28 Guevara wrote in his diary:

> A day of anguish which, at times, seemed to be our last. Water was brought in at dawn and almost immediately Inti and Willy left to explore another possible way to go down to the canyon, but they came back right away because there is a trail all along the hill in front of us and a farmer on horseback was traveling on it. At 10, 46 soldiers carrying their knapsacks crossed in front of us, taking centuries to go on. Another group appeared at 12, this time 77 men, and to top it off, a shot was heard at that moment and the soldiers took positions. The officer ordered a descent, no matter what, to the ravine, which appeared to be ours, but at last they communicated by radio and he seemed to be satisfied and resumed the march. Our refuge has no defense against an attack from above and had we been discovered our possibilities of escape would have been remote.[44]

A number of basic factors were working inexorably against the rebels. The peasants displayed virtually no interest in aiding them. Guevara repeatedly remarked upon this in his Bolivian diary, noting at the end of September, 1967, that "the mass of peasants does not help us at all and they become informers." Over a dozen years previously Bolivia had gone through an agrarian reform, and most of the peasants now owned their own land. Guevara had nothing to offer them. The lack of peasant support was a major element in the eventual defeat of the guerrillas: Guevara himself, in his writings on guerrilla warfare, had emphasized the necessity of basing this type of conflict on peasant assistance.

Another difficulty was that Guevara and others of his hard-core nucleus were Cubans—in a word, foreigners. Even the local Bolivian Communist parties failed to provide support. The diary of a doctor with the guerrillas noted on December 31:

> Today there arrived Mario Monje, secretary-general of the Communist Party of Bolivia. He conversed with "Ramón." He made known three conditions for remaining with the guerrillas. First, he would resign his position because his party did not support the guerrilla movement. Second, to be recognized as political and military chief of the guerrillas, as long as they operated in Bolivian territory; and third, freedom to talk with all parties in order to obtain their support. To the second condition "Ramón" told Monje, "I am the chief." Later Monje left the camp.[45]

How good a guerrilla, in fact, was Guevara? In Cuba he was brave, he persevered, he was evidently a good leader of men, and he fought well. But it must not be overlooked that Batista military commanders all but stood aside to permit Guevara to make his famous march across the island without interference. In Bolivia Guevara violated a number of the basic precepts he had enumerated in his own guerrilla textbook. He had said that "the guerrilla soldier should preferably be an inhabitant of the zone." Yet he and the other Cubans were complete outsiders. He chose to be the operational leader of the guerrillas despite the fact that his age (39) and ill health (severe asthma) were hardly in accord with the requirements of campaigning, and he himself had said that a warrior should have "health of iron" and "the best age of the guerrilla fluctuates between twenty-five and thirty-five." He had written, "Fundamental characteristic of a guerrilla group is mobility,"[46] but he persisted, during the early days of the campaign, in remaining at the finca, "read[ing] all day in his hammock," as Bustos later recalled.

Guevara believed in the guerrilla mystique. Despite the discouragement reflected in his diary in the last months, there is no evidence that he ever doubted that final victory would be his. Well might he have heeded the admonition Karl Marx had written long ago:

> Hegel remarks somewhere that all facts and personages of great importance in world history occur, as it were, twice. He forgot to add: the first time as tragedy, the second as farce.[47]

Guevara undoubtedly imagined that the Bolivian army was a carbon copy of the inept, corrupt army that crumbled in Cuba in 1958. The Bolivian army, with the specter of what had happened to the Cuban army at the hands of the Castroites before it, poured troops into the troubled area. Although Bolivia had no forces specifically prepared for counter-insurgency operations, the Second Ranger Battalion (about 640 men) entered, with the assistance of American advisers, into a four-month period of training for jungle fighting.

Sent into action upon completion of their training, the Rangers patrolled aggressively. The guerrillas already were on the run. The climax came with a relentless five-day pursuit by 120 Rangers seeking to catch Guevara and the sixteen men who were with him. The guerrilla movement had splintered, and most were dead or had deserted, and this group with Guevara were all that were left.

On October 7 Guevara noted in his diary:

> We completed eleven months of our guerrilla operation without complications . . . until 12:30 o'clock, at which time an old woman leading goats came into the canyon where we were camped, and we had to pressure her. The woman has not given any trustworthy word about the soldiers, answering to everything that she does not know, that it is a long time since she has been there, but she gave information about the roads. As a result of the report by the old woman, we figure that we are approximately one league from Higueras and another from Jagüey and about two from Pucará. . . . The seventeen of us left under a very small moon and the march was very tiresome and we left many traces in the canyon where we were, which has no houses nearby but there are some potato fields irrigated by canals of the same creek. At 2:00 we stopped to rest as it was now useless to continue advancing.

The next day, October 8, in mid-morning, government troops caught up with Guevara and his men. In the attacking group were two Ranger companies, with a third in reserve. The Rangers, commanded by Captain Gary Prado Salmon, had Guevara trapped in the Yuro Canyon a few miles from La Higuera. In the first exchange of fire two soldiers were killed. The guerrillas, however, were forced into making an attempt to break through the Rangers' lines.

The first to brave the Rangers' fire were Guevara and a former union leader from the mining town of Huanuni named Simón Cuba (nom de guerre: Willy). Guevara fell almost instantly with a bullet in the leg, his shattered carbine shot out of his grasp. Simón Cuba tried to pull Guevara back to safety but succeeded only in dragging his leader to a spot where four Rangers were concealed. Guevara is reported to have gasped: "Stop! I'm Che! I'm worth more to you alive than dead."[48]

The forward troops radioed their colonel, "Hello, Saturn, we have 'Papa.'"

Incredulous, the colonel radioed back, "Ask 'Skinny' [Captain Prado] to confirm that news."[49]

The news was confirmed. "Che" Guevara had been captured.

Placed on a blanket, he was carried by four soldiers to the town school-house at La Higuera. Simón Cuba had also been captured, as was a third guerrilla, Aniceto Reynaga Gordillo (nom de guerre: Aniceto), a member of the National Executive Committee of the Bolivian Communist Youth. Cuba and Reynaga were also taken to La Higuera.

In the town, the three guerrillas were quickly separated. Cuba and Reynaga were put in a shed adjoining the schoolhouse where Guevara was imprisoned. Having identified himself to his captors, Guevara became the object of considerable interest. He parried an inevitable barrage of questions with noncommittal replies, giving little satisfaction to his captors. When the opportunity presented itself, he directed the cleaning and dressing of the bullet wound, a relatively superficial injury, in the calf of his left leg. Guevara was interrogated almost continuously by Bolivian officers. He took out his pipe and asked the officers to fill it with tobacco from Astoria cigarettes which he carried in his pockets. He pipe-smoked one cigarette after another.

An officer asked him what he was thinking. Guevara did not reply, barely moving his head.

A second officer came up and asked what was the matter. The former replied, referring to a Spanish story, that Guevara "must be thinking about the immortality of the burro."

Slowly, in a low voice, Guevara said, "No, no, I'm thinking of the immortality of the revolution."[50]

Guevara, however, was not immortal.

Sometime in the late morning, a short burst of gunfire from Sergeant Bernardo Huanca's carbine terminated the guerrilla career of Simón Cuba and grimly announced the beginning of executions. Guevara blanched; he finally understood that he was not to be spared, that it was the end of the road. This realization was emphatically punctuated a few minutes later by the sound of a single shot coming from the shed; Aniceto Reynaga had been dispatched. Guevara's ordeal continued for another hour until, at last, Sergeant Mario Teran, who had fortified himself by downing several bottles of beer, entered the schoolhouse with carbine raised. Recognizing Teran's intention, Guevara stood up to face his executioner, his hands still bound. There was a brief exchange of angry words. Guevara declared: "You are killing an hombre." Teran fired a burst of bullets that ended the life of Ernesto "Che" Guevara. Teran left the schoolhouse and went and got another beer.

Time may well show that the death of "Che" Guevara marked a historic turning point. Not only was this the first occasion that a major Communist leader had been captured in battle—it was also the first time that a leading theoretician and advocate of guerrilla warfare had been captured. Since Castro came to power in 1959, he and Guevara had launched or encouraged more than a dozen guerrilla operations throughout Latin America. Not one of these has succeeded in overthrowing a democratic government; several have been wiped out completely (notably in Peru, Argentina, and the Dominican Republic); and a number still sputter along (Venezuela, Colombia, and Guatemala). When Guevara personally entered the lists of battle, this was the master himself engaging in combat. Now he had failed. Would this not be a deterrent to others who might think of taking to the field of combat?

Far off in Cuba, where Guevara might have lived out a life of power and prestige, his friend and former comrade in arms, Fidel Castro, stated: "Who could deny the significance to the revolutionary movement of the blow of Che's death? . . . It is a fierce blow, a very hard one . . ."[51]

There is, however, another side to the matter, the full import of which cannot yet be judged: the buildup of a "Che" Guevara myth.

The reality of "Che" Guevara is one thing; the growing fiction quite another. The real Guevara came out of an unproductive obscurity, shared, through an accident of history, in a successful uprising against a corrupt and inept dictatorship that was in the process of collapsing of its own weight, and played a large—perhaps decisive—role in the imposition of a Communist system on Cuba and the voluntary submission of Cuba to a colonial-like status as against the USSR. He then failed in a succession of assignments and personal undertakings, including management of the Cuban economy, the use of Cuba as a base and lever to get a viable revolutionary movement underway throughout Latin America, a direct effort to influence the rise of a revolutionary tide in black Africa, and finally as leader of a guerrilla war in Bolivia. In real world terms, the near comic opera circumstances of Guevara's last days and the decidedly unheroic appearance presented by his lifeless body sprawled on a bare table would have seemed the best antidotes to any romanticizing about him. The world of fantasy, however, can make a mockery of the real world. Viewed subjectively, photographs of the frail warrior lying in death could be made to take on a saintly hue. And the ill-conceived and poorly executed brigand-like foray in the wilds of Bolivia could be reshaped in the imagination so as to provide a bold new dimension to the Guevara figure.

Within weeks after the news of Guevara's death, placards proclaiming "Che is alive" and "Viva Che," together with appropriate portraits, became standard features of protest demonstrations everywhere. In Rimini, Italy, two priests presided over a mass for Guevara; a Brazilian bishop asked for prayers "for our brother Che Guevara," and a Brazilian archbishop declared, "I find that Che Guevara was sincere." In Lima, Peru, grammar school children held hands, danced in a circle, and chanted, "Con cuchillo y con cuchara, que viva el Che Guevara" (With knife and with spoon, long live Che Guevara). In Santiago, Chile, a bookstore sold photographs of Guevara mounted on a wooden base at the rate of 500 per month, and in Italy close to 15,000 copies of Guevara's *Guerrilla Warfare* were sold in a fortnight. In the United States, adherents of the New Left adopted Guevara as their new symbol. In Rome and Milan Guevara clubs were organized by a Socialist party, in Naples activist students splintered from the regular Communist Party and formed a "Che Guevara Club," and in Paris a student group named itself the "Cercle Che Guevara," while Parisian advocates of black power incorporated "Guevarisme" in their credo. A poll published in Spain showed Guevara to be the "most popular international figure of the year," and the student bulletin of the medical school of the University of Salamanca declared: "There is a man of this century who looked above and beyond his political party. From the point of view of dedication to the sick, to the weak, to his fellow men, this Ernesto Guevara . . . doctor by profession and guerrillero by necessity, can be a lesson for us all." In Bolivia the commander of the army that had destroyed Guevara, General Alfredo Ovando Candia, declared, "He was a brave man but God was not with him."

The irony of the Guevara myth is that its strength appears to spring from yearnings the exact opposite of those that moved Guevara himself. He has become the symbol of those who profess hatred of war and violence, while his own life was dedicated to the principle and practice of both. Anti-militarists disregard his obsession with things military and see him as one of their own. He worshipped at the shrine of big technology and wanted to make Cuba a big mill town with its masses rushing in and out of bleak factories. Yet he is taken to heart by those who would escape the age of modernization with its automation, nuclear energy, space travel, laser beams, computerization and zip codes, and who would end the inequities of the world by turning all mankind back to an underdeveloped state. Guevara as a Communist was above all else a collectivist, but he is cherished as a staunch individualist. He is pictured as a dreamer, a romanticist who abdicated great power to follow his lonely destiny to a far corner of the world, while in fact power was his god and in leaving Cuba he was reaching for the far greater power that he believed was for the taking in the vast continent that lay beyond the tiny island in whose affairs he had become enmeshed, with little personal success or glory. He is even hailed as a good family man—a loving father who noted the birthdays of his children in his Bolivian diary—although he left those same children and his wife without means of support and in faith that his friend, Castro, would take care of them. He is treated as a lover of humanity, but he did not disguise his arrogant contempt for the blacks who spurned his leadership in Africa, and he flaunted in his diary his disgust with the peasants he sought to "liberate" in Bolivia. His lament to his executioner, "you are killing a man," is taken as epitomizing his life philosophy; ignored is the evident glee with which he recorded the deaths inflicted on Bolivian recruits in ambushes arranged by his professionally trained "guerrillas."

Given the recasting of Guevara the man in the mold of Guevara the myth, the influence of his writings regarding revolution will doubtless be far greater than their intellectual content would justify. Guevara wrote well, sometimes brilliantly, as will be apparent from a reading of the documents given in the remainder of this volume, even though their literary quality necessarily suffers from translation. But he was neither an original nor a profound thinker. Most students would argue that he had a poor understanding—in fact a large measure of naïveté—with regard to the world in which he lived and the great forces that shape its destiny. He knew nothing of economics, and his notion of history bordered on the grotesque. Most striking of all, he was ill-versed in the tenets of communism. He leaned heavily on what he thought to be the concepts of the leading theoreticians of the movement, but what came through in his own writings and speeches was heavily marred by oversimplifications, near-distortions, and ill-digested parrotings. He either did little homework or else lacked the capacity to understand much of what he read.

But how important are deficiencies such as these in a case like Guevara's? Historical happenstance and his own strange behavior are surrounding him with a charismatic mystique that for many, and particularly among the young of all lands, sets him above ordinary standards of judgment. For these, not the logic or truth or plausibility of what he says determines its worth: the decisive thing is that he has said it. It may well

Guevara in the jungles of Bolivia in what seems to be an observation post

be, of course, that this Guevara phenomenon is a peculiar product of this peculiar moment in history and will soon pass. On the other hand, the phenomenon may turn out to be more deeply based. In a sense, in romanticizing Guevara, the present generation of radicals—those who pride themselves on membership in the category, Under Thirty—has recreated him in its own image. Guevara and his writings may thus prove more acceptable and enduring as a hero figure for those-who-would-change-the-world in the last decades of the twentieth century than the somewhat shopworn hand-me-downs from previous generations such as Lenin, Stalin, Tito, Mao, and even Ho Chi Minh.

GUEVARA'S ACCOUNT OF GUERRILLA CAMPAIGN 1

Eighty-two expeditionaries landed on the southeast coast of Cuba early in December of 1956, and the guerrilla phase of the Cuban revolution was launched. Government forces rapidly decimated the rebels, but a small nucleus managed to escape into the Sierra Maestra Mountains. The survivors included the Castro brothers, Fidel and Raúl, as well as Guevara, who had joined the expedition as its doctor. Eventually Guevara's military abilities superseded his medical talents, and he became one of the leaders of the guerrilla movement. Guevara alone, of the top group, later wrote extensively about the difficult early days in the mountains, and the warfare that finally spread out across a good part of Cuba. The account that follows was originally published in the Brazilian magazine *O Cruzeiro*. Because Guevara was a leading participant in the events, the account is a valuable first-hand description of the campaign that put the Castro regime in power. The viewpoint is limited to the guerrilla movement, however, and thus it overlooks the substantial—perhaps decisive—role of the underground movements that operated in all Cuban cities. These clandestine organizations, through civic resistance and terrorism, helped to undermine the government of dictator Fulgencio Batista. And it was their support—particularly in the city of Santiago de Cuba—that helped the guerrillas survive their first dark, desperate days in the mountains.

GUEVARA'S ACCOUNT OF GUERRILLA CAMPAIGN

Beginning of a Revolution

THE HISTORY OF the military aggression consummated on March 10, 1952—"a bloodless coup directed by Fulgencio Batista"—does not begin, of course, the very day of the coup. Its antecedents must be sought far back in the history of Cuba, much before U.S. Ambassador Sumner Welles' intervention in 1933, even before the Platt Amendment in 1901, before the landing of hero Narciso López, special envoy of the U.S. annexationists, all the way back to its roots in the time of John Quincy Adams, who, at the beginning of the 18th [*sic*] century, announced the theme of his country's policy toward Cuba: an apple that, dropping from the Spanish tree, was predestined to fall into the hands of Uncle Sam. These are links in a long chain of continental aggression aimed not exclusively at Cuba.

This ebb and flow of the imperialist tide is marked now by the overthrow of democratic governments and again by the appearance of new governments as a result of the irresistible drive of the masses. History shows similar characteristics in all of Latin America. Dictatorial governments represent a small minority and come into power by means of coups d'etat; democratic governments with a broad popular base arise painfully and, often, before taking over power, are already stigmatized by a series of previous concessions which they have been forced to make in order to stabilize their position in the first place. And even though the Cuban Revolution is, in that sense, an exception in the Americas, it has been necessary to point out the antecedents to this whole process. The author, carried to and fro by the tides of the social events that are shaking the hemisphere, had an opportunity to meet, as a result of these events, another [Latin] American exile, Fidel Castro.

I met him one of those cold Mexican nights, and I remember that our first conversation dealt with the subject of international policy. Within a few hours of our meeting—in the early morning hours—I had already become one of his future expeditionaries. But I wish to clarify how and why I met in Mexico the present chief of the Government of Cuba.

This happened in 1954 during the ebb-tide of the democratic governments, when the last American revolutionary democracy—that of Jacobo Arbenz—still in power in this area failed as a result of the cold, premeditated aggression carried out by the United States, hiding behind the smokescreen of its continental propaganda. Its visible head was Secretary of State Dulles, a man who, through a rare coincidence, was also

stockholder and attorney of the United Fruit Company, the most powerful imperialist enterprise in Guatemala.

I left Guatemala then, defeated, united to the Guatemalan people by
a bond of common sorrow, waiting, seeking a way to rebuild a future
for that grief-stricken country, while Fidel had come to Mexico seeking
a neutral ground where he could prepare his men for the great push.
Internal dissension had already set in, following the assault on the Moncada garrison in Santiago de Cuba, resulting in the desertion of all the
weak-kneed, all those who for one reason or another joined political
parties or revolutionary groups expecting less sacrifice. Already the
first groups of new recruits were joining the ranks of the newly-born
26th of July Movement, named for the date that marked the attack on the
Moncada Garrison in 1953.

A most difficult task was ahead for those responsible for the training
of new recruits in the conditions of unavoidable secrecy essential in Mexico, having to struggle against the Mexican Government, against all
agents of the F.B.I. and those of Batista, against all those forces, which
at times combined their efforts in various ways, in a situation where
money and bribery played an important role. Moreover, we had to con-
tend with Trujillo's spies and the poor selection of men, especially in
Miami, and, after overcoming all these obstacles, we were to achieve what
was most important: our departure . . . and later . . . our landing and the
rest, which, at the time, seemed easy to us. Today we are able to evaluate
what all of that cost in effort, sacrifice, and lives.

Fidel Castro, assisted by a small team of trusted revolutionaries, devoted all his vocation and extraordinary working capacity to the task
of organizing the armed forces that were to sail for Cuba. He seldom
attended classes in military tactics, as he did not have enough time left
over for this. The rest of us were able to learn a good deal from General
Alberto Bayo. My almost immediate impression after attending the first
few classes was that victory was possible, something I had doubted when
I joined the rebel chief to whom, from the very beginning, I was tied
by a bond of romantic sympathy for adventure and the thought that
it would be worthwhile to meet death on a foreign beach for so pure an
ideal.

A few months went by. Our marksmanship improved, and our sharp-
shooters emerged. We found a ranch in Mexico where, under the direction of General Bayo and with myself as chief of personnel, we made the
last plans for departure in 1956. However, at that time, two different
Mexican units—both of them in Batista's pay—were hunting for Fidel
Castro, and one of them was lucky enough to arrest him, but committed

the absurdity—to their economic loss—of not killing him after taking him prisoner. Many of Fidel's followers were captured a few days later. Our ranch on the outskirts of Mexico City also fell into the hands of the police, and we all landed in jail.

This setback delayed the last part of the first stage. Some of us were in prison for fifty-seven days with the threat of extradition hanging over our heads. Major Calixto García and I are witnesses to this. However, at no time did we lose our personal confidence in Fidel Castro. We could almost say that Fidel's attitude at times jeopardized his position as a revolutionary in favor of friendship. I recall that I specifically explained my situation to him: an alien, illegally residing in Mexico, with a whole series of charges against me. I told him that on no account was the revolution to be stopped for my sake and that they could leave me behind, that I understood the situation and that I could join the struggle from whatever place I was ordered to do so. And that the only effort to be made was to have me sent to a nearby country and not to Argentina. I also recall Fidel's energetic reply: "I will not forsake you." As a result, it was necessary to spend precious time and money to get us out of the Mexican jail. Such personal gestures by Fidel toward those whom he loves are the key to the strong devotion created around him, where a feeling of loyalty based on principle is added to a loyalty based on friendship, making the Cuban rebel army an indivisible block.

The days went by as we worked in secrecy, hiding where we could, avoiding appearing in public as much as possible, seldom going out on the streets.

The "Granma" Landing

A few months later we learned that there was a traitor among us whose identity was still unknown to us. This man had sold the enemy one lot of weapons. We also learned that he had sold the yacht and a radio transmitter, although the "bill of sale" had not yet been made out. This first delivery served to prove to Cuban authorities that the traitor did, indeed, know our organization from within. His delivery of the weapons also saved us by tipping us off. From that moment on, we had to proceed with feverish haste: the yacht "Granma" was readied at full speed. We gathered together all the supplies we could get hold of—which were few indeed—as well as uniforms, rifles, equipment, and two anti-tank rifles with practically no ammunition for them. Finally, on November 25, 1956, at 2 A.M., Fidel's words, which had been treated as a joke by the official press: "In the year 1956, we will be free men or martyrs"—began to turn into reality.

We sailed from the port of Tuxpán with all lights out, in the midst of an infernal over-crowding of all sorts of supplies and men. The weather was bad, but, although navigation was prohibited, the waters of the estuary were calm. We crossed the entrance into the Gulf in the region of Yucatán and, a few moments later, turned on the ship's lights. Then began a frantic search for our anti-histamine tablets against seasickness, which we could not locate. We sang the Cuban National Anthem and the 26th of July Anthem for perhaps five minutes, after which the situation on the entire ship took on a ridiculously tragic aspect: men, seized by an attack of seasickness, held their stomachs while their faces reflected their anguish. Some had their heads buried in buckets while others were lying about, motionless, their clothes covered by vomit. With the exception of two or three experienced seamen and four or five others, all of the 83 men aboard were the victims of seasickness. After the fourth or fifth day, the general situation had improved somewhat. We discovered that what we thought was a leak was no such thing, but only an open faucet in the men's room, but by then we had already jettisoned all surplus weight to lighten the ship's load.

The route chosen included a wide sweep around the south coast of Cuba, skirting Jamaica and the island of Grand Cayman to a spot near the town of Niquero, in the province of Oriente. We were rather behind our time schedule. On the 30th, we heard via radio the news of the Santiago de Cuba riots organized by our comrade, Frank País, and which were to coincide with our landing in Cuba. The following night, December 1st, we made straight for the Cuban coast, searching frantically for the Cabo Cruz Light. We were running low on water, fuel and food. At 2 A.M., on a stormy, dark night, the situation was disquieting. Lookouts went to and fro searching for the beam of light, which could not be seen on the horizon. Roque, a former lieutenant in the Cuban Navy, climbing once more to the top bridge trying to make out the Cabo Cruz Light, tripped and fell overboard. Shortly after, starting again on our way, we finally saw the Light, but the slow pace of our vessel made the last few hours of sailing seem endless. It was daylight when we landed in Cuba in the vicinity of the place known as Belic, on the Coloradas Beach.

We had been spotted by a coastal vessel which telegraphed our position to Batista's army. Leaving the yacht, as hastily and with as little equipment as possible, we had scarcely entered the swamp when the attack of Batista's airplanes began. Naturally, marching through the swamps, under cover of the mangroves, we could not be spotted and harassed by the planes, but the army of the dictatorship was already at our heels.

We spent several hours getting out of the swamp, in which we had landed because of the irresponsibility of a comrade who had claimed to know it. We reached solid ground, lost, stumbling along like so many shadows or ghosts marching in response to some obscure psychic impulse. We had been through seven days of constant hunger and seasickness during the sea crossing, topped by three still more terrible days on land. Exactly ten days after our departure from Mexico, during the early morning hours of December 5, following a night-long march, interrupted by faintings and frequent rest periods, we reached a spot parodoxically known as Alegría de Pío. It was a small wooded area, bordered on one side by a canefield and on the remaining sides by valleys leading to thick woods in the distance. It was an ill-suited place to camp, but we called a halt to spend the day there and continue our march the following night.

At four o'clock that afternoon, without the slightest warning and to our complete surprise, we heard the first shot, followed by a symphony of lead over our heads. We were not as yet accustomed to such virile sports. One of our comrades fell and I personally felt the unpleasant sensation in my flesh of simultaneous baptism by fire and blood. We got out of there as best we could, every man for himself or in groups, not heeding our leader's orders, without contact with our captains, and in a state of complete confusion. I remember the push that Major Almeida gave me, at my lack of willingness to walk and it was only thanks to his imperious orders that I got up and kept going, believing all the time that I was near death. In a kaleidoscopic scene, men ran by shouting, the wounded called for help, some men tried to take cover behind slender stalks of sugarcane as if they were tree trunks while others signaled in terror for silence by placing a finger over their lips amidst the roar of battle. Suddenly, we heard the ominous cry of "the canefield is on fire!"

With Almeida in the lead, we made it through one of the lanes between the canefields and walked on until we reached the thick woods. We pushed on until darkness and the trees—which prevented us from seeing the stars—stopped us, still not far from the scene of our encounter with the army. We slept piled one against another. Everything was lost except our weapons and two canteens carried by Almeida and me. In these conditions, we went on for nine interminable days of suffering, without tasting cooked food, chewing grass or raw corn. Some of the more valiant, including Camilo Cienfuegos, ate raw crabs.

During those nine days our morale crumbled. Throwing all caution to the wind, we approached a countryman's bohío in search for food. Some of our men collapsed there. News was bad, on the one hand, but encouraging on the other. Together with reports of crimes supposedly committed by us, came the light of hope: Fidel was alive. Hair-raising accounts by the peasants prompted us to cache our rifles and try to cross a heavily-guarded highway armed with our pistols only. The result was that all the weapons left in the care of the peasants were lost while we made our way toward the Sierra Maestra, where Fidel was.

Approximately fifteen days after the disastrous landing, those of the 82 "castaways" of the *Granma*—as Comrade Juan Manuel Márquez had described us—who were still in fighting condition were reunited. There were some seventeen of us. Our list of casualties was long and depressing: Juan Manuel Márquez himself; "Ñico" López, a great comrade from the working class; Juan Smith, captain of our vanguard; and Cándido González, Fidel's aide, a revolutionary with a spotless record. It was a long list, to which new names were constantly being added, fulfilling Fidel's prediction: "In the year 1956 we will be free men or martyrs." Now we who were left, some 15 men led by Fidel Castro, had the responsibility of raising high the banner of insurrection and of turning the first part of that prediction—"we will be free men"—into reality in honor of the martyrs who fell there as well as of those who were dying day by day throughout Cuba, suffering torture or being murdered ruthlessly in an incredible holocaust of blood. It was equally incredible that this small group of men, still scarcely well-acquainted with one another, already spoke of victory, of taking the offensive.

All of us had become conscious of the unreserved affection felt for us by the peasants of the zone; they had taken care of us and had brought us, through a long chain of clandestine contacts, to our meeting place, the house of Crescencio Pérez's brother. But the one who had the greatest faith in the people, who at all times showed his extraordinary powers of leadership, was Fidel. Already during those nights, those long nights—since our activities ceased at nightfall—sitting under the trees anywhere, we began to draw plan after plan for the present, for the near future and for victory. Those were happy hours, during which I acquired a taste for my first cigars (which I learned to smoke as a way of driving away the overly-aggressive mosquitoes, until I was captured by the fragrance of the Cuban leaf), as projects for the future followed one another rapidly.

The days passed, and, little by little, new recruits came in. The first peasants started joining us, some unarmed, some with weapons that had been left by our comrades in the homes of friendly people, or abandoned in canefields as they fled. Our small troop had twenty-two rifles at the time we stormed La Plata on January 17, 1957, forty-five days after our landing. That action gave Cuba new hope, on learning of new encounters in the heart of the Sierra Maestra, though the operation was no more than a skirmish. We had caught by surprise an army post of 12 to 15 men, who surrendered after an hour of fighting. In those moments, an hour of fighting was an hour of tremendous suffering. Fidel and I, who were expert marksmen with rifles equipped with telescopic sights, had 70 shots each. Those with automatic rifles had 25 cartridges apiece; those with bolt-action guns, 15 each; while some of the machine gunners had 20 to 30 each. We took the small army post of La Plata with those weapons. Five days later, with the dozen new rifles obtained from that action, we were able to defeat the advance guard of a detachment sent after us, commanded by the then Lieutenant Sánchez Mosquera, a figure of sinister reputation. This was followed by an impasse caused by a traitor within our ranks who betrayed our position to the enemy, which very nearly liquidated us on three different occasions. It is worth mentioning that this man had been personally charged with the mission of killing Fidel. One night he and Fidel slept under the same blanket. The traitor wore a pistol, but could not gather enough courage to carry out the murder, preferring to take the easier way out of leaving our camp under different pretexts and guiding the enemy to our position. He was finally caught on his fourth try and executed. But the damage he had done was already great.

Herbert Matthews, a newsman from *The New York Times*, visited our camp in those days. He gave a full account to the world—especially Cuba—of our existence in the Sierra Maestra and the assurance that Fidel was alive. Nevertheless, our trials were far from over. Our dangerous life high up on inaccessible mountains, completely surrounded by soldiers of the dictatorship, continued, and we could not yet count on the unanimous support of the people. Many peasants still fled before us, fearing the reprisals taken by the government forces every time they learned of any contact, no matter how casual, between the people of the zone and our group.

One month later, about the middle of March, we were joined by a handful of men sent by Frank País from Santiago de Cuba. The incorporation of these men gave our revolution a new character.

The Revolution Advances

The weapons brought in by the new recruits were not in any way extraordinary, but they constituted a considerable strengthening of the column. We then initiated the march through new regions; we climbed the Turquino for the first time, the highest mountain in Cuba, leaving there signs of our passing, and we continued, walking for long days together, through the undergrowth of the Sierra Maestra, until we came close to the sawmills of Pino del Agua and Babún.

We patiently awaited the right opportunity, which presented itself on May 28, 1957, to take the military detachment of Uvero, situated on the coast, where the Sierra Maestra drops down almost vertical to the sea. This battle for Uvero was the fiercest of the war; of the 120 to 140 men that took part, 40 were put out of action, which meant that the dead and wounded amounted to approximately thirty percent of the total combatants. The political outcome of the battle was extraordinary, because it took place in one of the few moments—after the Granma invasion—when there was no press censorship in the island. The whole of Cuba spoke about Uvero. And, in spite of the weapons taken from the enemy—fifty guns and ammunition—we had to put up with serious contretemps. As doctor, I was in charge of seven wounded, and we had to hide with them in some bohíos not far away from the place of the combat.

The column continued its march towards the customary camping places, and we joined up again, in the following months, with the wounded who were fit by then. After the reincorporation I was made Major of another group, which we called for tactical reasons, the Fourth Column. The Fourth Column—that was actually the Second—passed over to take its place together with the First, headed by Fidel Castro. From that time on, we, much less harassed because of our lesser political importance, were able to form the bases of the first factories and more permanent camps and to end the nomadic life. We carried out some actions of little importance, but the most important thing was precisely that stabilization, carried out with great difficulty, carrying the materials from very distant regions on our shoulders.

We were able to install in this way a shoe factory and a saddlery, an armory with its electric lathe, a tinshop and smithy for the purpose, among other things, of filling small tin grenades to be fired from a gun— an invention of ours. It was fired with a blank cartridge and dubbed "M-26." We also built schools, recreation areas and ovens to bake bread. Later on, the Radio Rebelde transmitter had been installed, and our first clandestine newspaper, with the same name as the Mambi newspaper of wars of 1868 and 1895, *El Cubano Libre*, was published.

All these installations were in danger at times, in the face of the impact of enemy troops, but the place chosen in La Mesa Valley was never vulnerable to advancing troops and we were able to maintain the position safe until the end of the war.

The increase in our forces was continuous. We obtained weapons in victorious battles carried out on one front or another. The second battle fought at Pino del Agua, a positive triumph for our men and which also took place during a lapse in press censorship, had great political repercussions. That growth allowed us to establish the Second Eastern Front, and it was then that Major Raúl Castro took charge of Column Six Frank País—in honor of the veteran militant who fell in Santiago de Cuba in March 1958—and, crossing the Central Highway, buried himself in the hills of Mayarí, to the north of Oriente Province. This Second Eastern Front would afterwards have enormous importance in the development of the war, and it was the best organized in all ways, having seven departments that functioned like real ministries, where justice was carried out, public works were organized, revolutionary laws for the army made, and transport established. Great advances were taken in comparison with our modest tasks of the Sierra Maestra. It was a vigorous infant, and all the factories were built in an almost industrial sense, since abundant materials were at hand. All was done with more money, the product of taxes taken from big companies and sugar mills.

Major Almeida was also transferred from the old haunt, coming to a site close to Santiago de Cuba, and creating there another front with Column Three. There were now four columns in the Sierra Maestra, and there was fighting on one front or another with more or less intensity, but the whole of Oriente Province was up in arms. Small actions were then initiated in the region of the Escambray, in the center of the island, that had never been a source of worry to the regime until our arrival, and some uprisings took place in Camagüey Province, and in Pinar del Río.

The whole of the movement in the cities was intensely preparing for a general revolutionary strike. The organization Frente Obrero Nacional (FON) [National Workers' Front], led and controlled by the 26th of July, had been constituted but suffered from the beginning from the sin of sectarianism, and the workers reacted a little cooly to this organization that came to life completely saturated with the color of the 26th of July and with much too radical ideas for the reality of the moment. Fidel Castro, shortly before April 9, had issued a final declaration in which he issued a serious warning to all those who had not taken the path of the Revolution.

A little later, he issued another declaration to the workers, calling them to unite, inside or outside the FON, since he had now seen that this organism alone could not promote a general strike.

Our troops threw themselves into the struggle, and Camilo Cienfuegos,

captain of the Fourth Column at that time, went down to the plains of
Oriente in the region of Bayamo, where death and confusion were
quickly sown among the enemy. Nevertheless, April 9 arrived and all our
struggle was in vain; the national leadership of the Movement, completely
mistaking the principles of mass struggle, tried to initiate the strike without previous announcement, by surprise and sudden violence, thus pro-
voking a total contraction of the workers' support and the death of many
great comrades throughout the country. April 9 was a resounding failure
that at no time put the stability of the regime in danger. Not only that:
after this tragic date, the government could move troops and gradually
send them to Oriente and bring destruction to the Sierra Maestra. Our
defense had to move ever further inside the Sierra Maestra, and the government continued increasing the number of regiments that it placed
against our positions, until it reached the figure of 10,000 men, with
which the offensive was initiated on May 25, in the village of Las Mer-
cedes, which was our advance position.

The combative ineffectiveness of Batista's army was demonstrated
there, and also our scanty resources. Two hundred weapons to fight
against 10,000 weapons of all kinds was an enormous disadvantage. Our
boys fought valiantly during two days, at a proportion of one against
10 or 15; fighting, besides, against mortars, tanks and aviation, until the
small group had to abandon the village. It was commanded by Captain
Angel Verdecia, who a month later would die heroically in combat.

By this time Fidel Castro had already received a letter from the traitor
Eulogio Cantillo, who, true to his opportunistic politics, as Operations
Chief for the enemy, wrote to the Rebel Chief telling him that the offensive would take place anyway, but that good care should be taken of
"The Man" (Fidel) pending the final result of their negotiations. The
offensive did indeed take its course, and in two and a half months of hard
fighting the enemy lost more than a thousand men, including dead,
wounded, prisoners and deserters. It left in our hands 600 weapons, including a tank, twelve mortars, 12 tripod machine guns, twenty-odd hand
machine guns, and an enormous number of automatic arms, besides an
enormous quantity of ammunition and equipment of all kinds and 450
prisoners who were handed over to the Red Cross at the end of the
campaign.

The Batista army had its back broken after this last offensive in the
Sierra Maestra, but it was still not beaten. The struggle had to go on.
The final strategy was then established, attacking in three places: Santiago de Cuba, subjected to a flexible encirclement; Las Villas, where I
would have to go; and Pinar del Río, on the other end of the island, where

Camilo Cienfuegos, now commander of Column Two—named for Antonio Maceo—would go, to recall the historic invasion of the great leader
of '95 which in epic days traversed the whole territory of Cuba until it
reached Mantua. Camilo Cienfuegos could not complete the second part
of his program, since the necessities of the war obliged him to remain in
Las Villas.

When the regiments that attacked the Sierra Maestra had been liquidated, the front restored to its natural level and our troops increased in
effectiveness and morale, it was decided to initiate the march to Las
Villas, the central province. In the military order sent to me the principal
strategic plan indicated was that of systematically cutting the communications between the two extremes of the island. Further, I was ordered
to establish relations with all the political groups that were in the mountain parts of that region and was given ample prerogatives to govern
the zone under my charge militarily. Marching under these instructions
and expecting to arrive in four days, we started off by truck on August
30, 1958, but a freak accident interrupted our plans. That night a small
truck carrying uniforms and the gasoline necessary for the vehicles that
were now ready arrived, and a shipment of arms also arrived by air at an
airport close to the road. The plane was located on landing though it was
at night, and the airport was systematically bombed from 8:00 P.M. until
5 o'clock in the morning, when we burned the plane to prevent its falling
into enemy hands or being bombed by day, which would have had even
worse results. The enemy troops advanced on the airport; they inter-
cepted the truck with the gasoline, so that we had to go on foot. In this
way we began the August 31 march, without trucks or horses, hoping to
pick them up later on crossing the highway from Manzanillo to Bayamo.
We did, in fact, find the trucks on crossing it, but on the first of September we were hit by a devastating hurricane that destroyed all transit routes
except the Central Highway, the only paved highway in that region of
Cuba, obliging us to disregard motor transportation. From that time on,
it was necessary to utilize horses or go on foot. We were equipped with
sufficient ammunition, a bazooka with 40 projectiles, and everything
necessary for a long journey and the rapid setting up of a camp.

The succeeding days were difficult, even though we were in the
friendly territory of Oriente: crossing flooded rivers, canals and brooks
turned into rivers, struggling tirelessly to prevent the ammunition, the
arms, the shells from getting wet, looking for horses and leaving the tired-
out horses behind; fleeing from populated areas as we moved further
away from the eastern province.

We crossed over difficult, flooded terrain, attacked by a plague of mosquitoes that made our hours of rest unbearable, eating little and badly, drinking water from swampy rivers or simply from swamps. Our days seemed to grow longer and longer and to become truly horrible. It was now a week since we had left the camp, and our forces were in a pretty weakened condition as we crossed the Jobabo River that borders the provinces of Camagüey and Oriente. This river, like all the previous ones and those that we would have to cross later, had risen considerably. Also our men were beginning to suffer from lack of boots, and many of them went barefoot through the swamps of south Camaguey.

On the night of September 9, while entering a place known as La Federal, our advance party fell into an enemy ambush and two of our courageous comrades were killed. But the most unfortunate development was that we were located by enemy forces, who from then on never ceased attacking us. After a short combat the small garrison located there surrendered, and we took four prisoners. We had to move on with great caution, since the planes knew approximately how we were going. We arrived a day of two later at a place called Laguna Grande, together with the force led by Camilo, much better equipped than ours. This zone stands out in our memory for the extraordinary number of mosquitoes there. It was absolutely impossible to rest without mosquito netting, and not all of us had it.

Those were days of fatiguing marches across desolate areas with nothing but mud and water. We were hungry, we were thirsty, and we could hardly move ahead; our legs felt like lead, and our weapons weighed us down. We continued on with horses that Camilo had left us when he obtained trucks, but we had to leave the horses behind near the Macareño Sugar Mill. The scouts who were supposed to have been sent to us never arrived, so we set off on our own. Our advance column ran into an enemy post at a place known as Cuatro Compañeros, and a long battle began.

It was daybreak, and with considerable difficulty we managed to gather most of our men in the densest thicket in the area. But the army advanced on our flanks, and we were forced to fight harder in order to make it possible for some of our stragglers to cross a railroad line and reach the woods. When planes located us bombings began by B-26s, C-47s, the big C-3 observation planes, and smaller planes over an area not more than 200 meters wide. After this, we retreated.

One man had been killed by a bomb and several had been wounded, including Captain Silva, who went through the rest of the invasion with a fractured shoulder.

The picture looked somewhat less gloomy the next day, since several of the stragglers appeared and we were able to reunite the entire troop, except for ten men, who were to join Camilo's column and march with it to the north front of Las Villas Province (Yaguajay). In spite of all the difficulties, we always received aid from the people in the countryside. We always found someone to be our guide, our scout, or to provide us with the necessary food to go on. Naturally, it was not the unanimous support that we had in Oriente, but there were always people who would help us out. Sometimes people would inform on us, as we went across a farm. But this was not a direct act against us by the farmers but rather the result of their living conditions. These people had become slaves of the farm owners, and, fearing the loss of their daily sustenance, they told their masters of our presence in the region. The farm owners, in turn, were only too happy to pass this information on to the military authorities.

One afternoon we heard a report over our radio issued by General Francisco Tabernilla Dolz. In his killer tones he announced the destruction of the hordes led by Che Guevara, going into detail about the dead and wounded, giving names—which they obtained when they captured our knapsacks at the time of that disastrous encounter with enemy forces a few days earlier. All this was mixed with false information invented by Army Staff Headquarters.

This false news of our deaths made the troop rather light-spirited. However, a mood of pessimism came creeping in. Hunger and thirst, fatigue, a feeling of helplessness in the face of the enemy, which was encircling us more and more, and, above all, the terrible foot disease known in the countryside as *mazamorra*—which made each step taken by our soldiers intolerable torture—turned us into an army of shadows. It was difficult to keep on, extremely difficult. Day by day the physical condition of our troop was deteriorating. Having food every other day, and not always then, did nothing to ameliorate this state of misery we were facing. The worst days were when we were surrounded near the Baraguá Sugar Mill, in infested swamplands, without a drop of drinking water, continually under attack from the air, without a single horse to take the weakest men through inhospitable swamps, with our shoes completely destroyed by the muddy sea water, with plants cutting our bare feet. We were in a disastrous situation when we got out of that encircled area and made our way to the famous Trocha from Júcaro to Morón— a line that was the historic scene of so many fierce battles between the patriots and the Spanish in the War of Independence.

We had not even had time to recover slightly when a new storm broke out, inclement weather began, there were enemy attacks or reports of the enemy's presence, and we were once more on the march. The troop was increasingly exhausted and disheartened. However, when the situation was most tense, when the only way to keep the exhausted men going was by using insults, rebuffs, and pleadings of all kinds, a sight in the distance caused faces to brighten and filled the group with new hope. That was a blue patch in the west, a blue spot that was the mountain range of Las Villas, which our men were seeing for the first time.

From that moment on, the same or similar privations seemed much lighter; everything seemed much easier. We evaded the last encirclement swimming across the Júcaro River that divides Camagüey from Las Villas Province. Then, things looked brighter.

Two days later we were safely in the heart of the Trinidad-Sancti Spíritus range, ready to begin the next stage of the war. Our rest lasted just two days, for we needed to continue our march forward immediately to attempt to prevent the elections scheduled for November 3. We had arrived in the mountainous region of Las Villas on October 16. Time was short, and the task enormous. Camilo was doing his part in the north, planting fear in the hearts of supporters of the dictatorship.

Guerrillas Fight On

Our first job when we arrived in the Sierra del Escambray was clearly defined: to harass the dictatorship's military apparatus, above all in regard to communications. Our immediate objective was to prevent elections from being held. But work was made difficult by the short time before elections and by disunity among revolutionary factions, which had led to internal fighting and even resulted in the loss of lives.

We had to attack the neighboring towns to prevent elections from being held there; we drew up plans to take simultaneously the cities of Cabaiguán, Fomento, and Sancti Spíritus on the rich plains in the center of the island. Meanwhile, the small garrison at Güinía de Miranda —in the mountains—was taken, and later we attacked the one in Banao, but with poor results. The days preceding November 3, the date of elections, were ones of extraordinary activity: our columns mobilized in all directions, with the result that few voters in those areas cast ballots. Troops led by Camilo Cienfuegos in the northern part of the province paralyzed the electoral farce. In general, everything from the transport of Batista soldiers to the movement of merchandise came to a halt.

There was practically no voting in Oriente; in Camagüey, the percentage was a little higher; and in the west, despite everything, popular abstention from voting was noted. This abstention appeared in Las

Villas spontaneously, as there had been no time to organize synchronized, passive mass resistance and guerrilla activities.

One battle after another took place in Oriente on the First and Second Fronts, and also on the Third with the Antonio Guiteras Column exerting pressure on Santiago de Cuba, the provincial capital. Except for major urban centers, the government did not control anything in Oriente.

The situation was also growing serious in Las Villas as we stepped up attacks on communication lines. When we arrived, we completely changed the system of struggle in the cities. We lost no time in transferring the best militia men from the cities to the training camp for instruction in sabotage, a measure that proved effective in suburban areas.

In November and December of 1958, we gradually closed off the highways. Captain Silva completely cut off the Trinidad-Sancti Spíritus Highway, and the Central Highway was seriously damaged when the bridge over the Tuinicú River was partially, but not completely, destroyed. The central railway line was cut at several points, and the southern highway was cut by the Second Front, while the northern highway was cut by Camilo Cienfuegos' troops. And so the island was effectively divided.

The most turbulent area, Oriente, only received government assistance by air and sea, in an increasingly precarious way. There were steadily growing signs of enemy deterioration.

We had to undertake an intensive campaign for revolutionary unity in the Escambray, as in the region there was one group led by Major Gutiérrez Menoyo (National Second Front of the Escambray), another from the Revolutionary Directorate (headed by Majors Faure Chomón and Rolando Cubela), another small group from the *Organización Auténtica*, and another from the Popular Socialist Party (headed by Torres), and ourselves.* That is, there were five different organizations operating under different commands in the same province. Following lengthy conversations which I held with leaders of the various groups, a series of agreements were reached, and we set about organizing a more or less united front.

After December 16, the systematic destruction of bridges and of all means of communication placed the dictatorship in a difficult situation for defending its outposts or even those posts on the Central Highway.

* The names of Majors Gutiérrez Menoyo and Rolando Cubela appeared in the original Spanish version published in 1959 in *O Cruzeiro Internacional*. However, they were deleted from both the Spanish and English versions published by *Granma* in October, 1967. Both men are imprisoned in Cuba for participating in anti-government activities.

At dawn that day, the Falcón River bridge on the Central Highway was destroyed, and communications between Havana and the cities east of Santa Clara, capital of Las Villas, were practically all cut. Our forces surrounded and attacked a number of towns, the southernmost of which was Fomento. The commander of the garrison conducted a more or less efficient defense for several days, but despite aerial attacks against our Rebel Army, the demoralized land troops of the dictatorship did not advance in support of their comrades. Realizing the futility of resistance, the garrison surrendered, and more than a hundred rifles were added to the liberation forces' supplies.

Without giving the enemy a chance to recover, we decided to immediately paralyze the Central Highway. On December 21, we simultaneously attacked Cabaiguán and Guayos, both on the highway. Within a few hours the latter surrendered, and two days later, the former, with its 90 soldiers, followed suit. (The garrisons surrendered on the agreement that the troops would go free, provided that they abandon the liberated territory. In that way they had the opportunity to turn over their weapons and save their lives.) In Cabaiguán we again saw the inefficiency of the dictatorship, which at no time sent in infantry reinforcements to back up the surrounded troops.

Camilo Cienfuegos took a number of small towns in the northern area of Las Villas and step by step surrounded Yaguajay, the last stronghold of the tyranny's troops. The commander, a captain of Chinese background, resisted for 11 days, preventing the mobilization of revolutionary forces of the region, while our men continued along the Central Highway, advancing toward the capital city, Santa Clara.

Cabaiguán fell, and we set our sights on Placetas. The latter surrendered after one day of fighting, conducted with the active cooperation of members of the Revolutionary Directorate. After taking Placetas, we liberated Remedios and Caibarién (an important port on the northern coast) in rapid succession. Things began to look grim for the dictatorship, with the rebels winning continued victories in Oriente, the Second Front of the Escambray capturing small garrisons, and Camilo Cienfuegos controlling the north.

When the enemy withdrew from Camajuaní without offering any resistance, we were ready for the decisive assault on the capital of the province of Las Villas. (Santa Clara, the focal point of the island's central plain, has a population of 150,000 and is the nation's rail and communications nerve center. It is surrounded by small, barren rises that had been taken by Batista forces.)

At the time of the attack, our forces had considerably augmented their supply of weapons by taking several points; we also had some heavy weapons that lacked ammunition. We had a bazooka without shells and we had to face a dozen enemy tanks. We realized that to fight effectively we had to get to the populated areas of the city, where the efficiency of a tank is drastically reduced.

Troops from the Revolutionary Directorate were charged with taking rural guard outpost number 31, and we turned our efforts toward besieging nearly all the strong points of Santa Clara. Basically, however, we aimed our struggle against troops defending an armored train located at the entrance to the Camajuaní road. The army tenaciously defended its position with excellent weapons in comparison to our own.

On December 29 we began the fight. At first we used the university as our base of operations. Next we set up headquarters closer to the center of the city. Our forces fought against troops supported by armored units, routing them, but many of our men paid for their daring with their lives; the dead and wounded filled improvised cemeteries and hospitals.

I recall an incident that demonstrated the spirit of our forces in those days. I had reprimanded a soldier for sleeping out a battle, and he replied that he had been disarmed for having accidentally fired a shot. I replied with my habitual dryness, "Get another rifle by going into the front line unarmed . . . if you dare to do it." At Santa Clara, when I was cheering up some wounded men in a makeshift hospital, a dying man touched my hand and said, "Remember me, Major? You sent me to get a gun at Remedios . . . and I got one here." It was the man who had accidentally fired his gun. He died a few minutes later. He seemed to me content at having demonstrated his bravery. That is what our Rebel Army is like.

The enemy was firmly entrenched in the Capiro hills. We fought there the entire day of December 30; we were also gradually taking various points of the city. At that time communications had been cut between the center of Santa Clara and the armored train. Its occupants, seeing themselves surrounded in the Capiro hills, tried to escape over the railroad tracks. But they and their valuable cargo went into the stretch of tracks that we had previously torn up; the engine and several cars were derailed. The battle changed form, and the occupants of the train were flushed out with Molotov cocktails. They had been magnificently protected, although only willing to fight at a safe distance, from comfortable positions and against a practically defenseless opponent, much the same way as the colonizers had fought the Indians in the American West.

With our men throwing Molotov cocktails from nearby points and from railroad cars, the train—thanks to the protective sheet metal plates— became a veritable oven for the soldiers within. In a few hours, the entire body had surrendered, with 22 cars of anti-aircraft guns, machine guns and a fabulous amount of ammunition—fabulous in comparison to our scanty supplies, naturally.

We had taken the electric power plant and the entire northwest section of the city. We announced over the radio that Santa Clara was nearly in the hands of the Revolution. In that report, which I issued as Commander in Chief of the Armed Forces in Las Villas, I recall that I had the sad duty of telling the people of Cuba of the death of Captain Roberto Rodríguez, nicknamed *El Vaquerito*, the short, young head of the "Suicide Squad" who had flirted with death a thousand and one times in the struggle for liberation. The "Suicide Squad" was an example of revolutionary morale; it was composed only of specially selected volunteers. However, whenever one of the men died—and that happened in every battle—and his replacement was selected, those rejected showed deep disappointment and even grief. It was strange to see these brave, battle-hardened veterans showing their youth by tears at not having been selected for the honor of being in the first line of combat and death.

Later on the police station fell, with the surrender of the tanks that were defending it. In rapid succession outpost 31 surrendered to Major Cubela, while the jail, the courthouse, the headquarters of the provincial government, and the Gran Hotel fell to our forces. On the tenth floor of the latter, snipers continued shooting almost until the end of the battle.

The only remaining stronghold was the Leoncio Vidal Garrison, the largest fortress in central Cuba. But it was already January 1, 1959, and there were symptoms of growing weakness among the defending forces. On the morning of that day we sent Captains Núñez Jiménez and Rodríguez de la Vega to discuss the surrender of the garrison. The news was contradictory and extraordinary. Batista had fled that day, and the leadership of his armed forces had fallen apart. Our two delegates established radio contact with Cantillo, inviting him to surrender, but he stated he could not accept the offer because it constituted an ultimatum; he announced that he had taken over command of the army following precise instructions of Fidel Castro. We immediately made contact with Fidel and reported the news to him, giving our opinion on Cantillo's traitorous attitude; his opinion coincided with ours. (During these decisive moments Cantillo allowed all the responsible figures of the Batista government to flee. His attitude was the more unfortunate considering that he was an officer who had made contact with us and whom we trusted as a military man of honor.)

The following results are familiar to all: Castro's refusal to recognize Cantillo, and his order to march on the city of Havana; Colonel Barquín's taking over as army chief after leaving the Isle of Pines prison; the taking of Camp Columbia by Camilo Cienfuegos, and the taking of La Cabaña fortress by our Column Eight; and within a few days, the final installation of Fidel Castro as Prime Minister of the provisional government.* All of this belongs to the country's present political history.

We are now in a position in which we are much more than simple actors in the history of one nation; we constitute at this moment the hope of Unredeemed America. All eyes—those of the great oppressors and those of the hopeful—are fixed upon us. The development of popular movements in America depend to a great extent on our future attitude and on our ability to solve manifold problems. Every step we take is closely watched by the omnipresent eyes of the great creditor and by the optimistic eyes of our brothers of America.

With our feet firmly on the ground, we are setting to work to produce the first fruits of the revolution, and coming up against the first difficulties. But what is Cuba's fundamental problem if not that of all America, the same even as that of huge Brazil, with its millions of square kilometers, a land of wonders that is a whole continent?—monoproduction. In Cuba we are the slaves of sugar cane, the umbilical cord that ties us to the great northern market. We must diversify our farm production, stimulate industry, and guarantee suitable markets, accessible through our own transportation system, for our agricultural and mining production—and our industrial production, in the not too distant future.

The government's first great battle will be the Agrarian Reform: it will be daring and inclusive, but flexible: it will destroy the latifundium in Cuba, but not Cuban means of production. This battle will absorb a good share of the strength of the people and the government during the coming years. Land will be given free to the peasant, and anyone who shows that he owned his land honestly will be paid in long-term bonds. In addition, the peasants will be given technical aid, farm products will have guaranteed markets, and production will be channelled so as to benefit the nation, joined in the great battle of the Agrarian Reform, which will allow Cuba's incipient industries, within a short time, to compete with the huge industries of countries where capitalism has reached its fullest degree of development.

Along with the creation of a new domestic market achieved by the Agrarian Reform, and the distribution of new products to satisfy an incipient market, the necessity of exporting some products will emerge and we will need a suitable means of delivering them to various parts of

* Actually, Castro officially became Prime Minister on February 16 [1959].

the world. This will be a merchant fleet, as provided in the already passed Maritime Development Law. With these elemental weapons, we Cubans will undertake the struggle for complete liberation of our soil. We all know that it will not be easy, but we are all conscious of the enormous historic responsibility of the 26th of July Movement, of the Cuban Revolution, of the nation in general as an example for all peoples of the Americas, whom we must not disappoint.

Our friends from the unbowed continent can rest assured that, if necessary, we will fight to the last economic consequence of our acts. And if the battle is carried still further, we will fight to the last drop of our rebel blood to make this land a sovereign republic, with the genuine attributes of a nation that is happy, democratic, and fraternal to the other American nations.

"SOCIAL PROJECTIONS OF THE REBEL ARMY" 2

The Castro regime had been in power less than a month when Guevara delivered this talk before a Communist cultural society in Havana. He set forth the social and economic paths that he believed the new government would take. The accuracy of Guevara's predictions, seen now in retrospect, are a measure of the wide influence he later exercised in the actions of the regime. He called for agrarian reform, increased industrialization, and nationalization of the telephone company. It would be months before the first elements of a militia would be established, but already Guevara was urging that "every Cuban should learn how to handle weapons and when they should be used in his defense." Guevara called for the "restructuring of the Rebel Army," and the Cuban army would indeed grow into one of the largest and most modern in the hemisphere. Guevara was already germinating his guerrilla theories (". . . a small group of determined men, supported by the people and without fear of death . . . can . . . overcome a disciplined regular army and definitively defeat it"). And Guevara also foresaw the spread of the Cuban revolution to other lands: ". . . Our brothers of America . . . must make revolutions. . . . The Revolution is not limited to the Cuban nation . . ." The Cuban revolution, declared Guevara, must be "the first step of the victory of America."

SOCIAL PROJECTIONS OF THE REBEL ARMY
Speech delivered by Major Ernesto Guevara January 27, 1959

Tonight we honor the memory of Martí, as was fittingly stated by the man who introduced me, and I believe that upon speaking of the social projections of the Rebel Army, I shall refer concretely to the dream that Martí would have made come true. And as this is a night of remembrance, before entering fully into the theme in its historical significance, I will briefly review what this Movement has been and what it is.

I cannot begin by speaking of the attack on Moncada Barracks on July 26, 1953. I wish to refer only to the phase in which I was involved due to my participation in the series of events that resulted in the triumph of the Revolution on the first of January.

We, therefore, begin this history as I began it in Mexico.

For all of us it is very important to know the present thinking of those who make up our Rebel Army, the thinking of that group that embarked on the adventure of the Granma and the evolution of that thinking born in the heart of the July 26th Movement, as well as its successive changes through the stages of the Revolution, arriving at the final lessons of the last chapter with which the insurrectional phase has terminated.

I was saying that I became acquainted with the first members of the July 26th Movement in Mexico. Very different was the social projection those men had before the Granma phase, before there occurred the first schism in the July 26 when it still contained the entire surviving nucleus of the attack on Moncada Barracks. I remember that during an intimate discussion in a house in Mexico I explained the necessity of offering the people of Cuba a revolutionary program, and one of the Moncada attackers—who fortunately left the July 26th—answered me with words which I always remember, saying: "The thing is very simple. What we must do is to launch a coup. Batista staged a coup and seized power in one day; there must be another coup to take power away from him. . . Batista has made 100 concessions to the North Americans; let us give them 101." The thing was to seize power. I explained that we had to launch a coup based on principles, that it was also important to know what we were going to do once we were in power. That was the idea of a member of the first phase of the July 26th who, fortunately for us, as I said, left our revolutionary movement, together with others who held those beliefs, and took another path.

From that moment, the group that would later come here on the

Granma began to be shaped. This was formed with difficulty because we suffered the continuous persecution of Mexican authorities, which endangered the success of the expedition. A series of internal factors, such as individuals who at first seemed to want to go on the adventure and later, under one pretext or another, began to quit, limited the number of expeditionaries. Finally, there remained the 82 men who boarded the Granma. The rest of the story is well known by the Cuban people.

What interests me and what I believe is important was the social thinking of the survivors of Alegría de Pío. That was the first and the only disaster that the rebel arms suffered during the course of the insurrection. Some fifteen men, physically destroyed, even their morale ruined, joined together and were only able to go forward because of the enormous confidence of Fidel Castro in those decisive moments, because of his unwavering stature as a revolutionary leader and his unbreakable faith in the people. We were a group of men of civilian extraction who were set in, but not grafted onto, the Sierra Maestra. We went from hut to hut. It is true that we did not touch anything that did not belong to us; we did not eat anything that we could not pay for, and many times we went hungry because of this principle. We were a group viewed with tolerance, but it was not an integrated group. And thus, much time went by . . .

There were several months of roving life on the highest peaks of the Sierra Maestra, launching sporadic blows and then halting again. We went from one peak to another; there was no water there, and living was extraordinarily difficult.

Little by little a change favorable to us began among the campesinos. It was furthered by the action of the repressive forces of Batista, who devoted themselves to murdering people and to destroying their homes, and who were hostile in every way to those who, even occasionally, had had the slightest contact with our Rebel Army. That change resulted in the inclusion among our guerrillas of the *yarey** sombrero, and thus our army of civilians began converting into a campesino army. Simultaneous to the incorporation of the campesinos to the armed struggle as a result of their grievances and their longing for freedom and social justice, there arose the great magic word that began mobilizing the oppressed masses of Cuba in the struggle for possession of land: Agrarian Reform. Thus took form the first great social plan which would later be the banner and the predominant design of our movement, although we went through a stage of much uneasiness due to the natural preoccupations related to the policy and the conduct of our great neighbor to the north. At those mo-

* Hat made of palm leaves.

ments, we felt to be more important the presence of a foreign journalist, preferably North American, than a military victory. More important than the incorporation into the struggle of campesinos, who brought to the Revolution their ideals and their faith, was that there should be North American combatants who would serve to export our revolutionary propaganda.

At that time in Santiago de Cuba there occurred a very tragic event: the murder of our campañero Frank País. This marked a change in the entire structure of the revolutionary movement. Responding to the emotional impact produced by the death of Frank País, the people of Santiago de Cuba went out into the streets spontaneously, producing the first attempt at a political general strike. The strike, although it had no leadership, completely paralyzed Oriente, reverberating in similar form in Camagüey and Las Villas. The dictatorship liquidated this movement, which had occurred without preparation and without revolutionary control. This popular phenomenon served to make us aware that it was necessary to incorporate into the struggle for the liberation of Cuba the workers as a social element, so we began immediately our clandestine activity in the workers' centers in order to prepare a general strike that would help the Rebel Army to achieve power.

That was the beginning of a campaign by clandestine organizations carried out with an insurrectional mentality, but those who encouraged these activities did not really know the significance and the tactics of mass struggle. The organizations were directed on completely erroneous paths because neither revolutionary spirit nor unity of the combatants were created and an attempt was made to direct the strike from above without effective ties with the base of strikers.

Victories of the Rebel Army and courageous clandestine efforts agitated the country and created so great a state of effervescence that it provoked the calling of a general strike last April 9. But it failed precisely because of errors of organization, among them, principally, the lack of contacts between the working masses and the leadership, and the latter's erroneous attitude. But the experience was utilized, and there arose an ideological struggle in the bosom of the July 26th Movement that provoked a radical change in its outlook of conditions in the country and of the action groups. The July 26th emerged stronger from the abortive strike, and the experience taught its leaders a precious truth, which was —and is—that the Revolution did not belong to this or that group, but rather should be the work of the entire Cuban people, and toward this goal were channeled all the energies of the militants of our movement, in the plain [i.e., the cities] as well as in the Sierra.

Precisely at that time there began in the Rebel Army the first steps to give theory and doctrine to the Revolution, providing palpable demonstration that the insurrectional movement had grown and, therefore, had arrived at political maturity. We had passed from the experimental to the constructive stage, from rehearsals to definitive deeds. We launched immediately the operation of "small industries" in the Sierra Maestra. A change occurred which our ancestors had seen many years before: We moved from nomadic life to sedentary life; we created production centers in accordance with our most urgent needs. Thus we set up our own shoe factory, our weapons factory, even a shop in which we reconstructed the bombs that the tyranny dropped on us in order to return them to Batista's own soldiers in the form of land mines.

The men and women of the Rebel Army never forgot their fundamental mission in the Sierra Maestra and elsewhere, which was the betterment of the campesinos. This was carried out through incorporation of the Rebel Army in the struggle for land and through schools set up by improvised teachers in the most inaccessible areas of the Sierra Maestra. There the first test was made of the distribution of land through agrarian regulations formulated basically by Dr. Humberto Sorí Marín* and by Fidel Castro, and in which I had the honor of collaborating. The lands were revolutionarily given to the campesinos, large farms of servants of the dictatorship were occupied and distributed, and all the lands of the State began to be turned over to the possession of the campesinos in that zone. The moment had arrived in which we were fully identified as a campesino movement closely bound to the land and with the Agrarian Reform as our banner.

Later we suffered the consequences of the abortive strike of April 9, because the savage repression of Batista was felt toward the end of May, causing in all of our fighting ranks very serious dejection which could have had catastrophic consequences for our cause. The dictatorship prepared its fiercest offensive. Around the twenty-fifth of May of last year, 10,000 well-equipped soldiers attacked our positions, centralizing their offensive against Column Number One, personally led by our commander in chief, Fidel Castro. The Rebel Army occupied a very small area, and it was almost incredible that we opposed that mass of 10,000 soldiers with only 300 rifles of freedom, the only ones that there were in the Sierra Maestra at that moment. Correct tactical leadership in that campaign resulted in the end of the Batista offensive around the thirtieth of July, with the Rebels moving from the defensive to the offensive. We captured 600

* Dr. Sorí Marín was executed in 1961 for conspiring against the Castro government.

new weapons, more than double the number of rifles with which we began that action, and we inflicted on the enemy more than 1,000 casualties, including dead, wounded, deserters, and prisoners.

The Rebel Army emerged from that campaign ready to initiate an offensive on the plain, a tactical and psychological offensive because our armaments could not compete in quality and even less in quantity with those of the dictatorship. This was a war in which we always counted on that imponderable ally of such extraordinary value—the people. Our columns were able continuously to mock the enemy and place themselves in the best positions, thanks not only to tactical advantages and to the morale of our militia, but also, to an important degree, to the great assistance of the campesinos. The campesino was the invisible collaborator who did all that the Rebel soldier could not do: he provided us with information, watched the enemy, discovered his weak points, rapidly brought urgent messages, spied within the very ranks of the government army. And this was not due to any miracle, but rather because we had already energetically initiated our policy of land and livestock recoveries. As a result of the bitterness engendered by the army attack and the siege of hunger around the Sierra Maestra, 10,000 cattle belonging to all the landholders in the adjoining areas were taken up into the mountains, and they went not only to supply the Rebel Army, but were also distributed among the campesinos. For the first time the *guajiros** of the Sierra, in that region that is particularly pauperized, enjoyed well-being; for the first time the campesino children drank milk and ate beef. And for the first time, also, they received the benefits of education, because the Revolution brought the school with it. Thus all the campesinos came to decisions favorable to our rule.

On the other side, what the dictatorship systematically had for them was the burning of their houses, eviction from land, and death; and not only death on land, but also death from the sky with the napalm bombs that the democratic neighbors to the north graciously supplied to Batista in order to terrorize civilian populations, bombs that weigh 500 kilograms and which, when they fall, extend their area of destruction to more than 100 meters. A napalm bomb dropped on a coffee plantation means total destruction—with its years of accumulated labor—throughout an area of 100 meters, and five or six years are needed to restore what was destroyed in one minute.

At this time the march on Las Villas began. It is important to mention this not because I was a participant in the march, but because upon

* Rural folk

arriving in Las Villas we found a new political-social panorama of the Revolution.

We arrived with the banner of the July 26th [Movement] in Las Villas, where the Revolutionary Directorate, groups of the Second Front of the Escambray, groups of the Popular Socialist Party, and small groupings of the Authentic Organization were already fighting against the Dictatorship. Important political work had to be carried out, and it was seen then more than ever that unity was a preponderant factor of the revolutionary struggle. The July 26th, with the Rebel Army at the fore, had to negotiate the unity of different elements who were angry at each other, and who found the work of the Sierra Maestra to be the only agglutinative factor. The first task was to plan that unity, and it had to be undertaken not only among the combatant groups but also among the urban organizations. We had to do the very important work of classifying all the labor groups that existed in the province. It was a task that was carried out in the face of much opposition, even within the ranks of our movement, which still suffered the illness of sectarianism.

We had just arrived in Las Villas and our first act of government—before establishing the first school—was to issue a revolutionary proclamation establishing the Agrarian Reform, which ordered, among other things, that the occupants of small parcels of land cease paying rent until the Revolution made a decision in each case. In fact, we advanced with the Agrarian Reform as the spearhead of the Rebel Army. And this was not a demagogic maneuver, but rather it occurred because in the course of one year and eight months of revolution the intermixture of the leaders and the campesino masses had become so extensive that very often the Revolution was led to do what it had not previously thought of doing. Agrarian Reform was not our invention; it was the demand of the campesinos. We convinced them that with weapons in hand, with an organization, and with loss of fear of the enemy, victory was certain. And the campesino, who had within him powerful reasons to do so, imposed the Agrarian Reform on the Revolution and imposed the confiscation of cattle and all the social measures that were adopted in the Sierra Maestra.

In the Sierra Maestra, Law Number Three was enacted during the days of the electoral farce of November 3, and this law established a true Agrarian Reform. Although it was not complete, it had very positive provisions: it distributed the lands of the state, of the servants of the dictatorship, and of those who were in possession through ownership rights acquired by deceitful means, like the land-grabbers who have swallowed up thousands of hectares along property boundaries. The law granted ownership to all small sugar planters who worked no more than two *caballerías** and on which they paid rent. All this was free. The principle was very revolutionary. The Agrarian Reform will benefit more than 200,000 families. But the Agrarian Revolution has not been completed with Law Number Three. For that it is necessary to enact rules against latifundia, as ordered by the Constitution. The concept of latifundium must be defined exactly; it characterizes our agrarian structure and is the indisputable source of the stagnation of the country and of all the ills suffered by the great campesino majorities. The latifundia have not yet been touched.

It will be the task of the organized campesino masses to impose the law that proscribes latifundia, just as they compelled the Rebel Army to enact the beginning of the Agrarian Reform contained in Law Number Three. There is another aspect that should be taken into account. The Constitution establishes that all expropriations of land should be paid for in cash before being carried out. If the Agrarian Reform is undertaken in accord with that principle, it may be a bit slow and burdensome. Also necessary is the collective action of the campesinos, who have won the right to freedom since the triumph of the Revolution, democratically to demand the enforcement of the Agrarian Reform and be able to go directly to a true and ample reform.

The Rebel Army is already into its social projections: we have an armed democracy. When we plan the Agrarian Reform and respect the demands of the new revolutionary laws which complement it and which will make it viable and complete, we are thinking of the social justice signified by the redistribution of the land and also of the creation of an extensive internal market and of the diversification of crops—two cardinal, inseparable objectives of the revolutionary government which cannot be postponed, because popular interest is implicit in them.

All economic activities are connected. We must increase the industrialization of the country, without ignoring the many problems that that process brings with it. But a policy of industrial development demands certain tariff measures that will protect the budding industry and a domestic market capable of absorbing the new merchandise. We cannot expand that market further except by providing the great campesino masses with access to it—the guajiros who do not have purchasing power but do have the needs to be filled and who cannot buy today.

It does not escape us that we are determined upon pursuing aims that demand an enormous responsibility on our part, and these are not our only goals. We must await the reaction against them on the part of

* Caballería [Cuba]: 13.43 hectares.

those who are dominant in more than 75% or our trade interchange and our market. In the face of that danger, we must prepare ourselves with the application of countermeasures, among which tariffs and the multiplication of foreign markets stand out. We need to create a Cuban merchant fleet to transport our sugar, tobacco, and other products, for having this fleet will very favorably influence freight charges, upon which depends to a large degree the progress of underdeveloped countries like Cuba.

If we are moving toward the development of a program of industrialization, what is most important in order to achieve it? Why, the raw materials which the Constitution so wisely defended and which the Batista dictatorship handed over to foreign consortiums. We must move to the rescue of our subsoil, of our minerals. Another element of industrialization is electricity. We must be able to rely on it. We are going to insure that electrical energy is in Cuban hands. We should also nationalize the Telephone Company because of the poor service it gives and the high price it charges.

On what resources can we count in order that a program like the one set forth can be carried out? We have the Rebel Army, and this should be our first instrument of battle, the most positive and most vigorous weapon, and we must destroy all that remains of the Batista army. And understand well that that liquidation is not to be carried out for vengeance, or only because of the sense of justice, but because of the necessity of assuring that all those gains of the people will be achieved in the most minimal time.

We destroyed a numerically much superior army with the assistance of the people, with the right tactics, and with revolutionary morale. But now we must face the reality that our army is not yet qualified for newly acquired responsibilities, such as defending fully the territory of Cuba. We must move rapidly toward the restructuring of the Rebel Army, because we created, without planning, an armed corps of campesinos and workers, many of them illiterate, uncultured, and without technical preparation. We must prepare that army for the high tasks its members must undertake, and we must train them technically and culturally.

The Rebel Army is the vanguard of the Cuban people, and upon referring to its technical and cultural progress, we must understand the significance of these things in a modern sense. We have already symbolically begun its education with a recital presided almost exclusively by the spirit and the teachings of José Martí.

National recuperation must destroy many privileges, and we must, therefore, be prepared to defend the nation from its declared or disguised enemies. In line with that, the new army must adapt itself to the new atmosphere which has resulted from this war of liberation, because we know that if we are attacked by a small island,* the attack will have the support of a power that is almost a continent; we would have to suffer on our soil an aggression of immense proportions. And for that reason we should make ourselves ready and prepare our forward positions with guerrilla spirit and strategy, so that our defenses will not disintegrate under the first attack, but will maintain their central unity. The entire Cuban people should convert themselves into a guerrilla army: the Rebel Army is a growing corps whose capacity is limited only by the number of the republic's six million Cubans. Every Cuban should learn how to handle weapons and when they should be used in his defense.

With wide strokes I have set forth the social projection of the Rebel Army after the victory and its role in urging the government to make revolutionary aspirations evident.

There is something more of interest to say in order to end this talk: the example that our Revolution has set forth for Latin America, and the lessons that are implied as a result of having destroyed all the drawing room theories. We have shown that a small group of determined men, supported by the people and without fear of death, can if necessary overcome a disciplined regular army and decisively defeat it. That is the fundamental lesson. There is another that should be realized by our brothers of America, economically situated in the same agrarian category as ourselves, and that is that they must make agrarian revolutions; there must be struggle in the fields, in the mountains, and from there the revolution must be taken to the cities—but it should not be attempted in the cities without an integral social content.

Now, in the face of the experiences that we have had, the question is asked, what is to be our future, so closely linked to that of all underdeveloped countries of Latin America? The Revolution is not limited to the Cuban nation, for it has touched the conscience of America and has gravely alerted the enemies of our peoples. For that reason we have clearly warned that any attempt at aggression will be repulsed with weapon in hand. The example of Cuba has increased effervescence in all of Latin America and in the oppressed countries. The Revolution has placed the Latin American tyrants on the spot, because they are enemies of popular regimes just as foreign monopolistic companies are. As we

* Guevara evidently was referring to the Dominican Republic, at that time ruled by Generalissimo Rafael Trujillo.

are a small country we need the support of all the democratic nations and aspecially of Latin America.

We should fully state the noble goals of the Cuban Revolution to the entire world and issue a call to the friendly peoples of this Continent, to the North Americans and the Latin Americans. We should create a spiritual union of all our countries, a union which goes beyond mere words and bureaucratic association and is translated into effective aid to our brothers, offering them our experience.

Finally, we should open new paths which lead to the identification of the common interests of our underdeveloped countries. We must be alert against the attempts and designs to divide us; we must fight against those who seek to sow the seed of discord among us, those who, ensconced in known purposes, try to take advantage of our political disagreements and to incite impossible prejudices in this country.

Today all the people of Cuba are on a war footing, and they must remain thus united so that the victory against the dictatorship will not be transitory, and this will be the first step of the victory of America.

"THE CADRE, SPINAL COLUMN OF THE REVOLUTION" 3

When the Castro government began to carry out radical changes within Cuba's political and economic structure, the regime faced what Guevara in this article called "a real hunger for technicians" because a good part of the country's technical pool was fleeing abroad. This article, published in *Cuba Socialista*, detailed how the government was selecting and preparing—preparing ideologically, that is—the "cadres" who would manage official machinery in the fields of administration and economic production. The cadres, said Guevara, were to be picked from among outstanding members of "the masses" and given special political training. Their primary functions would be to transmit to the "masses" the guidance (and, presumably, orders) of the country's leaders, and to transmit to the leaders the wishes and feelings of the "masses." The cadre, however, was more than a mere transmission belt. Guevara saw him as a person "with his own ability to analyze," his own "creative initiative"—providing, of course, that this did not clash with party discipline. The cadre was "a creator, a leader of high stature, a technician of good political level"—in a word, the Communist ideal of an "exemplary human."

THE CADRE, SPINAL COLUMN OF THE REVOLUTION

I T IS UNNECESSARY to dwell upon the characteristics of our Revolution —upon the original manner, with some flashes of spontaneity, by which the transition from a national liberating revolution to a socialist revolution was produced—nor upon the number of rapid stages that occurred in the course of this development. Led by the same actors of the initial epic of Moncada, the process moved through the Granma episode and terminated in the declaration of the socialist character of the Cuban Revolution. New sympathizers, cadres, organizations joined the frail organic structure of the initial movement until they became the flood of people which characterized our Revolution.

When it became evident that in Cuba a new social class was definitively taking command, there also became apparent the great limitations that this class would have in exercising power. The conditions in which we found the state made it difficult – without–cadres to develop the enormous accumulation of tasks that should have been carried out within the state apparatus, in the political structure, and on the entire economic front.

In the period following the assumption of power, bureaucratic posts were filled haphazardly. But there were no big problems; in fact, there were none because the old structure was not yet broken. The apparatus functioned with the slow and tired movement of an old thing, almost without life, but it did have an organization and, in it, sufficient coordination to maintain itself by inertia, disdaining the political changes that were being produced as a prelude to the change in the economic structure.

The July 26th Movement, deeply wounded by the internal struggles between its left and right wings, could not devote itself to constructive tasks; and the Popular Socialist Party, having suffered fierce attacks and illegality for years, had not been able to develop intermediate cadres to face the new approaching responsibilities.

When the first state interventions in the economy took place, the task of seeking cadres was not very complicated and selections could be made among many people who had some minimal base for exercising the duties of management. But, upon the acceleration of the process with the nationalization of the North American companies and, later, of the large Cuban companies, there was a great need of administrative technicians. The same anguished need for technicians was felt also in production, due to the exodus of many of them, attracted by better positions offered by the imperialist companies in other parts of the continent or in the United States itself. The political apparatus had to subject itself to an intense effort in the midst of the tasks of structurization in order to give ideological attention to the masses who were coming into contact with the Revolution, filled with a desire to learn.

All of us carried out our roles as best we could, but not without pains and troubles. Many errors were committed in the administrative side of the Executive; enormous faults were committed by the new managers of enterprises with too great responsibilities in their hands; and we also committed large and costly errors in the political apparatus, which, little by little, was falling into a tranquil and pleasant bureaucracy, virtually taken as a springboard for promotions and for bureaucratic positions of greater or lesser rank, totally disconnected from the masses.

The central axis of our errors has lain in our being out of touch with reality at a given moment, but the tools that we lacked—what was dulling our perceptive capacity and converting the party into a bureaucratic entity, putting the administration and production in danger—were cadres developed at the middle level. Policy of cadres was obviously synonymous with policy of masses; to establish contact again with the masses, as it had been tightly maintained by the Revolution in the first stages of its life, was the watchword. This contact, however, was to be established through some kind of apparatus that should render the best fruits. It should be useful in perceiving all the pulsations of the masses as well as in the transmission of all political orientations, which in many cases were provided only through statements made personally by Prime Minister Fidel Castro or some other leaders of the Revolution.

At this point, we can ask ourselves, what is a cadre? We can say that a cadre is an individual who has achieved sufficient political development to be able to understand the important directives emanating from the central power, to make these decisions his own, and to transmit them as orientation to the masses; in addition, he must be capable of perceiving the manifestations by which the masses express their desires and their most intimate motivations. He is an individual with ideological and administrative discipline who knows and practices democratic centralism and can evaluate the contradictions that exist in the method in order to make use to the maximum of its multiple facets; he knows how to practice in production the principle of collective discussion and individual decision and responsibility. A cadre is an individual whose loyalty has been proved and whose physical and moral valor has grown as much as his ideological development, so that he is always ready to face any debate and to respond, even with his life, to the forward march of the Revolution. He is, in addition, an individual with his own ability to analyze, which enables him to make necessary decisions and to utilize creative initiative in a manner that does not clash with discipline.

The cadre, therefore, is a creator, a leader of high stature, a technician of good political level who can, reasoning dialectically, carry forward his production section or guide the masses from his political post of leadership.

This exemplary human, seemingly encircled by virtues difficult to achieve, is, nevertheless, present among the people of Cuba, and we meet him day after day. It is essential to take advantage of all opportunities to develop him to the maximum and to educate him, taking from each personality the best qualities and converting these into' the most useful values for the nation.

The development of a cadre is achieved in everyday affairs; but the task, in addition, should be carried out in a systematic manner in special schools, where competent proféssors, examples to the students, will promote the most rapid ideological ascent.

In a regime that begins the construction of socialism, one cannot imagine a cadre who does not have high political development. Political development, however, should not be understood to mean only the learning of Marxist theory. The individual must also show responsibility for his acts, discipline that overcomes any transitory weakness and which is not in conflict with a large dose of initiative, and constant concern for all the problems of the revolution. To develop the cadre it is necessary to begin by establishing the selective principle among the masses; that is where to look for the emerging personalities who have been tested in sacrifice or who have now begun to show their concern. They must be taken to special schools or, in the absence of these, given positions of greater responsibilities so as to test them in practical work.

We have thus found and developed a multitude of new cadres in these years; but their development has not been the same in all cases because the young comrades have faced the reality of revolutionary creation without adequate party orientation. Some have triumphed fully, but there are many who could not make the grade and remained halfway on the path, or who, simply, were lost in the bureaucratic labyrinth or in the temptations that power provides.

In order to assure the triumph and total consolidation of the Revolution we must develop different types of cadres. The political cadre will be the foundation of our mass organizations, the one who orients them through the action of the United Party of the Socialist Revolution. (This foundation is already being established by means of the provincial and national schools of Revolutionary Instruction and by means of studies and study circles at all levels.) Also needed are military cadres; they can be obtained from the selection the war made among our young combatants. A large number survived, without much theoretical knowledge but tested in the fire and under the most difficult conditions of the struggle, and having a loyalty beyond reproach toward the revolutionary regime with whose birth and development they have been so intimately united since the first guerrillas were in the Sierra. We must also advance economic cadres that dedicate themselves specifically to the difficult tasks of planning and of organizing the socialist State in these moments of creation. It is necessary to work with the professionals and encourage the youths to follow some of the most important technical careers, aiming to give the sciences the tone of ideological enthusiasm that guarantees accelerated development. And it is imperative to create the administrative machinery that can make use of and join together the specific technical skills of people, at the same time managing the state enterprises and other organizations and linking them to the strong rhythm of the Revolution.

For all of the cadres, the common denominator is political clarity. This does not consist in unconditional but rather in reasoned support of the postulates of the Revolution, in a great capacity for sacrifice, and in a dialectical capacity for analysis. All this permits continuous contributions at all levels to the rich theory and practice of the Revolution. These comrades should be selected from among the masses, the only principle applied being that the best stand out and that to the best be given the major opportunities for development.

In all these categories the function of the cadres, although they may occupy different fronts, is the same. The cadre is the key part of the ideological motor that is the United Party of the Revolution. He is what we might call a dynamic screw of that motor—a screw in that he is a functional piece that assures correct operation, dynamic in not being a simple transmitter, upwards or downwards, of slogans or demands, but rather a creator who, serving as a contact point, will assist in the development of the masses and add to the information of the leaders. He has an important mission of vigilance in seeing that the great spirit of the Revolution is not liquidated, that the Revolution does not sleep, and that its rhythm does not abate. It is a sensitive spot: to transmit what comes from the masses and to infuse in them the orientation of the Party.

To develop the cadres is, therefore, a task of this moment that cannot be delayed. The development of the cadres has been undertaken with great determination by the Revolutionary Government: with its programs of scholarships, using selective principles; with the programs of studies for the workers, providing different opportunities for technological development; with the establishment of special technical schools; with the promotion of secondary schools and with the universities opening new fields of study; with the launching, finally, of study, work, and revolutionary vigilance as mottoes of our entire fatherland. All this is based fundamentally on the Union of Communist Youths, from whence should come the cadres of all kinds and even the leadership cadres of the Revolution in the future.

Closely tied to the concept of the "cadre" is capacity for sacrifice, for showing through one's own example the truths and principles of the Revolution. The cadre, as a political leader, should win the respect of the workers with his actions. It is indispensable that he have the consideration and the affection of the compañeros whom he is to guide on the forward paths.

Because of all this, there is no better cadre than the one whose election is effected by the masses at the meetings at which the exemplary workers are designated. These cadres will be taken into the P.U.R.S. [United Party of the Socialist Revolution] together with the former members of the ORI [Integrated Revolutionary Organizations] who pass all the required selective tests. At first they will constitute a small group, but their influence among the workers will be immense. Later the group will grow larger when the development of the socialist conscience converts work for, and total dedication to, the cause of the people into a necessity.

With middle-level leaders of this kind, the difficult tasks that we have before us will be carried out with less mishaps. After a period of disorder and bad methods, the right policy has been arrived at, and it will never be abandoned. With the ever-renewed thrust of the working class, its inexhaustible fountain nourishing the ranks of the future United Party of the Socialist Revolution, and with the leadership provided by our party, we enter fully into the shaping of cadres that guarantee the spirited development of our Revolution. We must triumph in this endeavor.

"GUERRILLA WARFARE: A METHOD" 4

In this article Guevara projects his theories on guerrilla warfare beyond Cuba's borders. The article provides basic instructions on this type of conflict; it also contains Guevara's theoretical views on the utilization of guerrilla warfare. Guevara sees this kind of combat as the means for conquest of other nations in the Western Hemisphere—and, by implication, as a means for Communist conquest elsewhere in the world, as well. This work is considered to be the most important of Guevara's theoretical writings. It has been widely reprinted in Cuba, and, as an indication of its international importance, it was reprinted in Peking's *Renmin Ribao* and an English version was issued in pamphlet form by the Foreign Languages Press, official outlet of the Chinese Communist government. Guevara foresaw guerrilla uprisings as not being purely local matters in each country, but as part of an overall continental plan. He stated, "It does not matter, for the final result, that one movement or another may be momentarily defeated." The struggle would continue, anyway. Presumably this is the way Guevara would have viewed his own defeat in Bolivia. It is the way the Cuban government views that defeat: it continues to try to develop guerrilla warfare in Bolivia, as well as elsewhere in Latin America.

GUERRILLA WARFARE: A METHOD

G UERRILLA WARFARE has been used innumerable times in history under various conditions and for different ends. Lately it has been used in various wars of people's liberation where the people's vanguard has chosen the path of unconventional armed struggle against enemies with greater military potential. Asia, Africa, and America have been the sites of these activities when power was sought in the struggle against feudal, neocolonial, or colonial exploitation. In Europe it was used as a complement to the regular armies themselves or allies.

In America recourse has been made to guerrilla warfare on different occasions. The closest precedent is the experience of César Augusto Sandino, fighting against the Yankee expeditionary forces in the Nicaraguan Segovia. And recently, the revolutionary war of Cuba. Since then, the problems of guerrilla warfare have arisen in America in the theoretical discussions of the progressive parties of the Continent, and the possibility and appropriateness of using it is the subject of heated controversies.

These notes will be an attempt to express our ideas on guerrilla warfare and what would be its correct use.

Above all it must be made clear that this type of struggle is a method; a method to achieve an end. That end, essential and inescapable for any revolutionary, is the gaining of political power. Therefore, in the analyses of the specific situations in the various countries of America, the guerrilla concept, reduced to the simple category of a method of struggle to achieve that end, should be used.

Almost immediately the question arises: Is the guerrilla warfare method the only formula for the seizure of power throughout America? or will it, in any case, be the predominant form? or simply will it be one more formula among all those employed for the struggle? and, in the final analysis, is asked, will the example of Cuba be applicable to other continental realities? By way of argument, it is customary to criticize those who want to use guerrilla warfare, adducing that they forget the struggle of the masses, almost as if they were opposing methods. We reject the concept that embraces that position; guerrilla warfare is a people's war, it is a struggle of the masses. To try to wage this type of warfare without the support of the people is a prelude to inevitable disaster. The guerrilla is the fighting vanguard of the people, located in a specific place in some given area, armed, ready to carry out a series of warlike activities leading to the only possible strategic end: the seizure of power. It is supported by the peasant and working masses of the zone and the entire territory involved. Without these conditions guerrilla warfare cannot be permitted.

"In our American situation, we believe that the Cuban Revolution made three fundamental contributions to the mechanics of the revolutionary movements in America; they are: first, popular forces can win a war against an army; second, it is not always necessary to wait for all the conditions for revolution to exist—the insurrectionary focal point can at times create them; third, in underdeveloped America the field of armed struggle should be principally the countryside" (*La Guerra de Guerrillas*, Guerrilla Warfare).

Such are the contributions for waging the revolutionary struggle in America, and they can be applied to any of the countries of our continent in which a guerrilla war is going to be waged.

The Second Declaration of Havana indicates: "In our countries an underdeveloped industry exists side by side with a feudal agrarian system. It is for that reason that, despite the unbearable living conditions of the urban workers, the rural populace lives under even more horrible conditions of oppression and exploitation; but it is also, with some exceptions, the absolute majority, in proportions sometimes surpassing 70 percent of the Latin American populations.

"Not counting the landowners, who often live in the cities, the rest of that great mass eke their sustenance working as peons on the farms for wretched wages or work the land under conditions of exploitation that give the Middle Ages no room to boast. These circumstances are those that cause the poor country population in Latin America to constitute a tremendous potential revolutionary force.

"The armies, which are the force on which the power of the exploiting classes is sustained, organized and equipped for conventional warfare, are absolutely powerless when they have to face the unconventional warfare of the peasants on their territory. They lose ten men for every revolutionary fighter who falls, and demoralization spreads rapidly in them on having to face an invisible and invincible enemy who gives them no chance to display their academic tactics and sword rattling, of which they make so much ostentation to repress the workers and students in the cities.

"The initial struggle of small fighting nuclei is fed unceasingly by new forces, the movement of the masses begins to be unleashed, the old order cracks little by little into a thousand pieces: that is the moment when the working class and the urban masses decide the battle.

"What is it that from the very beginning of the struggle of those first nuclei makes them invincible regardless of the number, power, and resources of their enemies? The support of the people, and they will count on the support of the masses to an ever increasing degree.

"But the peasant is a type that, because of the uncultured state in which he is kept and the isolation in which he lives, needs the revolutionary and political leadership of the working class and the revolutionary intellectuals, without which he could not by himself plunge into the struggle and gain victory.

"Under the present historical conditions of Latin America, the national bourgeoisie cannot head the antifeudal and anti-imperialist struggle. Experience shows that in our nations that class, even when its interests are opposed to those of Yankee imperialism, has been incapable of confronting it, paralyzed by the fear of social revolution and frightened by the clamor of the exploited masses" (Second Declaration of Havana).

Completing the scope of these assertions, which constitute the heart of the revolutionary declaration of America, the Second Declaration of Havana expresses in other paragraphs the following: "The subjective conditions of each country—that is to say, awareness, organization, leadership—can accelerate or retard the revolution according to its greater or lesser degree of development; but sooner or later in each historical epoch, when the objective conditions mature, awareness is acquired, organization is attained, leadership comes forth, and the revolution is produced.

"Whether the revolution takes place through peaceful passages or whether it will come into the world after a painful birth, does not depend on the revolutionaries, it depends on the reactionary forces of the old society, which refuse to allow the birth of the new society, engendered by the contradictions held by the old society. The revolution plays the same part in history as does the doctor who assists in the birth of a new life. He does not use instruments of force unless they are necessary, but he uses them without hesitation each time that they may be necessary to aid the birth. It is a birth which brings the hope of a better life to the enslaved and exploited masses.

"The revolution is inevitable today in many Latin American countries. That fact is not determined by the will of anyone. It is determined by the frightening conditions of exploitation in which the American man lives, the development of the revolutionary awareness of the masses, the world crisis of imperialism, and the universal movement of struggle of the subjugated people" (Second Declaration of Havana).

We shall start from these bases for an analysis of the entire guerrilla problem in America.

We have established that it is a method of fighting to obtain an end. It is of interest, first, to analyze the end and to see if it is possible to succeed in the conquest of power in a manner other than by armed struggle here in America.

The peaceful struggle can be carried out by means of mass movements, and it can—in special situations of crises—force governments to yield, and eventually the popular forces would hold the power and establish the dictatorship of the proletariat. This is theoretically correct. Upon analyzing previous events in the panorama of America, we have to arrive at the following conclusions: On this continent in general there exist objective conditions which impel the masses to violent actions against the bourgeois and landowner governments; power crises exist in many other countries and some subjective conditions also exist. It is clear that, in the countries in which all the conditions are found, it would even be criminal not to act for the takeover of power. In those other countries in which this is not the case, it is permissible to consider different alternatives, and for a decision applicable to each country to spring from theoretical discussion. The only thing that history does not permit is for the analysts and executors of the policy of the proletariat to err. No one can seek to be part of the vanguard as he would seek an official diploma given by the university. To be a member of the vanguard is to be at the head of the working class in the struggle for the seizure of power, to know how to guide it to the capture, and even to lead it through short cuts. That is the mission of our revolutionary parties and the analysis ought to be profound and exhaustive so that there may be no equivocation.

Day by day, a state of unstable balance between the oligarchic dictatorship and the popular pressure is seen in [Latin] America. We call it oligarchy with the idea of trying to define the reactionary alliance between the bourgeoisie of each country and the landowning classes, with the greater or lesser preponderance of the feudal structures. These dictatorships occur within certain frameworks of legality which they themselves set up for their own convenience during the whole unrestricted period of class domination. But we are passing through a stage in which the popular pressure is very strong; the people are knocking at the doors of bourgeois legality, which must be violated by its own authors in order to hold back the drive of the masses. The shameless violations, contrary to all previously enacted legislation—or legislation enacted a posteriori to justify the event—put more tension on the popular forces. Therefore, the oligarchic dictatorship tries to use the old legal arrangements to change the constitutionality and to oppress the proletariat even more, without the collision being head-on. In spite of that, here is where the contradiction takes place. The people no longer support the

old nor, still less, the new coercive measures established by the dictatorship, and try to break them. We should never forget the class, authori-
tarian, and restrictive character of the bourgeois state. Lenin referred
to it in this manner: "The state is the product and the manifestation of
the irreconcilable character of class contradictions. The state appears
in the place, in the moment, and to the extent in which the contradictions
of class cannot be objectively reconciled. And vice versa: the existence
of the state demonstrates that the contradictions of class are irreconcilable." (*The State and the Revolution.*)

This means that we should not admit that the word democracy, used
in an apologetic form to represent the dictatorship of the exploiting
classes, loses its depth of concept and acquires the concept of certain more
or less optimal liberties given to the citizen. To struggle only to obtain
the restoration of certain bourgeois legality without raising, on the other
hand, the problem of revolutionary power, is to struggle to return to a
certain dictatorial order previously established by the dominant social
classes; it is, in any case, to struggle for the establishment of some chains
with a ball at the end somewhat less heavy for the convict.

Under these conditions of conflict, the oligarchy breaks its own
contracts, its own appearance of "democracy," and attacks the people,
although it always tries to use the methods of the superstructure it has
created for oppression. The dilemma is stated again at that moment:
What must be done? We answer: Violence is not the patrimony of the
exploiters, the exploited can use it and, what is more, they ought to use
it at the opportune time. Martí said: "He who promotes a war which
can be avoided is a criminal; and he who fails to promote an inevitable
war is also a criminal."

Lenin, on the other hand, said: "Social-democracy has never viewed,
nor does it view now, war from a sentimental point of view. It condemns,
absolutely, war as a savage means of settling differences between men,
but it knows that wars are inevitable as long as society is divided into
classes, as long as the exploitation of man by his fellow men exists. And
to do away with that exploitation we cannot disregard wars always and
everywhere begun by the very classes that exploit, dominate, and oppress." He said this in 1905; later, in *The Military Program of the Proletarian Revolution*, profoundly analyzing the character of the class
struggle, he affirmed: "He who accepts the class struggle cannot help but
accept civil wars, which in any society of classes represent the continua-
tion, the development, and the outbreak—which are natural and, under
certain circumstances, inevitable—of the class struggle. All the great
revolutions confirm it. To deny civil wars or to forget them would be
to fall into an extreme opportunism and to deny the socialist revolution."

This means that we should not fear violence, the midwife of new societies; the only thing is that the violence ought to be unleashed at the exact moment when the leaders of the people have found the most favorable circumstances.

Which will these be? They depend, subjectively, on two conditions that complement each other and that in turn continue to intensify during the struggle: the awareness of the need for change and the certainty of the possibility of this revolutionary change. These objective conditions —which are tremendously favorable in almost all of [Latin] America for carrying out the struggle—together with a firm will to achieve the change and the new balances of power in the world, determine the way of action.

No matter how far away the socialist countries may be, their beneficial influence will always be felt by the struggling peoples, and their enlightening example will give them more strength. Fidel Castro said last 26 of July: "And the duty of the revolutionary, above all at this moment, is to be able to discern, to be able to make use of the changes in the balance of power that have taken place in the world, and to understand that change promotes the struggle of the peoples. The duty of the revolutionaries, of the Latin American revolutionaries, is not to wait for the change in the balance of power to work the miracle of social revolutions in Latin America but to take full advantage of everything that the changed balance of power presents to the revolutionary movement and 'make revolutions!' "

There are those who say, "We accept revolutionary warfare as a suitable measure, in certain specific cases, to achieve the seizure of political power. Where do we get the great leaders, the Fidel Castros to bring us to victory?" Fidel Castro, as every human being, is a product of history. The military and political leaders who may direct the insurrectionary struggles in [Latin] America, united, if it were possible, in a single person, will learn the art of warfare in the practice of war itself. There is no occupation or profession which one can learn from textbooks alone. In this case, the struggle is the great teacher.

It is obvious that the task is not easy nor free of grave dangers throughout its course.

During the waging of the armed struggle two moments of extreme danger for the future of the revolution appear. The first arises during the preparatory stage, and the manner in which it is resolved determines the decision to struggle and the clear understanding that the popular forces have of the ends. When the bourgeois state advances against the positions of the people, obviously a defensive process against the enemy must be created which, once it achieves superiority, attacks. If minimum objective and subjective conditions have already developed, the defense should be armed, but in such a way that the popular forces are not converted into mere recipients of the blows of enemies; nor should the stage for armed defense simply be a last refuge for the persecuted. The guerrilla, the people's defensive movement at a given moment, has in itself, and constantly should develop, its ability to attack the enemy. In time, this ability is what will determine its nature as a catalyst of the popular forces. It merits being said that guerrilla activity is not passive self-defense; it is defense with attack, and from the moment it establishes itself as such, its final goal is the conquest of political power.

This moment is important. In the social processes, the difference between violence and non-violence cannot be measured by the number of shots that are exchanged; it yields to concrete and fluctuating situations. And it is necessary to be able to see the instant in which the popular forces, aware of their relative weakness but, at the same time, of their strategic strength, must force the enemy to take the necessary steps so that the situation does not retrocede. The balance between the oligarchic dictatorship and popular pressure must be upset. The dictatorship constantly tries to operate without the showy use of force. Forcing the dictatorship to appear undisguised—that is, in its true aspect of violent dictatorship of the reactionary classes—will contribute to its unmasking, which will intensify the struggle to such extremes that then there is no turning back. The manner in which the people's forces, dedicated to the task of making the dictatorship define itself—holding back or unleashing the battle—carry out their function depends on the firm beginning of a long-range armed action.

Escape from the other dangerous moment depends on the power of growing development which the popular forces possess. Marx always maintained that once the revolutionary process had begun, the proletariat had to strike and strike unceasingly. Revolution that does not constantly become more profound is a regressive revolution. Tired soldiers begin to lose faith and then some of the maneuvers to which the bourgeoisie has so accustomed us may appear. These can be elections with the transfer of power to another gentleman with a more mellifluous voice and a more angelic countenance than the current dictator, or a coup by reactionaries generally led by the army and, directly or indirectly, supported by progressive forces. There are others, but we do not intend to analyze tactical stratagems.

Principally, we are calling attention to the maneuvers of the military coup that was previously mentioned. What can the military give to the true democracy? What loyalty can one ask of them if they are mere tools of the domination of the reactionary classes and of the imperialist monopolies, and, as a caste, whose value depends upon the weapons it possesses, aspire merely to maintain their privileges?

In situations difficult for oppressors, when the military plot and oust a dictator who de facto has already been beaten, it must be supposed that they do it because the dictator is not capable of preserving their class privileges without extreme violence, which, in general, now does not suit the interest of oligarchies.

This in no way means rejecting the use of the military as individual fighters, separated from the social milieu in which they have operated and, in fact, rebelled against. But this use must be made in the framework of the revolutionary course to which they will belong as fighters and not as representatives of a caste.

In times past, in the preface to the third edition of *The Civil War in France*, Engels said, "After each revolution, the workers were armed; for that reason, the disarmament of the workers was the first order of the bourgeoisie who headed the State. Hence, after each revolution won by the workers, a new struggle developed that culminated with their overthrow . . ." (Quoted from Lenin, *The State and the Revolution*).

This game of continual struggles, in which formal changes of any type are attained only to strategically regress, has been repeated for decades in the capitalist world. But still, permanent deception of the proletariat in this aspect has been going on periodically for more than a century.

It is also dangerous that, moved by the desire to maintain for some time the conditions most favorable for revolutionary action by means of the use of certain aspects of bourgeois legality, the leaders of the progressive party confuse the terms—which is very common during the course of the action—and forget the final strategic objective: seizure of power.

These two difficult moments of the revolution, which we have briefly analyzed, are obviated when the leading Marxist-Leninist parties are able to see clearly the implications of the moment and to mobilize the masses, to the greatest extent, by correctly leading them to resolve fundamental contradictions.

In discussing the subject, we have assumed that, eventually, the idea of armed struggle and also the formula of guerrilla warfare as a method of combat will be accepted. Why do we estimate that guerrilla warfare is the correct method under the present conditions in America? There are basic arguments which, to our mind, determine the necessity of guerrilla action in America as the central axis of the struggle.

First: Accepting as a truth the fact that the enemy will struggle to keep himself in power, it is necessary to consider the destruction of the oppressing army; but to destroy it, it is necessary to oppose it with a popular army. This army is not created spontaneously but must arm itself from its enemy's arsenal, and this causes a hard and very long struggle in which the popular forces and their leaders would be continually exposed to attack from superior forces without suitable conditions for defense and maneuverability.

On the other hand, the guerrilla nucleus, settled in terrain favorable to the struggle, guarantees the security and permanence of the revolutionary command. The urban forces, directed from the general staff of the army of the people, can carry out actions of incalculable importance. The possible destruction of these groups would not kill the soul of the revolution; its leadership, from its rural fortress, would continue to catalyze the revolutionary spirit of the masses and organize new forces for other battles.

Furthermore, the organization of the future state apparatus begins in this zone. It is in charge of efficiently guiding the class dictatorship during the entire transition period. The longer the battle, the greater and more complex will be the administrative problems, and in solving them, cadres will be trained for the difficult task of consolidating power and economic development in a future stage.

Second: We have to look at the general situation of the Latin American peasants and the progressively more explosive nature of their struggle against feudal structures in the framework of a social situation of alliance between local and foreign exploiters.

Returning to the Second Declaration of Havana: "The peoples of America freed themselves from Spanish colonialism at the beginning of the last century, but they did not free themselves from exploitation. The feudal landlords took over the authority of the Spanish governors, the Indians continued in grinding slavery, the Latin American man in one form or another followed in the steps of the slave, and the slightest hopes of the people crumbled under the power of oligarchies and the yoke of foreign capital. This has been the situation in [Latin] America, in one form or another. Today Latin America is under an even more ferocious imperialism, far more powerful and ruthless than Spanish colonial imperialism.

"And faced with the objective and historically inexorable reality of the Latin American revolution, what is the attitude of Yankee imperialism? To prepare to begin a colonial war with the peoples of Latin America; to create an apparatus of force, political pretexts, and pseudo-legal instruments signed with the representatives of reactionary oligarchies to repress by blood and fire the struggle of the Latin American peoples."

This objective situation demonstrates the force that slumbers, unproductive, in our peasants and the need for using it for the liberation of America.

Third: The continental character of the struggle.

Could this new stage of the emancipation of America be conceived as the meeting of two local forces struggling for power in a given territory? Only with difficulty. The struggle will be to the death between all the popular forces and all the forces of repression. The paragraphs quoted above also predict it.

The Yankees will intervene out of solidarity of interests and because the struggle in America is a decisive one. In fact, they are already intervening in the preparation of repressive forces and in the organization of a continental fighting apparatus. But, from now on, they will do it with all their energies; they will punish the popular forces with all the destructive weapons at their disposal; they will not permit the revolutionary power to consolidate, and if anyone should do so, they will again attack, they will not recognize it, they will try to divide the revolutionary forces, they will introduce saboteurs of every kind, they will create border problems, they will turn other reactionary states against them, they will try to smother the economy of the new state, in one word, to annihilate it.

With this American panorama, it is difficult to achieve and consolidate victory in an isolated country. The unity of repressive forces must be answered with the unity of popular forces. In all countries where oppression reaches unbearable levels, the banner of rebellion must be raised, and this banner will have, because of historical need, continental features. The Andes Cordillera is called on to be the Sierra Maestra of America, as Fidel has said, and all the vast territories of the continent are called to be the scene of the struggle to the death against the imperialist power.

We cannot say when it will achieve these continental features, nor how long the struggle will last; but we can predict its coming and its success, because it is the result of inevitable historical, economic, and political circumstances, and the course cannot be turned aside. To begin it when conditions are propitious, regardless of the situation in other countries, is the task set for the revolutionary force in each country. The waging of the struggle will continue to control the general strategy. The prediction on the continental character is the fruit of the analysis of the forces of each contender, but this does not exclude, not by a long shot, an independent outburst. Just as the beginning of the struggle at a point in a country is intended to carry it throughout the country, the beginning of the revolutionary war contributes to the development of new conditions in neighboring countries.

The development of revolutions has come about normally by inversely proportional ebbs and flows. The revolutionary flow corresponds to the counterrevolutionary ebb, and vice versa, at the moment of the revolutionary decline, there is a counterrevolutionary rise. At times like this, the situation of the popular forces becomes difficult and they must resort to the best means of defense to suffer the least damage. The enemy is extremely strong, continentally. For this reason, the relative weaknesses of the local bourgeoisie cannot be analyzed for purposes of making decisions of a limited scope. Even more remote is the possible alliance of these oligarchies with the people under arms. The Cuban Revolution has sounded the alarm. The polarization of forces will be total: exploiters from one side and the exploited from another; the masses of the petty bourgeoisie will lean toward one or the other, depending on their interests and the political skill with which they are handled. Neutrality will be an exception. This is what the revolutionary war will be like.

Let us think about how a guerrilla focus could begin.

Relatively small nuclei of people choose favorable places for guerrilla warfare, either to begin a counterattack, or to weather the storm, and thus they begin to act. The following must be clearly established: at first, the relative weakness of the guerrilla movement is such that it must work only to settle in the terrain, establishing connections with the populace and reinforcing the places that will possibly become its base of support.

There are three conditions for the survival of a guerrilla movement that begins its development under the situation just described: constant mobility, constant vigilance, constant distrust. Without the adequate use of these three elements of military tactics, the guerrilla will survive only with difficulty. It must be remembered that the heroism of the guerrilla warrior at this moment consists in the extent of his established ends and the enormous sacrifices he must make to achieve them.

These sacrifices will not be the daily combat, or face-to-face fighting with the enemy. They will take forms that are more subtle and more difficult to resist for the body and mind of the individual who is in the guerrilla movement.

These guerrillas will perhaps be severely punished by the enemy armies. Sometimes they will be divided into groups; those who have been made prisoners, martyrized; persecuted like hunted animals in those areas where they have chosen to operate, with the constant worry of having the enemy one step behind; with the constant distrust of everyone since the frightened peasants will hand them over, in some cases, to be rid of the repressive troops; with no other alternative but death or victory, at times when death is an ever present thought, and victory is the myth about which only a revolutionary can dream.

That is the heroism of the guerrilla. That is why it is said that walking is a form of fighting, that retreat from combat at a given moment is but another form of combat. Faced with the general superiority of the enemy, the plan is to find the tactical form of achieving a relative superiority at a selected point, whether it be to concentrate more effectives than the enemy, or to assure an advantage in making use of the terrain, thus upsetting the balance of forces. Under these conditions a tactical victory is assured. If the relative superiority is not clear, it is preferable not to act. Combat that will not lead to victory should not be carried out, as long as the "how" and the "when" can be chosen.

In the framework of the large political and military action of which it is a part, the guerrilla movement will grow and consolidate. Bases of support, a basic element for the prosperity of the guerrilla army, will then appear. These bases of support are points which the enemy's army can penetrate only with great losses. They are bastions of the revolution, the refuge and springboard of the guerrilla for excursions which are farther away and more daring.

This moment arrives if the tactical and political difficulties have been simultaneously overcome. The guerrillas can never forget their function as the vanguard of the people, a mandate which they personify, and consequently, they must create the necessary political conditions for the establishment of a revolutionary power based on the total support of the masses. The great claims of the peasants must be satisfied to the extent and in the way circumstances warrant, making the population a compact and decided unit.

If the military situation will be difficult at first, the political will be no less ticklish. And if one single military error can liquidate the guerrilla movement, a political error can stop its development for long periods.

The struggle is political and military. That is the way it must be waged and, consequently, understood.

The guerrilla movement, in its growth period, reaches a point where its capacity for action covers a specified region for which there is a surplus of men and an overconcentration in the zone. The bee swarming begins when one of the leaders, an outstanding guerrilla, moves to another region and repeats the chain of developments of guerrilla warfare, subject, of course, to a central command.

Now, it is necessary to point out that it is not possible to aspire to victory without the formation of a popular army. The guerrilla forces can expand only to a certain size; the popular forces in the cities and other penetrable zones of the enemy can inflict damages on him but the military potential of the reaction could still remain intact. It must always be remembered that the final result must be the annihilation of the enemy. Therefore, every new zone which is created, plus the zones of penetration of the enemy behind his lines, plus the forces that operate in the principal cities, must be subordinate to the [central] command. It cannot be claimed that the tight chain of command that characterizes an army exists, but certainly there must be a strategic chain of command. Within determined conditions of freedom of action, guerrilla units must obey all strategic orders from the central command, set up in one of the most secure and strongest posts, preparing the conditions for the union of the forces at a given moment.

Guerrilla warfare or war of liberation will, in general, have three stages: the first, a strategic defense, in which a small hunted force bites the enemy; it is not protected for a passive defense in a small circle, but its defense consists in limited attacks which it can carry out. After this, a state of equilibrium is reached in which the possibilities of action of the enemy and the guerrilla unit are stabilized; and later the final moment of overrunning the repressive army that will lead to the taking of the great cities, to the great decisive encounters, to the total annihilation of the enemy.

After the point of equilibrium is reached, when both forces respect one another, guerrilla warfare acquires new characteristics along the way of its development. The concept of the maneuver begins to appear. Large columns attack strong points. It is a war of movement with a transfer of forces and means of attack of relative strength. But, due to the capacity for resistance and counterattack that the enemy still has, this war of maneuvers does not definitely replace the guerrilla units. It is merely another way they act. It is a greater magnitude of the guerrilla forces until finally a popular army crystallizes into army corps. Even at this moment, marching at the head of the action of the main forces, the guerrilla units will go in their state of "purity," destroying communications, sabotaging the enemy's entire defensive apparatus.

We had predicted that the war would be continental. This means also that it will be prolonged; there will be many fronts, it will cost much blood, innumerable lives for a long time. But, even more, the phenomena of polarization of forces that are occurring in America, the clear division between exploiters and exploited that will exist in future revolutionary wars, means that when power is taken over by the armed vanguard of the people, the country, or countries, that obtain it will have liquidated simultaneously, in the oppressor, the imperialist and the national exploiters. The first stage of socialist revolution will have crystallized; the peoples will be ready to stanch their wounds and begin the construction of socialism.

Will there be other possibilities less bloody?

Sometime ago the last partition of the world was made in which the United States took for itself the lion's share of our continent; today the imperialists of the old world are expanding and the power of the European Common Market frightens the North Americans themselves. All this would seem to indicate that it would be possible to watch an inter-imperialist fight as a spectator and then to make gains, perhaps in alliance with the strongest national bourgeoisie. Without mentioning that a passive policy never brings good results in the class struggle, and alliances with the bourgeoisie, however revolutionary they may seem at a given moment, have only a transitory character, there are reasons of time that lead to taking another position. The sharpening of the fundamental contradiction appears to be so rapid in America that it is disturbing the "normal" development of the contradictions in the imperialist camp in the their struggle for markets.

Most of the national bourgeoisie have joined North American imperialism and must suffer the same fate as the latter in each country. Even in the cases where there are pacts or identity of contradictions between the nationalist bourgeoisie and other imperialisms with the North American, this happens in the framework of a fundamental struggle that necessarily, in the course of its development, will include *all the exploited and all the exploiters*. The polarization of antagonistic forces of class adversaries is, until now, more rapid than the development of the contradictions among the exploiters over the division of the spoils. There are two camps: the alternative is becoming clearer for each individual and for each special stratum of the population.

The Alliance for Progess is an attempt to check the uncheckable.

But if the advance of the European Common Market, or any other imperialist group, on the American markets were more rapid than the development of the fundamental contradiction, the only thing remaining would be to introduce the popular forces as a wedge into the open breach, the latter leading the entire struggle and using the new intruders with full awareness of their final intentions.

Not one position, not one weapon, not one secret can be surrendered to the class enemy, under pain of losing all.

In fact, the birth of the American struggle has begun. Will its vortex be in Venezuela, Guatemala, Colombia, Peru, or Ecuador . . . ? Will these present skirmishes be only manifestations of an unrest that does not bear fruit? It does not matter what may be the outcome of today's struggle. It does not matter, for the final result, that one movement or another may be momentarily defeated. What counts is the decision to struggle that ripens day by day; the awareness of the need for revolutionary change, the certainty of its possibility.

This is a prediction. We make it with the conviction that history will prove us right. The analysis of objective and subjective factors of America and of the imperialist world indicate to us the certainty of these statements based on the Second Declaration of Havana.

PROLOGUE TO GENERAL GIAP'S BOOK 5

China's Mao Tse-tung, Viet Nam's Vo Nguyen Giap, and Cuba's Ernesto Guevara rank as the leading warrior-theoreticians of communism. The prologue to the Cuban edition of Giap's book, *People's War, People's Army*, is a unique and interesting document in that it is one of the rare instances in which one of these men discusses the work and writings of one of the others. Guevara's comments on Giap are, naturally, entirely complimentary, but nevertheless of value in that they—to use a favorite Guevara word—"synthesize" the thinking of both men in regard to un-conventional warfare, for which they prefer the semantic label "people's war." "People's war," to Guevara, is basically rural, or guerrilla, warfare. In what was once French Indochina, the struggle at first included "the entire people," and this, in Guevara's view, was not particularly good, but "little by little the opposing camps were defined, and thus began the anti-feudal struggle, achieving then its true anti-imperialist, anti-colonialist, anti-feudal character, resulting in the establishment of a so-cialist revolution." In the Communist view, nationalism—the ousting of the French from Indochina—was less important than the setting up of a Communist state. Guevara discusses the tactics of guerrilla warfare—the need for "mobility" and "dynamism," the use of "armed propaganda," the creation of "self-defense" zones—and he draws parallels between the guerrilla campaigns in Indochina and Cuba.

PROLOGUE BY GUEVARA TO THE BOOK
"PEOPLE'S WAR, PEOPLE'S ARMY"

W E CONSIDER IT a high honor to write the prologue for this book based on the writings of General Vo Nguyen Giap, present Deputy Prime Minister, Minister of National Defense, and Commander in Chief of the Popular Army of the Democratic Republic of Viet Nam. General Giap speaks with the authority conferred by his long personal experience and that of the Party in the battle for liberation. The book, which has in itself permanent actuality, has even more interest, if possible, due to the tumultuous series of events which have occurred in recent times in that region of Asia, and due to the controversies which have arisen regarding the adequate use of armed struggle as a means of resolving the insolvable contradictions between exploiters and the exploited under certain historic conditions.

The battles which were fought successfully for long years by the heroic armies and the entire people of Viet Nam are now being repeated; South Viet Nam is on a war footing; that part of the country snatched away from its legitimate owner, the Vietnamese people, is ever closer to victory. Even while the imperialist enemies threaten to send thousands of men, the outlaws speak of using the tactical atomic bomb, and General Taylor is named Ambassador in the so-called "Republic of South Viet Nam" and, tacitly, Commander-in-Chief of the armies that will try to liquidate the people's war, nothing will prevent the defeat of these armies. Very nearby, in Laos, civil war has been ignited, also provoked by the maneuvers of the North Americans, supported in one way or another by their usual allies; and the neutral kingdom of Cambodia, a part, like its brothers Laos and Viet Nam, of what was previously called French Indochina, is subject to violations of its borders and to permanent attacks due to its righteous position in defending its neutrality and its right to live as a sovereign nation.

Because of all this, the book for which we write the prologue goes beyond the limits of a set historic episode and acquires meaning for the entire area; but, in addition, the problems which it delineates have particular importance for the greater portion of the peoples of Latin America subjected to the domination of North American imperialism. And this is apart from the fact that knowledge of this book would be of extraordinary interest for the peoples of Africa who day after day engage in struggles ever more difficult—but also repeatedly victorious—against the different kinds of colonialists.

Viet Nam has special characteristics: a very old civilization and a long tradition as an independent kingdom with its own peculiarities and autochthonic culture. Within its millenary history, the French colonial period was hardly a drop of water. Nevertheless, the country's fundamental qualities and the opposing qualities of the aggressor are the same, in general terms, as the insolvable contradictions that are present in the entire dependent world. The manner of resolving these contradictions is the same, too. Cuba, without knowing these writings nor others on the same subject which had been written on the experiences of the Chinese revolution, set out on the path toward its liberation through similar methods, with the resultant success that is today visible to all.

This book, therefore, brings up questions of general interest for the world battling for its liberation. These can be summarized thus: The feasibility of armed conflict in special conditions in which the pacific methods of liberation struggle have failed; and the type of struggle that should be adopted in places with great expanses of terrain favorable to guerrilla warfare and having a majority or an important peasant population.

Although the book is based on a compilation of articles, it has a good narrative thread, and certain repetitions do no more than give greater vigor to the whole.

The book deals with the liberation war of the Vietnamese people; of the definition of that struggle as a people's war and of its operating arm as a people's army; of the interpretation of the great experiences of the Party in the direction of armed struggle and the organization of the revolutionary armed forces. The last chapter deals with the conclusive episode of the conflict, Dienbienphu, in which the liberation forces now have gained in quality and pass to a war of positions, defeating the imperialist enemy in that type of war, as well.

The book begins by telling how, after the end of the world war with the triumph of the Soviet Union and of the Western allied powers, France mocked all agreements and took all of Viet Nam to a situation of extreme tension. The peaceful and rational methods of resolving controversies were proving to be useless, and so the people took the path of armed struggle. In this, because of the characteristics of the country, the main burden fell on the rural population. It was a typically peasant war because of the nature of the places of action and the special composition of the army, but it was directed by the ideology of the proletariat, thus once more validating the worker-peasant alliance as the basic factor of victory. In the first moments, however, because of the characteristics of an anti-colonialist and anti-imperialist struggle, this was a war of the entire people, and a great number of persons whose origins did not fit exactly into the classic definitions of the poor peasant or of the worker also incorporated themselves into the struggle for liberation. Little by little the opposing camps were defined, and thus began the anti-feudal struggle, achieving then its true anti-imperialist, anti-colonialist, anti-feudal character, and resulting in the establishment of a socialist revolution.

Mass struggle was utilized during the entire course of the war by the Vietnamese Party. It was utilized, in the first place, because guerrilla warfare is but an expression of mass struggle, and cannot be given consideration if it is isolated from its natural medium, the people. Guerrillas mean, in this case, the numerically inferior vanguard of the great majority of the people who do not have weapons but who through this means express their will to triumph. Mass struggle was also utilized in the cities at all moments as an indispensable weapon in the development of the conflict. It is very important to state that never during the course of the action for the liberation of the Vietnamese people did the mass struggle give up any of its rights in order to receive certain concessions from the regime; it did not discuss mutual concessions, but rather stated the necessity of obtaining specified liberties and guarantees, without making any counter-offers, thus avoiding, in many sectors, having the war become even more cruel than the French colonialists were making it. This significance of the mass struggle in its dynamic character, without compromises, makes understanding of the problem of the struggle for liberation in Latin America fundamentally important.

Marxism was, therefore, applied to the concrete historic situation of Viet Nam, and that is why, guided by a vanguard Party loyal to its people and in accord with its doctrine, so celebrated a victory was achieved against the imperialists.

The characteristics of the struggle made it a prolonged war: there were fluctuations, rising and ebbing tides, territory had to be yielded, and many years went by before the final victorious result.

During the entire course of the struggle it could be said that the front was where the enemy was. At first the enemy occupied almost the entire country, and the front spread to wherever he was. Later there occurred a delimitation of lines of combat and there was a principal front, although the enemy rearguard constantly constituted another area for the combatant bands. Therefore the war was total and the colonialists could never comfortably mobilize their soldiers of aggression from a secure base against the liberated zones.

The watchwords, "dynamism, initiative, mobility, rapid decisions in the face of new situations," are the total synthesis of guerrilla tactics, and in those few words is expressed all the very difficult art of popular war.

At certain moments the new guerrillas, in arms under the leadership of the Party, were still in places where French penetration was very strong and the population was terrorized. In those cases, they constantly carried out what the Vietnamese call "armed propaganda." Armed propaganda is simply the presence in certain places of liberation forces who demonstrate their power and their fighting spirit while submerged in the great sea of people, like fish in water. Armed propaganda, upon perpetuating itself in a zone, catalyzed the masses with its presence and immediately revolutionized the region, adding new territories to those already obtained by the people's army. Thus it was that the guerrilla bases and zones proliferated in all Vietnamese territory. The tactic, in this case, was summed up in a principle expressed this way: If the enemy concentrates, it loses terrain; if it spreads out, it loses strength. When the enemy concentrates in order to hit hard, there must be counterattacks in all the places where he ceased dispersing his forces. If the enemy again occupies certain places with small groups, the counterattack will be made in accordance with the existing correlation in each place—the basic shock force of the enemy, however, will have been weakened once more. This is another of the fundamental lessons of the liberation war of the Vietnamese people.

The struggle has passed through three stages which characterize, in general, the development of a people's war. The struggle begins with small guerrilla groups which have great mobility and are completely concealable in the physical and human geography of the region. Upon the passage of time, quantitative processes take place that, at a given moment, lead to the great qualitative jump to the war of movements. Here the groups that act are more compact, controlling entire zones. Although their means are greater and their capacity for striking the enemy is much stronger, mobility is their fundamental characteristic. After another period of time, when conditions ripen, the final stage of the struggle is reached in which the army consolidates and even goes into a war of positions, as happened at Dienbienphu, the final kick to the colonial dictatorship.

In the course of the conflict—developing dialectically until it culminates in the attack on Dienbienphu, in a war of positions—zones liberated or semi-liberated from the enemy are created which constitute self-defense territories. Self-defense is conceived by the Vietnamese also in an active sense as participation in a unitary struggle against the enemy;

the self-defense zones can defend themselves against limited attacks, supply men to the people's army, maintain internal security in the region, maintain production, and assure supplies for the front. Self-defense is nothing more than a minimal part of the whole, with special characteristics; a self-defense zone can never be conceived as a whole in itself, that is to say, a region where the popular forces attempt to defend themselves from the enemy's attack while all the territory outside of said zone remains calm. If that were to happen, the focus would be localized, torn apart, and demolished, unless it went immediately into the first phase of people's war, that is, into guerrilla warfare.

As we have already said, the entire process of the Vietnamese struggle should have been based fundamentally on the peasantry. At first, though, without a clear definition of the lines of struggle, the war was carried out solely in the interests of national liberation. Little by little, however, the camps were defined, the struggle was transformed into a typical peasant war, and the agrarian reform was established in the course of the conflict when the antagonisms became more profound, as did in turn the power of the people's army. That is the mark of class struggle within a society at war. The struggle was directed by the Party with the aim of annulling the largest possible number of enemies and of utilizing to the maximum the contradictions between colonialism and its less resolute friends. Thus, making opportune use of the contradictions, the Party could take advantage of all the forces emanating from these clashes and achieve victory in the least possible time.

Compañero Vo Nguyen Giap also tells us of the tight bond which exists between the Party and the army—how, in this struggle, the army is but a component of the guiding Party of the struggle. He tells of the tight bond which exists in turn between the army and the people; how army and people are but the same thing, which once again is seen corroborated in the magnificent synthesis stated by Camilo: "The army is the people uniformed." The armed corps, during the conflict and after it, has had to acquire new abilities which permit it to overcome the new weapons of the enemy and to repulse any kind of offensive.

The revolutionary soldier has a conscientious discipline. Throughout the entire process he is characterized fundamentally by his self-discipline. In turn, within the people's army, while respecting all the rules of the military codes, there should be great internal democracy and great equality in the procurement of the goods necessary for the man in battle.

In all these statements, General Nguyen Giap points out what we know through our own experience, experience that we gained some years after the Vietnamese popular forces achieved their triumph. Our experience, however, reinforces the concept of the necessity for profound analysis of the historic processes of the present moment. This should be done in the light of Marxism, utilizing all its creative capacity in order to be able to adapt it to the changing circumstances of countries which differ in all the exterior aspects of their conformation but are alike in their colonized structure, with the existence of oppressive imperialist powers and of classes associated with those powers through very tight bonds. After an accurate analysis, General Giap reaches the following conclusion: "In the present state of the world, a nation, although it be small and weak, which rises in arms as one man under the direction of the working class in order to resolutely battle for its independence and for democracy, has the moral and material potential to defeat all aggressors, no matter who they are. Under certain historical conditions, this struggle for national liberation may go through an armed conflict of long duration, with prolonged resistance, in order to achieve triumph."

These words synthesize the general characteristics that the war of liberation ought to assume in dependent territories.

We believe that the best statement to conclude the prologue is the same one used by the editors of this book and with which we agree: "We hope that all our friends who, like ourselves, still suffer the attacks and the threats of imperialism can find in *People's War, People's Army* what we ourselves have found: new reasons for faith and hope."

SPEECH BEFORE THE UNITED NATIONS 6

Guevara had moved from the Cuban stage to international conferences for the expression of his views, and now, late in 1964, he used the United Nations itself as a sounding-board. He utilized the opportunity to cover a wide spectrum of topics dealing with Cuba's foreign relations— Guevara, the international revolutionist, giving his views before the entire world. He assailed—inevitably—the United States, he called for the seating of Communist China at the United Nations, he talked of Laos and Basutoland, of Taiwan and Costa Rica, of Puerto Rico and Viet Nam. Guevara even touched on the Negro problem in the United States, stating that the day would come when the General Assembly would "demand guarantees from the United States Government for the lives of the Negro and Latin American populations that reside in that country." Guevara deftly managed to place Cuba ideologically within both the Communist and non-aligned camps, at the same time dutifully echoing the claims of both to being "partisans" of peace. He asserted:

> We want to build socialism; we have declared ourselves partisans of those who strive for peace; we have declared ourselves as falling within the group of nonaligned countries although we are Marxist-Leninists, because the nonaligned countries, like ourselves, fight imperialism.

He failed to indicate how nations could be fighting and "nonaligned" at the same time.

SPEECH DELIVERED BY GUEVARA
BEFORE THE GENERAL ASSEMBLY OF THE UNITED
NATIONS ON DECEMBER 11, 1964

Mr. President,
Messrs. Delegates,

THE CUBAN DELEGATION to this Assembly has pleasure, first of all, in fulfilling the pleasant duty of welcoming three new nations to the large number of nations whose representatives are discussing the problems of the world. We therefore greet through their Presidents and Prime Ministers the people of Zambia, Malawi, and Malta, and express the hope that from the outset these countries will be added to the group of nonaligned countries which struggle against imperialism, colonialism, and neocolonialism.

We also wish to convey our congratulations to the President of this Assembly whose elevation to so high a post is of special significance since it reflects this new historic stage of resounding triumphs for the peoples of Africa, until recently subject to the colonial system of imperialism, and, today, in their immense majority, in the legitimate exercise of self-determination, have become citizens of sovereign States. The last hour of colonialism has struck and millions of inhabitants of Africa, Asia, and Latin America rise to meet a new life and assert their unrestricted right to self-determination and to the independent development of their nations.

We wish you, Mr. President, the greatest success in the tasks entrusted to you by Member States.

Cuba comes here to state its position on the most important controversial issues and will do so with the full sense of responsibility which the use of this rostrum implies, while at the same time responding to the unavoidable duty of speaking out clearly and frankly.

We should like to see this Assembly shake itself out of complacency and move forward. We should like to see the Committees begin their work and not stop at the first confrontation. Imperialism wishes to convert this meeting into an aimless oratorical tournament, instead of using it to solve the grave problems of the world. We must prevent their doing so. This Assembly should not be remembered in the future only by the number 19 which identifies it.

Our efforts are geared to obtain that goal. We feel that we have the right and the obligation to try to make this meeting effective because our country is a constant point of friction; one of the places where the principles supporting the rights of small nations to sovereignty are tested day by day, minute by minute; and at the same time our country is one of the barricades of freedom in the world, situated a few steps from United States imperialism, showing with its actions, its daily example, that people can liberate themselves, can keep themselves free, in the existing conditions of the world.

Of course, there is now a socialist camp which becomes stronger day by day and has more powerful weapons of struggle. But, additional conditions are required for survival: the maintenance of internal cohesion, faith in one's destiny, and the irreversible decision to fight to the death for the defense of one's country and revolution. These conditions exist in Cuba.

Of all the burning problems to be dealt with by this Assembly, one which has special significance for us and whose solution we feel must be sought first, so as to leave no doubt in the minds of anyone, is that of peaceful coexistence among States with different economic and social systems. Much progress has been made in the world in this field. But, imperialism, particularly United States imperialism, has tried to make the world believe that peaceful coexistence is the exclusive right of the great powers on earth. We repeat what our President said in Cairo, and which later took shape in the Declaration of the Second Conference of Heads of State or Government of Nonaligned Countries: that there cannot be peaceful coexistence only among the powerful if we are to ensure world peace. Peaceful coexistence must be practiced by all States, independent of size, of the previous historic relations that linked them, and of the problems that may arise among some of them at a given moment.

At present, the type of peaceful coexistence to which we aspire does not exist in many cases. The Kingdom of Cambodia, merely because it maintained a neutral attitude and did not submit to the machinations of United States imperialism has been subjected to all kinds of treacherous and brutal attacks from the Yankee bases in South Viet Nam.

Laos, a divided country, has also been the object of imperialist aggressions of every kind. The conventions concluded at Geneva have been violated, Laos' people have been massacred from the air, and part of its territory is in constant danger from cowardly attacks by imperialist forces.

The Democratic Republic of Viet Nam, which knows the histories of aggressions as few people on earth, once again has seen its frontier violated, its installations attacked by enemy bomber and fighter planes, its naval posts attacked by United States warships violating territorial waters.

At this moment there hangs over the Democratic Republic of Viet Nam the threat that the United States warmongers may openly extend to its territory the war that, for many years, they have been waging against the people of South Viet Nam.

The Soviet Union and the People's Republic of China have given serious warning to the United States. Not only the peace of the world is in danger in this situation, but also the lives of millions of human beings in this part of Asia are being constantly threatened and subjected to the whim of the United States invader.

Peaceful coexistence has also been put to the test in a brutal manner in Cyprus, due to pressures from the Turkish Government and NATO, compelling the people and the Government of Cyprus to make a firm and heroic stand in defense of their sovereignty.

In all these parts of the world imperialism attempts to impose its version of what coexistence should be. It is the oppressed peoples in alliance with the socialist camp which must show the meaning of true coexistence, and it is the obligation of the United Nations to support them.

We must also say that it is not only in relations between sovereign States that the concept of peaceful coexistence must be clearly defined. As Marxists we have maintained that peaceful coexistence among nations does not encompass coexistence between the exploiters and the exploited, the oppressor and the oppressed.

Furthermore, a principle proclaimed by this Organization is the right to full independence, as against all forms of colonial oppression. That is why we express our solidarity with the colonial peoples of so-called Portuguese Guinea, Angola, and Mozambique, who have been massacred for the crime of demanding their freedom, and we are prepared to help them to the extent of our ability in accordance with the Cairo Declaration.

We express our solidarity with the people of Puerto Rico and its great leader, Pedro Albizu Campos, who has been set free in another act of hypocrisy, at the age of seventy-two, after spending a lifetime in gaol, now paralytic and almost without the ability to speak. Albizu Campos is a symbol of the still unredeemed but indomitable America. Years and years of prison, almost unbearable pressures in gaol, mental torture, solitude, total isolation from his people and his family, the insolence of the conqueror and lackeys in the land of his birth: nothing at all broke his will. The delegation of Cuba, on behalf of its people, pays a tribute of admiration and gratitude to a patriot who bestows honor upon America.

The North Americans for many years have tried to convert Puerto Rico into a reflection of hybrid culture—the Spanish language with an

English inflection, the Spanish language with hinges on its backbone, the better to bend before the United States soldier. Puerto Rican soldiers have been used as cannon-fodder in imperialist wars, as in Korea, and even have been made to fire at their own brothers, as in the massacre perpetrated by the United States army a few months ago against the helpless people of Panama—one of the most recent diabolical acts carried out by Yankee imperialism. Yet, despite that terrible attack against their will and their historic destiny, the people of Puerto Rico have preserved their culture, their Latin character, their national feelings, which, in themselves, give proof of the implacable will for independence that exists among the masses on the Latin American island.

We must also point out that the principle of peaceful coexistence does not imply a mockery of the will of the peoples, as is happening in the case of so-called British Guiana. Here the Government of Prime Minister Cheddi Jagan has been the victim of every kind of pressure and maneuver while the achievement of independence has been delayed by the search for methods that would allow for the flouting of the will of the people. They want to ensure the docility of a government different from the present one, put in by underhanded tactics, later to grant a curtailed freedom to this piece of American soil. Whatever roads Guiana may be compelled to follow to obtain independence, the moral and militant support of Cuba goes to its people.

Furthermore, we must point out that the islands of Guadaloupe and Martinique have been fighting for a long time for their autonomy without obtaining it. This state of affairs must not continue.

Once again we raise our voice to put the world on guard against what is happening in South Africa. The brutal policy of "apartheid" is being carried out before the eyes of the whole world. The people of Africa are being compelled to tolerate in that continent the concept, still official, of the superiority of one race over another, and in the name of that racial superiority the murdering of people with impunity. Can the United Nations do nothing to prevent this? I should like specifically to refer to the painful case of the Congo, unique in the history of the modern world, which shows how, with absolute impunity, with the most insolent cynicism the rights of peoples can be flouted. The prodigious wealth of the Congo, which the imperialist nations wish to maintain under their control, is the direct reason for this. In his speech on his first visit to the United Nations, Compañero Fidel Castro, said that the whole problem of coexistence among peoples was reduced to the illicit appropriation of another's wealth. He said: "When this philosophy of despoilment disappears, the philosophy of war will have disappeared." The philosophy of despoilment not only has not ceased, but rather it is stronger than ever, and that is why those who used the name of the United Nations to commit the murder of Lumumba, today in the name of the defense of the white race are assassinating thousands of Congolese. How can one forget how the hope that Patrice Lumumba placed in the United Nations was betrayed? How can one forget the machinations and maneuvers which followed in the wake of the occupation of that country by United Nations troops, under whose auspices the assassins of this great African patriot acted with impunity? How can we forget that he who flouted the authority of the United Nations in the Congo, and not exactly for patriotic reasons, but rather by virtue of conflicts between imperialists, was Moise Tshombe, who initiated the secession in Katanga with Belgian support? And how can one justify, how can one explain that at the end of all United Nations activities there, Tshombe, dislodged from Katanga, returned as lord and master of the Congo? Who can deny the abject role that the imperialists compelled the United Nations to play?

To sum up, dramatic mobilizations were made to avoid the secession of Katanga, but today that same Katanga is in power, the wealth of the Congo is in imperialist hands and the expenses must be paid by honest nations. The merchants of war certainly do good business. That is why the Government of Cuba supports the just attitude of the Soviet Union in refusing to pay the expenses of this crime.

And, if this were not enough, we now have flung in our faces recent events which have filled the world with horror and indignation. Who are the perpetrators? Belgian paratroopers, transported by United States planes, who took off from British bases. We remember as if it were yesterday that we saw a small country in Europe, a civilized and industrious country, the Kingdom of Belgium, invaded by the hordes of Hitler. We learned with bitterness about these people being massacred by the German imperialists, and our sympathy and affection went out to them. But the other side of the imperialist coin many did not then perceive. Perhaps the sons of Belgian patriots who died defending their country are now assassinating thousands of Congolese in the name of the white race, just as they suffered under the German heel because their blood was not purely Aryan. But the scales have fallen from our eyes and they are now open upon new horizons and we can see what yesterday, in our conditions of colonial servitude, we could not observe—that "Western civilization" disguises under its showy front a scene of hyenas and jackals. That is the only name that can be applied to those who have gone to fulfill "humanitarian" tasks in the Congo. Bloodthirsty butchers who feed on helpless people! That is what imperialism does to men; that is what marks the "white" imperialists. The free men of the world must be prepared to avenge the crime committed in the Congo. It is possible that many of those soldiers who were converted into "sub-men" by imperialist machinery believe in good faith that they are defending the rights of a superior race, but in this Assembly those peoples whose skins are darkened by a different sun, colored by different pigments, constitute the majority, and they fully and clearly understand that the difference between men does not lie in the color of their skins, but in the ownership of the means of production and in the relationships of production.

The Cuban delegation extends greetings to the peoples of Southern Rhodesia and South-West Africa, oppressed by white colonialist minorities; to the peoples of Basutoland, Bechuanaland, Swaziland, French Somaliland, the Arabs of Palestine, Aden and the Protectorates, Oman, and to all peoples in conflict with imperialism and colonialism; and we reaffirm our support.

I express also the hope that there will be a just solution to the conflict facing our sister republic of Indonesia in its relations with Malaysia.

Mr. President, one of the essential items before this conference is general and complete disarmament. We express our support of general and complete disarmament. Furthermore, we advocate the complete destruction of thermonuclear devices and the holding of a conference of all the nations of the world in order to fulfill this aspiration of all peoples. In his statement before this Assembly, our Prime Minister said that arms races have always led to war. There are new atomic powers in the world, and the possibilities of a confrontation are grave.

We feel that a conference is necessary to obtain the total destruction of thermonuclear weapons and, as a first step, the total prohibition of tests. At the same time, there must be clearly established the obligation of all States to respect the present frontiers of other States and to refrain from indulging in any aggression, even with conventional weapons.

In adding our voice to that of all peoples of the world who plead for general and complete disarmament, the destruction of all atomic arsenals, the complete cessation of thermonuclear devices, and atomic tests of any kind, we feel it necessary to stress, furthermore, that the territorial integrity of nations must be respected and the armed hand of imperialism, no less dangerous with conventional weapons, must be held back. Those who murdered thousands of defenseless citizens in the Congo did not use atomic weapons. They used conventional weapons, and it was conventional weapons, used by imperialists, which caused so many deaths.

Even if the measures advocated here were to become effective, thus making it unnecessary to say the following, we must still point out that we cannot adhere to any regional pact for denuclearization so long as the United States maintains aggressive bases on our territory, in Puerto Rico, and in Panama, and in other American states where it feels it has the right to station them without any restrictions on conventional or nuclear weapons. This, apart from the recent resolutions of the Organization of American States against Cuba, which, on the basis of the Treaty of Rio, might permit aggression. If such a conference to which we have just referred should achieve all these objectives—which, unfortunately, would be rather difficult to do—it would be one of the most important developments in the history of mankind. To ensure this, the People's Republic of China must be represented, and that is why such a conference must be held. But it would be much simpler for the peoples of the world to recognize the undeniable truth that the People's Republic of China exists, that its rulers are the only representatives of the Chinese people, and to give it the place it deserves, which is, at present, usurped by a clique which controls the province of Taiwan with United States aid.

The problem of the representation of China in the United Nations cannot, in any way, be considered as a case of a new admission to the Organization, but rather as the restitution of their legitimate rights to the people of the People's Republic of China.

We repudiate strongly the concept of "two Chinas." The Chiang Kai-Shek clique of Taiwan cannot remain in the United Nations. It must be expelled and the legitimate representative of the Chinese people put in.

We warn, also, against the insistence of the United States Government in presenting the problem of the legitimate representation of China in the United Nations as an "important question" so as to require a two-thirds majority of Members present and voting.

The admission of the People's Republic of China to the United Nations is, in fact, an important question for the entire world, but not for the mechanics of the United Nations, where it must constitute a mere question of procedure.

Thus will justice be done, but almost as important as attaining justice would be the fact that it would be demonstrated, once and for all, that this august Assembly uses its eyes to see, its ears to hear, its own tongue to speak with, and correct judgment to make decisions.

The proliferation of atomic weapons among the member States of NATO and, especially, the possession of these devices of mass destruction by the Federal Republic of Germany would make the possibility of an agreement on disarmament even more remote, and linked to such an agreement is the problem of the peaceful reunification of Germany. So long as there is no clear understanding, the existence of two Germanys must be recognized: that of the Democratic Republic of Germany and the Federal Republic. The German problem can only be solved with the direct participation of the Democratic Republic of Germany with full rights in negotiations.

We shall touch lightly on the question of economic development and international trade, which takes up a good part of the agenda. This year, 1964, the Conference of Geneva was held and a multitude of matters relating to these aspects of international relations were dealt with. The warnings and forecasts of our delegations have been clearly confirmed, to the misfortune of the economically dependent countries.

We wish only to point out that insofar as Cuba is concerned the United States of America has not implemented the explicit recommendations of that Conference, and recently the United States Government also prohibited the sale of medicine to Cuba, thus divesting itself, once and for all, of the mask of humanitarianism with which it attempted to disguise the aggressive nature of its blockade against the people of Cuba.

Futhermore we once more state that these colonial machinations which impede the development of the peoples are not only expressed in political relations. The so-called deterioration of the terms of trade is nothing less than the result of the unequal exchange between countries producing raw materials and industrial countries which dominate markets and impose the apparent "justice" of an equitable exchange of values.

So long as the economically dependent peoples do not free themselves from the capitalist markets and, as a bloc with the Socialist countries, impose new terms of trade between the exploited and the exploiters, there will be no sound economic development and, in certain cases, there will be retrogression, the weak countries again falling under the political domination of imperialists and colonialists.

Finally, it must be made clear that, in the area of the Caribbean, maneuvers and preparations for aggression against Cuba are taking place; off the coast of Nicaragua above all, in Costa Rica also, in the Panama Canal Zone, in the Vieques Islands of Puerto Rico, in Florida, and possibly in other parts of the territory of the United States and, perhaps, also in Honduras, Cuban mercenaries are training, as well as mercenaries of other nationalities, with a purpose that cannot be peaceful.

After an open scandal, the Government of Costa Rica—it is said—has ordered the elimination of all training fields for Cuban exiles in that country. No one knows whether this attitude is sincere, or whether it is simply a maneuver because the mercenaries training there are about to commit some offense. We hope that full cognizance will be taken of the actual existence of those bases for aggression, which we denounced long ago, and that the world will think about the international responsibility of the government of a country which authorizes and facilitates the training of mercenaries to attack Cuba.

We must point out that news of the training of mercenaries at different places in the Caribbean and the participation of the United States Government in such acts is news that appears openly in United States newspapers. We know of no Latin American voice that has been raised officially in protest against this. This shows the cynicism with which the United States moves its pawns.

The shrewd Foreign Ministers of the OAS had eyes to "see" Cuban emblems and find "irrefutable proof" in the Yankee weapons displayed by Venezuela, but do not see the preparations for aggression in the United States, just as they did not hear the voice of President Kennedy, who explicitly declared himself to be the aggressor against Cuba at Playa Girón. In some cases, it is a blindness provoked by the hatred of the ruling classes of the Latin American people against our revolution; in others, and these are even more deplorable, it is the result of the blinding light of Mammon.

As everyone knows, after the terrible upheaval called the "Caribbean crisis," the United States went into certain commitments with the Soviet Union which culminated in the withdrawal of certain types of weapons that the continued aggressions of that country—such as the mercenary attack against Playa Girón and threats of invasion against our country —had compelled us to install in Cuba as a legitimate act of defense.

The Americans claimed, furthermore, that the United States should inspect our territory, which we refused emphatically since Cuba does not recognize the right of the United States, or of anyone else in the world, to determine what type of weapons Cuba may maintain within its borders.

In this connection we would only abide by multilateral agreements, with equal obligations for all parties concerned. Fidel Castro declared that "so long as the concept of sovereignty exists as the prerogative of nations and of independent peoples, and as a right of all peoples, we shall not accept the exclusion of our people from that right; so long as the world is governed by these principles, so long as the world is governed by those concepts which have universal validity because they are universally accepted by peoples, we shall not accept the attempt to deprive us of any of those rights and we shall renounce none of those rights."

The Secretary-General of the United Nations, U Thant, understood our reasons. Nevertheless, the United States presumed to establish a new prerogative, an arbitrary and illegal one, that of violating the air space of any small country. Thus, we see crossing over our country U-2 aircraft and other types of espionage apparatus which fly in our airspace with impunity. We have issued all the necessary warnings that these violations cease, as well as the provocations of the American navy against our sentry posts in the zone of Guantanamo, the "buzzing" by aircraft over our ships or ships of other nationalities in international waters, the piratical attacks against ships sailing under different flags, and the infiltration of spies, saboteurs, and weapons in our island.

We want to build socialism; we have declared ourselves partisans of those who strive for peace; we have declared ourselves as falling within the group of nonaligned countries although we are Marxist-Leninists, because the nonaligned countries, like ourselves, fight imperialism. We want peace; we want to build a better life for our people, and that is why we avoid answering, so far as possible, the planned provocations of the Yankees. But we know the mentality of their rulers; they want to make us pay a very high price for that peace. We reply that that price cannot go beyond the bounds of dignity.

And Cuba reaffirms once again the right to maintain on its territory the weapons it wishes and its refusal to recognize the right of any power on earth—no matter how powerful—to violate our soil, our territorial waters, or our airspace.

If, in any assembly, Cuba assumes obligations of a collective nature, it will fulfill them to the letter. So long as this does not happen, Cuba maintains all its rights, just as any other nation.

In the face of the demands of imperialism, our Prime Minister posed the five necessary points for the existence of a sound peace in the Caribbean. They are as follows:

1. Cessation of the economic blockade and all economic and trade pressures by the United States in all parts of the world against our country.

2. Cessation of all subversive activities, launching and landing of weapons and explosives by air and sea, organization of mercenary invasions, infiltration of spies and saboteurs, all of which are carried out from the territory of the United States and some accomplice countries.

3. Cessation of piratical attacks carried out from bases in the United States and Puerto Rico.

4. Cessation of all the violations of our airspace and our territorial waters by aircraft and warships of the United States.

5. Withdrawal from the Guantánamo naval base and restitution of the Cuban territory occupied by the United States.

None of these fundamental demands has been met, and our forces are still being provoked from the naval base of Guantánamo. That base has become a nest of malefactors and the point from which they are introduced into our territory.

We would bore this Assembly were we to give a detailed account of the large number of provocations of all kinds. Suffice it to say that, including the first days of December, the number amounts to 1,323 in 1964 alone. The list covers minor provocations such as violation of the dividing line, launching of objects from the territory controlled by the North Americans, the commission of acts of sexual exhibitionism by North Americans of both sexes, verbal insults; others which are graver such as shooting off of small-caliber weapons, the manipulation of weapons directed against our territory and offenses against our flag. The more serious provocations are those of crossing the dividing line and starting fires in installations on the Cuban side, seventy-eight rifle shots this year, and the death of Ramón López Peña, a soldier, from two shots fired from the United States post three and a half kilometers from the coast on the boundary to the northwest. This grave provocation took place at 19:07 hours on July 19, 1964, and our Prime Minister publicly stated on July 26 that, if the event were to recur, he woud give orders for our troops to repel the aggression. At the same time orders were given for the withdrawal of the advance line of Cuban forces to positions farther away from the dividing line and construction of the necessary casements.

One thousand three hundred and twenty-three provocations in 340 days amount to approximately four per day. Only a perfectly disciplined army with a morale such as ours could resist so many hostile acts without losing its self-control.

Forty-seven countries, which met at the Second Conference of Heads of State or Government of the Nonaligned Countries at Cairo, unanimously agreed that:

> The Conference, noting with concern that foreign military bases are, in practice, a means of bringing pressure on nations and retarding their emancipation and development based on their own ideological, political, economic and cultural ideas, declares its full support to the countries that are seeking to secure the evacuation of foreign bases on their territory and calls upon all States maintaining troops and bases in other countries to remove them forthwith.
>
> The Conference considers that the maintenance at Guantánamo (Cuba) of a military base of the United States of America, in defiance of the will of the Government and people of Cuba and in defiance of the provisions embodied in the Declaration of the Belgrade Conference, constitutes a violation of Cuba's sovereignty and territorial integrity.

Noting that the Cuban Government expresses its readiness to settle its dispute over the base at Guantánamo with the United States on an equal footing, the Conference urges the United States Government to start negotiations with the Cuban Government for the evacuation of this base.

The Government of the United States has not responded to the above request of the Cairo Conference and presumes to maintain indefinitely its occupation by force of a piece of our territory from which it carries out acts of aggression such as those we mentioned earlier.

The Organization of American States—also called by the people the United States Ministry of Colonies—condemned us "vigorously" although it had excluded us from its midst, and ordered its members to break off diplomatic and trade relations with Cuba. The OAS authorized aggression against our country at any time under any pretext, violating the most fundamental international laws and completely disregarding the United Nations. Uruguay, Bolivia, Chile, and Mexico opposed that measure, and the Government of the United States of Mexico refused to comply with the sanctions that had been approved. Since then we have had no relations with any Latin American countries other than Mexico; thus the imperialists have carried out one of the stages preliminary to a plan of direct aggression.

We want to point out once again that our concern over Latin America is based on the ties that link us—the language we speak, our culture, and the common master we shared. But we have no other reason for desiring the liberation of Latin America from the colonial yoke of the United States. If any of the Latin American countries here decides to re-establish relations with Cuba, we shall be prepared to do so on the basis of equality, not with the idea that it is a gift to our Government that we be recognized as a free country in the world, because we won the recognition of our freedom with our blood in the days of our struggles for liberation. We acquired it with our blood in the defense of our shores against the Yankee invasion.

Although we reject any attempt to attribute to us interference in the internal affairs of other countries, we cannot deny that we sympathize with those people who strive for their freedom, and we must fulfill the obligation of our Government and people to state clearly and categorically to the world that we morally support and feel as one with people anywhere who struggle to make a reality of the rights of full sovereignty proclaimed in the United Nations Charter.

It is the United States of America which intervenes. It has done so throughout history in America. Since the end of the last century Cuba has known very well the truth of the matter; but it is known, too, by Colombia, Venezuela, Nicaragua, Central America in general, Mexico, Haiti, and Santo Domingo. In recent years, besides our people, Panama has also known direct aggression when the "Marines" of the Canal opened fire against defenseless people; Santo Domingo, whose coast was violated by the Yankee fleet to avoid an outbreak of the righteous fury of the people after the death of Trujillo; and Colombia, whose capital was taken by assault as a result of a rebellion provoked by the assassination of Gaitán.

There are masked interventions through military missions which participate in internal repression organizing forces designed for that purpose in many countries, and also in coups d'état, so-called *gorilazos*, which have been so frequently repeated on the American continent during the past few years. Specifically, United States forces take part in the repression of the peoples of Venezuela, Colombia, and Guatemala, who carry on an armed struggle for their freedom. In Venezuela not only do the Americans advise the army and the police, but they also direct acts of genocide from the air against the peasant population in vast rebel-held areas, and the United States companies established there exert pressures of every kind to increase direct interference.

The imperialists are preparing to repress the peoples of [Latin] America and are setting up an "international" of crime. The United States interferes in [Latin] America while invoking the "defense of free institutions." The time will come when this Assembly will acquire greater maturity and demand guarantees from the United States Government for the lives of the Negro and Latin American population residing in this country, most of whom are native-born or naturalized United States citizens.

How can they presume to be the "guardians of liberty" when they kill their own children and discriminate daily against people because of the color of their skin, when they not only free the murderers of the colored people, but even protect them, while punishing the Negro population because they demand their legitimate rights as free men? We understand that today the Assembly is not in a position to ask for explanations of these acts, but it must be clearly established that the Government of the United States is not the gendarme of freedom, but rather the perpetrator of exploitation and oppression of the peoples of the world and of a large part of its own population.

To the equivocal language with which some delegates have painted the case of Cuba and the Organization of American States, we reply with blunt words that the peoples of the Americas will make their surrendering Governments pay for their treason.

Cuba, a free and sovereign state, with no chains binding it to anyone, with no foreign investments on its territory, with no proconsuls orienting its policy, can speak proudly in this Assembly, proving the justice of the phrase with which Cuba was named, "Free Territory of America."

Our example will bear fruit in our continent, as it is already doing to a certain extent in Guatemala, Colombia, and Venezuela. There is no longer either a small enemy or a contemptible force, since the people are no longer isolated. As is laid down in the Second Declaration of Havana:

> No people of Latin America is weak, because they are part of a family of 200 million brothers beset by the same miseries, who harbor the same feelings, have the same enemy, while they all dream of the same better destiny and have the support of all honest men and women in the world.
>
> Future history will be written by the hungry masses of Indians, of landless peasants, of exploited workers; it will be written by the progressive masses, by the honest and brilliant intellectuals who abound in our unfortunate lands of Latin America, by the struggle of the masses and of ideas: an epic that will be carried forward by our peoples who have been ill-treated and despised by imperialism, our peoples who have until now gone unrecognized but who are awakening. We were considered an impotent and submissive flock; but now there is fear of that flock, a gigantic flock of 200 million Latin Americans whom the Yankee monopolistic capitalists already see as their gravediggers.
>
> The hour of vindication, the hour Latin America chose for itself, is now striking from one end to the other of the continent. This anonymous mass, this America of races, sombre, adamant, which sings throughout the continent the same sad, mournful song, now that mass is beginning definitely to enter into its own history, it is beginning to write it with its blood, to suffer and to die for it. Because now, in the fields and in the mountains of America, in its plains and in its forests, in the solitude and in the bustle of cities, on the shores of the great oceans and rivers, it is beginning to shape a world full of quickening hearts who are ready to die for what is theirs, to conquer their rights, which have been flouted for almost 500 years. History will have to tell the story of the poor of America, of the exploited of Latin America, who have decided to begin to write for themselves, forever, their own odyssey. We see them already walking along those roads, on foot, day after day, in long and endless marches, hundreds of kilometers, until they reach the ruling "Olympus" and wrest back their rights. We see them armed with stones, with sticks, with machetes, here, there, everywhere, daily occupying their lands, and taking root in the land that is theirs and defending it with their lives; we see them carrying banners, their banners, we see these banners streaming in the wind on the mountains and on the plains. And that wave of heightening fury, of just demands, of rights that have been flouted, is rising throughout Latin America, and no one can stem that tide; it will grow day by day because it is made up of the majority in

every respect, those who with their work create the riches of the earth, and turn the wheel of history, those who are now awakening from their long, stupefying sleep.

For this great mass of humanity has said "enough" and has started to move forward. And their march, the march of giants, cannot stop and will not stop until they have conquered their true independence, for which have already died uselessly more than once. In any event, those who now die will die like those in Cuba, at Playa Girón; they will die for their only true and never to be renounced independence.

All this, Messrs. Delegates, this new will of a whole continent, of America, shows itself in the cry proclaimed daily by our masses as the irrefutable expression of their decision to fight, to grasp, and to deter the armed hand of the invader. It is a cry that has the understanding and support of all the peoples of the world, and, especially, of the socialist camp, headed by the Soviet Union.

That cry is: "Fatherland or Death."

"SOCIALISM AND MAN IN CUBA" 7

What is the role of the individual in a revolutionary Communist society? Guevara gave his views on this in a letter addressed to the editor of a Uruguayan publication. Guevara denied that the individual is completely submerged in "the masses" but rather he held that "the masses" are the collective expression of the thoughts and feelings of all citizens. He said:

> Looking at things from a superficial standpoint, it might seem that those who speak of the submission of the individual to the State are right; with incomparable enthusiasm and discipline, the mass carries out the tasks set by the government whatever their nature. . . . However, the State at times makes mistakes. When this occurs, the collective enthusiasm diminishes palpably as a result of a quantitative diminishing that takes place in each of the elements that make up the collective.

Guevara sees as one of the primary tasks of "socialist construction" the formation "of the new human being . . . the Twenty-First Century man." He states: "The institutionalization of the Revolution has still not been achieved. We are seeking something new that will allow a perfect identification between the government and the community as a whole . . ." Although Guevara emphasizes the collective nature of "socialist" society, he also speaks of the "vanguard group" which is "ideologically more advanced than the mass." The Party, says Guevara, "is a vanguard organization." Thus, he is saying in effect that society must be run by the Party elite.

LETTER TO CARLOS QUIJANO, EDITOR OF THE
MONTEVIDEO WEEKLY "MARCHA"

Dear compañero:

I AM FINISHING these notes while traveling through Africa, moved
by the desire to keep my promise, although after some delay. I
should like to do so by dealing with the topic that appears in the title.
I belive it might be of interest to Uruguayan readers.

It is common to hear how capitalist spokesmen use as an argument in
the ideological struggle against socialism the assertion that such a social
system, or the period of building socialism upon which we have embarked, is characterized by the extinction of the individual for the sake
of the State. I will make no attempt to refute this assertion on a merely
theoretical basis, but will instead establish the facts of the Cuban experience and add commentaries of a general nature. I shall first broadly
sketch the history of our revolutionary struggle both before and after
taking of power.

As we know, the exact date of the beginning of the revolutionary
actions which were to culminate on January 1, 1959, was July 26, 1953.
A group of men led by Fidel Castro attacked the Moncada military garrison in the province of Oriente, in the early hours of the morning of that
day. The attack was a failure, the failure became a disaster and the survivors were imprisoned, only to begin the revolutionary struggle all over
again, once they were amnestied.

During this process, which contained only the first seeds of socialism,
man was a basic factor. Man—individualized, specific, named—was
trusted and the triumph or failure of the task entrusted to him depended
on his capacity for action.

Then came the stage of guerrilla warfare. It was carried out in two
different environments: the people, an as yet unawakened mass that had
to be mobilized, and its vanguard, the guerrilla, the thrusting engine of
the movement, the generator of revolutionary awareness and militant
enthusiasm. This vanguard was the catalyst that created the subjective
condition necessary for victory. The individual was also the basic factor
in the guerrilla, in the framework of the gradual proletarianization of
our thinking, in the revolution taking place in our habits and in our minds.
Each and every one of the Sierra Maestra fighters who achieved a high
rank in the revolutionary forces has to his credit a list of noteworthy
deeds. It was on the basis of such deeds that they earned their rank.

The First Heroic Stage

It was the first heroic period in which men strove to earn posts of greater responsibility, of greater danger, with the fulfillment of their duty as the only satisfaction. In our work of revolutionary education we often return to this instructive topic. The man of the future could be glimpsed in the attitude of our fighters.

At other times of our history there have been repetitions of this utter devotion to the revolutionary cause. During the October Crisis and at the time of hurricane Flora, we witnessed deeds of exceptional valor and self-sacrifice carried out by an entire people. One of our fundamental tasks from the ideological standpoint is to find the way to perpetuate such heroic attitudes in everyday life.

The Revolutionary Government was established in 1959 with the participation of several members of the "sellout" bourgeoisie. The presence of the Rebel Army constituted the guarantee of power as the fundamental factor of strength.

Serious contradictions arose which were solved in the first instance in February, 1959, when Fidel Castro assumed the leadership of the government in the post of Prime Minister. This process culminated in July of the same year with the resignation of President Urrutia in the face of mass pressure.

With clearly defined features, there now appeared in the history of the Cuban Revolution a personage which will systematically repeat itself: the masses.

Full and Accurate Interpretation of the People's Wishes

This multifacetic being is not, as it is claimed, the sum total of elements of the same category (and moreover, reduced to the same category by the system imposed upon them) and which acts as a tame herd. It is true that the mass follows its leaders, especially Fidel Castro, without hesitation, but the degree to which he has earned such confidence is due precisely to the consummate interpretation of the people's desires and aspirations, and to the sincere struggle to keep the promises made.

The mass participated in the Agrarian Reform and in the difficult undertaking of the management of the state enterprises; it underwent the heroic experience of Playa Girón; it was tempered in the struggle against the groups of bandits armed by the CIA; during the October Crisis it lived one of the most important definitions of modern times and today it continues the work to build socialism.

Looking at things from a superficial standpoint, it might seem that those who speak of the submission of the individual to the State are right;

with incomparable enthusiasm and discipline, the mass carries out the tasks set by the government whatever their nature: economic, cultural, defense, sports, etc.

The initiative generally comes from Fidel or the high command of the revolution; it is explained to the people, who make it their own. At times, local experiences are taken up by the party and the government and are thereby made general, following the same procedure.

However, the State at times makes mistakes. When this occurs, the collective enthusiasm diminishes palpably as a result of a quantitative diminishing that takes place in each of the elements that make up the collective, and work becomes paralyzed until it finally shrinks to insignificant proportions; this is the time to rectify.

This was what happened in March, 1962, in the presence of the sectarian policy imposed on the Party by Aníbal Escalante.

Dialectical Unity Between Fidel and the Mass

This mechanism is obviously not sufficient to ensure a sequence of sensible measures; what is missing is a more structured relationship with the mass. We must improve this connection in the years to come, but for now, in the case of the initiatives arising on the top levels of government, we are using the almost intuitive method of keeping our ears open to the general reactions in the face of the problems that are posed.

Fidel is a past master at this; his particular mode of integration with the people can only be appreciated by seeing him in action. In the big public meetings, one can observe something like the dialogue of two tuning forks whose vibrations summon forth new vibrations each in the other. Fidel and the mass begin to vibrate in a dialogue of growing intensity which reaches its culminating point in an abrupt ending crowned by our victorious battle cry.

What is hard to understand for anyone who has not lived the revolutionary experience is that close dialectical unity which exists between the individual and the mass, in which both are interrelated, and the mass, as a whole composed of individuals, is in turn interrelated with the leaders.

Under capitalism, certain phenomena of this nature can be observed with the appearance on the scene of politicians capable of achieving popular mobilization, but if it is not an authentic social movement, in which case it is not completely accurate to speak of capitalism, the movement will have the same life span as its promoter or until the rigors of capitalist society put an end to popular illusions. Under capitalism, man is guided by a cold ordinance which is usually beyond his comprehension. The alienated human individual is bound to society as a whole by an invisible umbilical cord: the law of value. It acts upon all facets of his life, shaping his road and his destiny.

The Invisible Laws of Capitalism

The laws of capitalism, invisible and blind for most people, act upon the individual without his awareness. He sees only the broadness of an horizon that appears infinite. Capitalist propaganda presents it in just this way, and attempts to use the Rockefeller case (true or not) as a lesson in the prospects for success. The misery that must be accumulated for such an example to arise and the sum total of baseness contributing to the formation of a fortune of such magnitude do not appear in the picture, and the popular forces are not always able to make these concepts clear. (It would be fitting at this point to study how the workers of the imperialist countries gradually lose their international class spirit under the influence of a certain complicity in the exploitation of the dependent countries and how this fact at the same time wears away the militant spirit of the masses within their own national context, but this topic is outside the framework of the present notes.)

In any case we can see the obstacle course which may apparently be overcome by an individual with the necessary qualities to arrive at the finish line. The reward is glimpsed in the distance and the road is solitary. Furthermore, it is a race of wolves: he who arrives does so only at the expense of the failure of others.

I shall now attempt to define the individual, the actor in this strange and moving drama that is the building of socialism, in his two-fold existence as a unique being and a member of the community.

I believe that the simplest approach is to recognize his un-made quality: he is an unfinished product. The flaws of the past are translated into the present in the individual consciousness, and constant efforts must be made to eradicate them. The process is two-fold: on the one hand society acts upon the individual by means of direct and indirect education, while on the other hand, the individual undergoes a conscious phase of self-education.

Compete Fiercely with the Past

The new society in process of formation has to compete very hard with the past. This makes itself felt not only in the individual consciousness, weighed down by the residues of an education systematically oriented towards the isolation of the individual, but also by the very nature of this transition period, with the persistence of commodity relations. The commodity is the economic cell of capitalist society; as long as it exists, its effects will make themselves felt in the organization of production and therefore in man's consciousness.

Marx's scheme conceived of the transition period as the result of the explosive transformation of the capitalist system torn apart by its contradictions; subsequent reality has shown how some countries, the weak limbs, detach themselves from the imperialist tree, a phenomenon foreseen by Lenin. In those countries, capitalism has developed sufficiently to make its effects felt upon the people in one way or another, but it is not its own contradictions that explode the system after exhausting all of its possibilities. The struggle for liberation against an external oppressor, the misery which has its origin in foreign causes, such as war, whose consequences make the privileged classes fall upon the exploited, the liberation movements aimed at overthrowing neocolonial regimes, are the customary factors in this process. Conscious action does the rest.

A Rapid Change Without Sacrifices Is Impossible

In these countries there still has not been achieved a complete education for the work of society, and wealth is far from being within the reach of the masses through the simple process of appropriation. Underdevelopment and the customary flight of capital to "civilized" countries make impossible a rapid change without sacrifices. There still remains a long stretch to be covered in the building of the economic base and the temptation to follow the beaten paths of material interest as the lever of speedy development, is very great.

There is a danger of not seeing the forest because of the trees. Pursuing the chimera of achieving socialism with the aid of the blunted weapons left to us by capitalism (the commodity as the economic cell, profitability, individual material interest as a lever, etc.), it is possible to come to a blind alley. And the arrival there comes about after covering a long distance where there are many crossroads and where it is difficult to realize just when the wrong turn was taken. Meanwhile, the adapted economic base has undermined the development of consciousness. To build communism, a new man must be created simultaneously with the material base.

That is why it is so important to choose correctly the instrument of mass mobilization. That instrument must be fundamentally of a moral character, without forgetting the correct use of material incentives, especially those of a social nature.

Society Must Be a Huge School

As I already said, in moments of extreme danger it is easy to activate moral incentives; to maintain their effectiveness, it is necessary to develop a consciousness in which values acquire new categories. Society as a whole must become a huge school.

The broad characteristics of the phenomenon are similar to the process of formation of capitalist consciousness in the system's first stage. Capitalism resorts to force but it also educates people in the system. Direct propaganda is carried out by those who are entrusted with the task of explaining the inevitability of a class regime, whether it be of divine origin or due to the imposition of nature as a mechanical entity. This placates the masses, who see themselves oppressed by an evil against which it is not possible to struggle.

This is followed by hope, which differentiates capitalism from the previous caste regimes that offered no way out. For some, the caste formula continues in force: the obedient are rewarded by the *post mortem* arrival in other wonderful worlds where the good are requited, and the old tradition is continued. For others, innovation: the division in classes is a matter of fate, but individuals can leave the class to which they belong through work, initiative, etc. This process, and that of self-education for success, must be deeply hypocritical; it is the interested demonstration that a lie is true.

In our case, direct education acquires much greater importance. Explanations are convincing because they are genuine; subterfuges are not needed. It is carried out through the State's educational apparatus in the form of general, technical and ideological culture, by means of bodies such as the Ministry of Education and the Party's information apparatus. Education takes hold among the masses and the new attitude that is advocated tends to become habit; the mass gradually takes it over and exerts pressure on those who have still not become educated. This is the indirect way of educating the masses, as powerful as the other one.

The Process of Individual Self-education

But the process is a conscious one; the individual receives continuously the impact of the new social power and perceives that he is not completely adequate to it. Under the influence of the pressure implied in indirect education, he tries to adjust to a situation that he feels to be just and that his own lack of development has kept him from doing so thus far. He is educating himself.

We can see the new man who begins to emerge in this period of the building of socialism. His image is as yet unfinished; in fact it will never be finished, since the process advances parallel to the development of new economic forms. Discounting those whose lack of education makes them tend towards the solitary road, towards the satisfaction of their ambitions, there are others who, even within this new picture of over-all advances, tend to march in isolation from the accompanying mass. What is important is that people become more aware every day of the need to incorporate themselves into society and of their own importance as motors of that society.

They no longer march in complete solitude along lost roads towards far-off longings. They follow their vanguard, composed of the Party, of the most advanced workers, who move along bound to the masses and in close communion with them. The vanguards have their eyes on the future and its recompenses, but the latter are not envisioned as something individual; the reward is the new society where human beings will have different characteristics: the society of communist man.

A Long and Difficult Road

The road is long and full of difficulties. At times, the route strays off course and it is necessary to retreat; at times, a too rapid pace separates us from the masses and on occasions the pace is slow and we feel upon our necks the breath of those who follow upon our heels. Our ambition as revolutionaries makes us try to move forward as far as possible, opening up the way before us, but we know that we must be reinforced by the mass, while the mass will be able to advance more rapidly only if we encourage it by our example.

In spite of the importance given to moral incentives, the existence of two principal groups (excluding, of course, the minority fraction of those who do not participate for one reason or another in the building of socialism) is an indication of the relative lack of development of social consciousness. The vanguard group is ideologically more advanced than the mass; the latter is acquainted with the new values, but insufficiently. While in the former a qualitative change takes place which permits them to make sacrifices as a function of their vanguard character, the latter see only by halves and must be subjected to incentives and pressures of some intensity; it is the dictatorship of the proletariat being exercised not only upon the defeated class but also individually upon the victorious class.

To achieve total success, all of this involves the necessity of a series of mechanisms, the revolutionary institutions. The concept of institutionalization fits in with the images of the multitudes marching towards the future as that of a harmonic unit of canals, steps, dams, well-oiled apparatuses that make the march possible, that permit the natural selection of those who are destined to march in the vanguard and who dispense rewards and punishments to those who fulfill their duty or act against the society under construction.

Perfect Identification Between Government and Community

The institutionalization of the Revolution has still not been achieved. We are seeking something new that will allow a perfect identification between the government and the community as a whole, adapted to special conditions of the building of socialism and avoiding to the utmost the commonplaces of bourgeois democracy transplanted to the society in formation (such as legislative houses, for example). Some experiments have been carried out with the aim of gradually creating the institutionalization of the Revolution, but without too much hurry. We have been greatly restrained by the fear that any formal aspect might separate us from the masses and from the individual, and make us lose sight of the ultimate and most important revolutionary aspiration: to see man freed from alienation.

Notwithstanding the lack of institutions, which must be overcome gradually, the masses now make history as a conscious aggregate of individuals who struggle for the same cause. In spite of the apparent standardization of man in socialism, he is more complete; his possibilities for expressing himself and making himself heard in the social apparatus are infinitely greater, in spite of the lack of a perfect mechanism to do so.

It is still necessary to accentuate his conscious, individual, and collective participation in all the mechanisms of direction and production and associate it with the idea of the need for technical and ideological education, so that the individual will realize that these processes are closely interdependent and their advances are parallel. He will thus achieve total awareness of his social being, which is equivalent to his full realization as a human being, having broken the chains of alienation.

This will be translated concretely into the reappropriation of his nature through freed work and the expression of his own human condition in culture and art.

Work Must Acquire a New Condition

In order for it to develop in culture, work must acquire a new condition; man as commodity ceases to exist and a system is established that grants a quota for the fulfillment of social duty. The means of production belong to society and the machine is only the front line where duty is performed. Man begins to free his thought from the bothersome fact that presupposed the need to satisfy his animal needs by working. He begins to see himself portrayed in his work and to understand his human magnitude through the created object, through the work carried out. This no longer involves leaving a part of his being in the form of labor power sold, which no longer belongs to him; rather, it signifies an emanation from himself, a contribution to the life of society in which he is reflected, the fulfillment of his social duty.

We are doing everything possible to give work this new category of social duty and to join it to the development of technology, on the one hand, which will provide the conditions for greater freedom, and to voluntary work on the other, based on the Marxist concept that man truly achieves his full human condition when he produces without being compelled by the physical necessity of selling himself as a commodity.

It is clear that work still has coercive aspects, even when it is voluntary; man has still not transformed all the coercion surrounding him into conditioned reflexes of a social nature, and in many cases, he still produces under the pressure of the environment (Fidel calls this moral compulsion). He is still to achieve complete spiritual recreation in the presence of his own work, without the direct pressure of the social environment but bound to it by new habits. That will be communism.

The change in consciousness does not come about automatically, just as it does not come about automatically in the economy. The variations are slow and not rhythmic; there are periods of acceleration, others are slow, and some even involve a retreat.

Communism's First Transition Period

We must also consider, as we have pointed out previously, that we are not before a pure transition period such as that envisioned by Marx in the "Critique of the Gotha Program," but rather a new phase not foreseen by him: the first period in the transition to communism or in the building of socialism.

Elements of capitalism are present within this process, which takes place in the midst of violent class struggle. These elements obscure the complete understanding of the essence of the process.

If to this be added the scholasticism that has held back the development of Marxist philosophy and impeded the systematic treatment of the period, whose political economy has still not been developed, we must agree that we are still in diapers. We must study all the primordial features of the period before elaborating a more far-reaching economic and political theory.

The resulting theory will necessarily give preeminence to the two pillars of socialist construction: the formation of the new human being and the development of technology. We still have a great deal to accomplish in both aspects, but the delay is less justifiable as far as the conception of technology as the basis is concerned; here, it is not a matter of advancing blindly but rather of following for a sizeable stretch the road opened up by the most advanced countries of the world. This is why Fidel harps so insistently on the necessity of the technological and scientific formation of all of our people and especially of the vanguard.

Division Between Material and Spiritual Needs

In the field of ideas that lead to nonproductive activities, it is easier to see the division between material and spiritual needs. For a long time man has been trying to free himself from alienation through culture and art. He dies daily in the eight and more hours during which he performs as a commodity to resuscitate in his spiritual creation. But this remedy itself bears the germs of the same disease: he is a solitary being who seeks communion with nature. He defends his environment-oppressed individuality and reacts to esthetic ideas as an only being whose aspiration is to remain immaculate.

It is only an attempt to escape. The law of value is no longer a mere reflection of production relations; the monopoly capitalists have surrounded it with a complicated scaffolding which makes of it a docile servant, even when the methods used are purely empirical. The artist must be educated in the kind of art imposed by the superstructure. The rebels are overcome by the apparatus and only exceptional talents are able to create their own work. The others become shame-faced wage-workers or they are crushed.

Artistic investigation is invented and is taken as the definition of freedom, but this "investigation" has limits which are imperceptible until they are clashed with, that is, when the real problems of man and his alienated condition are dealt with. Senseless anguish or vulgar pastimes are comfortable safety valves for human uneasiness; the idea of making art a weapon of accusation is combatted.

If the rules of the game are respected, all honors are obtained—the honors that might be granted to a pirouette-creating monkey. The condition is not attempting to escape from the invisible cage.

A New Impulse for Artistic Investigation

When the Revolution took power, the exodus of the totally domesticated took place; the others, revolutionaries or not, saw a new road. Artistic investigation took on new force. However, the routes were more or less traced and the concept of escape was the hidden meaning behind the word freedom. This attitude, a reflection in consciousness of bourgeois idealism, was frequently maintained in the revolutionaries themselves.

In countries that have gone through a similar process, endeavors were made to combat these tendencies with an exaggerated dogmatism. General culture became something like a taboo and a formally exact representation of nature was proclaimed as the height of cultural aspiration. This later became a mechanical representation of social reality created by wishful thinking: the ideal society, almost without conflicts or contradictions, that man was seeking to create.

Socialism is young and makes mistakes. We revolutionaries often lack the knowledge and the intellectual audacity to face the task of the development of a new man by methods different from the conventional ones, and the conventional methods suffer from the influence of the society that created them (once again the topic of the relation between form and content appears). Disorientation is great and the problems of material construction absorb us. There are no artists of great authority who also have great revolutionary authority.

The men of the Party must take this task upon themselves and seek the achievement of the principal aim: to educate the people.

Socialist Realism Based on the Art of the Last Century

What is then sought is simplification, what everyone understands, that is, what the functionaries understand. True artistic investigation is obliterated and the problem of general culture is reduced to the assimilation of the socialist present and the dead (and therefore not dangerous) past. Socialist realism is thus born on the foundation of the art of the last century.

But the realistic art of the 19th century is also class art, perhaps more purely capitalist than the decadent art of the 20th century, where the anguish of alienated man shows through. In culture, capitalism has given all that it had to give and all that remains of it is the foretaste of a bad-smelling corpse; in art, its present decadence. But why endeavor to seek in the frozen forms of socialist realism the only valid recipe? "Freedom" cannot be set against socialist realism because the former does not yet exist; it will not come into being until the complete development of the new society. But let us not attempt to condemn all post-mid-nineteenth century art forms from the pontifical throne of realism-at-all-costs; that would mean committing the Proudhonian error of the return to the past, and straitjacketing the artistic expression of the man who is born and being formed today.

An ideological and cultural mechanism must be developed which will permit investigation and clear out the weeds that shoot up so easily in the fertilized soil of state subsidization.

The Man We Must Create

The error of mechanical realism has not appeared in our country, but rather the contrary. This is so because of the lack of understanding of the need to create a new man who will represent neither 19th century ideas nor those of our decadent and morbid century. It is the twenty-first century man whom we must create, although this is still a subjective and unsystematic aspiration. This is precisely one of the basic points of our studies and work; to the extent that we make concrete achievements on a theoretical base or vice versa, that we come to broad theoretical conclusions on the basis of our concrete studies, we will have made a valuable contribution to Marxism-Leninism, to the cause of mankind.

The reaction against 19th century man has brought a recurrence of 20th century decadence. It is not a very serious error, but we must overcome it so as not to leave the doors open to revisionism.

The large multitudes of people are developing themselves, the new ideas are acquiring an adequate impetus within society, the material possibilities of the integral development of each and every one of its members make the task ever more fruitful. The present is one of struggle; the future is ours.

Intellectuals Not Authentically Revolutionary

To sum up, the fault of many of our intellectuals and artists is to be found in their "original sin": they are not authentically revolutionary. We can attempt to graft elm trees so that they bear pears, but at the same time we must plant pear trees. The new generations will arrive free of "original sin." The likelihood that exceptional artists will arise will be that much greater because of the enlargement of the cultural field and the possibilities for expression. Our job is to keep the present generation, maladjusted by its conflicts, from becoming perverted and perverting the new generations. We must not create salaried workers docile to official thinking nor "fellows" who live under the wing of the budget, exercising freedom in quotation marks. Revolutionaries will come to sing the song of the new man with the authentic voice of the people. It is a process that requires time.

In our society, the youth and the Party play a big role. The former is particularly important because it is the malleable clay with which the new man, without any of the previous defects, can be formed.

Youth receives treatment in consonance with our aspirations. Education is increasingly integral and we do not neglect the incorporation of the students into work from the very beginning. Our scholarship students do physical work during vacation or together with their studies. In some cases work is a prize, while in others it is an educational tool; it is never a punishment. A new generation is being born.

The Party: Vanguard Organization

The Party is a vanguard organization. The best workers are proposed by their comrades for membership. The Party is a minority but the quality of its cadres gives it great authority. Our aspiration is that the Party become one of masses but only when the masses reach the level of development of the vanguard, that is, when they are educated for communism. Our work is aimed at providing that education. The Party is the living example; its cadres must be full professors of assiduity and sacrifice; with their acts they must lead the masses to the end of the revolutionary task, which means years of struggle against the difficulties of construction, the class enemies, the defects of the past, imperialism . . .

I should now like to explain the role played by the personality, the man as the individual who leads the masses that make history. This is our experience, and not a recipe.

Fidel gave impulse to the Revolution in its first years, he has always set the tone, but there is a good group of revolutionaries developing in the same direction as the maximum leader and a large mass that follows its leaders because it has faith in them. It has faith in them because these leaders have known how to interpret the longings of the masses.

So That the Individual Feels More Fulfilled

It is not a question of how many kilograms of meat are eaten or how many times a year someone may go to enjoy the beaches or how many pretty imported things can be bought with present wages. It is rather that the individual feels greater fulfillment, that he has greater inner wealth and many more responsibilities. In our country the individual knows that the glorious period in which he has happened to live is one of sacrifice; he is familiar with sacrifice.

The first ones came to know sacrifice in the Sierra Maestra and wherever there was fighting; later, we have known it in all Cuba. Cuba is the vanguard of America and must make sacrifices because it occupies the advance position, because it points out to the Latin American masses the road to full freedom.

Within the country, the leaders have to fulfill their vanguard role; and it must be said with complete sincerity that in a true revolution, to which you give yourself completely without any thought for material retribution, the task of the vanguard revolutionary is both magnificent and anguishing.

Let me say, with the risk of appearing ridiculous, that the true revolutionary is guided by strong feelings of love. It is impossible to think of an authentic revolutionary without this quality. This is perhaps one of the great dramas of a leader; he must combine an impassioned spirit with a cold mind and make painful decisions without flinching. Our vanguard revolutionaries must idealize their love for the people, for the most hallowed causes, and make it one and indivisible. They cannot descend, with small doses of daily affection, to the terrain where ordinary men put their love into practice.

There Should Be a Large Dose of Humanity

The leaders of the revolution have children who do not learn to call their father with their first faltering words; they have wives who must be part of the general sacrifice of their lives to carry the revolution to its destination; their friends are strictly limited to their comrades of revolution. There is no life outside the revolution.

In these conditions, the revolutionary leaders must have a large dose of humanity, a large dose of a sense of justice and truth to avoid falling into dogmatic extremes, into cold scholasticism, into isolation from the masses. They must struggle every day so that their love of living humanity is transformed into concrete deeds, into acts that will serve as an example, as a mobilizing factor.

The revolutionary, ideological motor of the revolution within his party, is consumed by this uninterrupted activity that ends only with death, unless construction be achieved on a worldwide scale. If his revolutionary eagerness becomes dulled when the most urgent tasks are carried on a local scale and if he forgets about proletarian internationalism, the revolution that he leads ceases to be a driving force and it sinks into a comfortable drowsiness which is taken advantage of by imperialism, our irreconcilable enemy, to gain ground. Proletarian internationalism is a duty, but it is also a revolutionary need. This is how we educate our people.

Dangers of Dogmatism and Weaknesses

It is evident that there are dangers in the present circumstances. Not only that of dogmatism, not only that of the freezing up of relations with the masses in the midst of the great task; there also exists the danger of weaknesses in which it is possible to incur. If a man thinks that in order to devote his entire life to the revolution, he cannot be distracted by the worry that one of his children lacks a certain article, that the children's shoes are worn out, that his family lacks some necessary item, with this reasoning, the seeds of future corruption are allowed to filter through.

In our case, we have maintained that our children must have, or lack, what the children of the ordinary citizen have or lack; our family must understand this and struggle for it. The revolution is made by man, but man must forge his revolutionary spirit from day to day.

Thus we go forward. Fidel is at the head of the immense column— we are neither ashamed nor afraid to say so—followed by the best Party cadres, and right after them, so close that their great strength is felt, come the people as a whole, a solid bulk of individualities moving towards a common aim; individuals who have achieved the awareness of what must be done; men who struggle to leave the domain of necessity and enter that of freedom.

That immense multitude is ordering itself; its order responds to an awareness of the need for order; it is no longer a dispersed force, divisible in thousands of fractions shot into space like the fragments of a grenade, trying by any and all means, in a fierce struggle with their equals, to achieve a position that would give them support in the face of an uncertain future.

We know that we have sacrifices ahead of us and that we must pay a price for the heroic fact of constituting a vanguard as a nation. We the leaders know that we must pay a price for having the right to say that we are at the head of the people that is at the head of America.

Each and every one of us punctually pays his share of sacrifice, aware of being rewarded by the satisfaction of fulfilling our duty, aware of advancing with everyone towards the new man who is to be glimpsed on the horizon.

We are More Free Because We are More Fulfilled

Allow me to attempt to come to some conclusions:

We socialists are more free because we are more fulfilled; we are more fulfilled because we are more free.

The skeleton of our complete freedom is formed, but it lacks the protein substance and the clothes; we will create them.

Our freedom and its daily sustenance are the color of blood and swollen with sacrifice.

Our sacrifice is a conscious one; it is in payment for the freedom we are building.

The road is long and in part unknown; we are aware of our limitations. We will make the Twenty-first Century man; we ourselves.

We will be tempered in daily actions, creating a new human being with a new technology.

The personality plays the role of mobilization and leadership insofar as it incarnates the highest virtues and aspirations of the people and does not become detoured.

The road is opened up by the vanguard group, the best among the good, the Party.

The basic raw material of our work is the youth: in it we place our hopes and we are preparing it to take the banner from our hands.

If this faltering letter has made some things clear, it will have fulfilled my purpose in sending it.

Accept our ritual greetings, as a handshake or an *Ave María Purísima*.

FATHERLAND OR DEATH

GUEVARA'S FAREWELL LETTER 8

Ernesto Guevara had been missing for more than half a year. There had been speculation placing him in various parts of the world; there was a growing belief that he was dead. Then, in a speech delivered October 3, 1965, Castro referred to the Guevara affair, stating, ". . . The enemy has engaged in a thousand conjectures; the enemy has tried to confuse and disseminate discord and doubt . . ." Castro announced that he was about to read a letter from Guevara. Carrying no date, the letter, according to Castro, had been delivered on April 1 and was to be read publicly "at the moment we believed most convenient." Addressed to Castro, the document was a poignant farewell to Cuba by Guevara in which he announced that he was giving up all his official posts. Thus he relieved Castro and Cuba "of any responsibility" for his future actions, although "wherever I stand I will feel the responsibility of being a Cuban revolutionary and will act accordingly." The letter renewed speculation about Guevara, but it shed no light on his whereabouts or activities. Nor did it lay to rest the belief by some Cuba experts that Guevara was dead. In fact, on October 15, the Reuters news service, in a dispatch from Cairo, Egypt, reported:

> Ernesto "Che" Guevara, the former Cuban Industry Minister, and Congolese Rebel Leader Gaston Soumilot may have been killed in an ambush in the Congo, a reliable African source here said today.

FAREWELL LETTER FROM GUEVARA TO CASTRO

Havana, . . .Year of Agriculture.
   Fidel:

I N THIS HOUR I remember many things, of when I met you at María
Antonia's house, of when you proposed that I come, of all the tension during the preparations.
         One day someone came by asking who should be notified in case
of death, and the actual possibility of that happening hit us all. Afterward, we learned it was true, that in a revolution one either triumphs
or dies (if it is a true revolution). Many compañeros fell during the long
road to victory.

Today everything has a less dramatic ring, because we are more
mature, but the act repeats itself. I feel that I have fulfilled the obligation
which bound me to the Cuban Revolution in its territory, and I say goodbye to you, to the compañeros, to your country, which is now mine.

I formally resign my positions in the leadership of the Party, my post
as Minister, my rank of major, my Cuban citizenship. I have no legal
ties with Cuba, only bonds of another kind which cannot be broken
like appointments.

In making an inventory of my life I believe I have worked with sufficient honesty and dedication to consolidate the revolutionary victory.
My only somewhat serious fault was in not having had more confidence
in you from the first moments in the Sierra Maestra and not having understood soon enough your qualities as a leader and revolutionary. I have
lived magnificent days, and, by your side, I have felt the pride of belonging to our people during the enlightening and sad days of the Caribbean
Crisis. Seldom has a statesman shined so brilliantly as in those days. I am
also proud of having followed you without vacillations, identifying myself with your way of thinking, and learning and appraising the dangers
and the principles.

Other lands of the world demand my modest efforts. I can do what is
denied to you because of your responsibility as the leader of Cuba, and
the time has arrived for us to part.

Let it be known that I do this with mixed emotions of happiness and
sorrow. Here I leave my purest hopes as a builder, and the ones I love
most among my loved ones . . . I leave a country that took me in as a son;
this tears a part of my spirit. I shall carry with me on the new fields of
battle the faith you instilled in me, the revolutionary spirit of my people,

the feeling of fulfilling the most sacred of obligations: to struggle against imperialism wherever it may be. This comforts and cures more than enough any heartbreak.

I repeat once again that I am releasing Cuba of any responsibility, save that which emanates from its example. That if my final hour arrives under other skies my last thoughts will be of this country and especially of you. That I thank you for your teachings and your example, and I shall try to be loyal right up to the last consequences of my actions. That I was always identified with the foreign policy of our revolution, and I still am. That wherever I stand I will feel the responsibility of being a Cuban revolutionary and will act accordingly. That I am not leaving my wife and children anything material and I am not ashamed: I am glad this is so. That I do not ask anything for them, for the State will provide enough for their livelihood and education.

I would have many things to say to you and to our people, but I feel these are unnecessary; words cannot express what I would like to say, and it is not worthwhile to scribble on sheets of paper.

Until victory always. Fatherland or Death!

I embrace you with all revolutionary fervor.

CHE

MESSAGE TO "TRICONTINENTAL" 9

In January of 1966 the Tricontinental Conference was held in Havana, attended by pro-Castro delegates from Asia, Africa, and Latin America. The following year, as an offshoot of this parley on subversion, Cuba began publishing *Tricontinental* magazine, and the first issue, scheduled to appear in June, was to have contained an article by Guevara (who at that time was in Bolivia). Events in that country, however, may have been moving faster than planned—it was only a matter of time before Guevara's presence would become known—and so publication of the article was moved up and published in Cuban newspapers and magazines in April. Guevara reviewed the world situation, as he saw it, assailing the United States as his main target, but indirectly also hitting at Communist countries for not providing greater assistance to the Vietnamese Communists. Referring to Communist countries, he spoke of the "guilt" of those who "hesitated to make Viet Nam an inviolable part of the socialist world." Guevara, however, was primarily interested in "the struggle in Our America" which he said would reach "continental proportions" and would include "many great battles." Guevara perhaps expected to lead those battles—the Bolívar of the twentieth century.

MESSAGE TO *TRICONTINENTAL* MAGAZINE
("... To Create a Second or a Third Viet Nam ...")

The Executive Secretariat of the Organization of Solidarity of the Peoples of Africa, Asia and Latin America will start to publish the "Tricontinental" magazine in the month of June; it has requested the collaboration of outstanding revolutionary leaders of the world.

Major Ernesto Che Guevara was included among the first collaborators, and to this effect has sent our organization an article for publication. Due to the content of this article; the clarity with which it approaches problems of vital importance for the revolutionary movement; its vigorous denunciation of U.S. imperialism's policy of sending U.S. soldiers to repress revolutionary movements of liberation in any part of the world where they may arise, as has been done not only in Viet Nam and the Dominican Republic, but also in Guatemala, Colombia, Venezuela, and Bolivia, countries in which large numbers of "Green Berets" have already appeared; and also because of the article's strong appeal to the people to give a fitting answer to this criminal policy, the Executive Secretariat of the OSPAAAL has decided to give publicity to this outstanding message to the peoples of the world from the heroic and legendary fighter, without awaiting publication of the first issue of its magazine.

Executive Secretariat of the Organization of Solidarity
of the Peoples of Africa, Asia and Latin America
OSPAAAL
Havana, April 16, 1967.

*Now is the time of forges, and nothing
but light should be seen.*

JOSÉ MARTÍ

TWENTY-ONE YEARS have already elapsed since the end of the last world conflagration; numerous publications, in every possible language, celebrate this event, symbolized by the defeat of Japan. There is a climate of apparent optimism in many areas of the different camps into which the world is divided.

Twenty-one years without a world war, in these times of maximum confrontations, of violent clashes and sudden changes, appears to be a very high figure. However, without analyzing the practical results of this peace (poverty, degradation, increasing exploitation of enormous sectors of humanity) for which all of us have stated that we are willing to fight, we would do well to inquire if this peace is real.

It is not the purpose of these notes to detail the different conflicts of a local character that have been occurring since the surrender of Japan, neither do we intend to recount the numerous and increasing instances of civilian strife which have taken place during these years of apparent peace. It will be enough just to name, as an example against undue optimism, the wars of Korea and Viet Nam.

In the first of these, after years of savage warfare, the northern part of the country was submerged in the most terrible devastation known in the annals of modern warfare: riddled with bombs; without factories, schools or hospitals; with absolutely no shelter for housing ten million inhabitants.

Under the discredited flag of the United Nations, dozens of countries under the military leadership of the United States participated in this war with the massive intervention of U. S. soldiers and the use, as cannon fodder, of the drafted South Korean population. On the other side, the army and the people of Korea and the volunteers from the People's Republic of China were furnished with supplies and technical aid by the Soviet military apparatus. The U. S. tested all sorts of weapons of destruction, excluding the thermonuclear type, but including, on a limited scale, bacteriological and chemical warfare.

In Viet Nam, the patriotic forces of that country have carried on an almost uninterrupted war against three imperialist powers: Japan, whose might suffered an almost vertical collapse after the bombs of Hiroshima and Nagasaki; France, that recovered from that defeated country its Indo-China colonies and ignored the promises it had made in harder times; and the United States, in this last phase of the struggle.

There have been limited confrontations in every continent although in the American continent for a long time there were only incipient liberation struggles and military coups d'etat until the Cuban Revolution sounded the alert, signaling the importance of this region. This action attracted the wrath of the imperialists and Cuba was finally obliged to defend its coasts, first in Playa Girón, and again during the October Crisis.

This last incident could have unleashed a war of incalculable proportions if a U.S.-Soviet clash had occurred over the Cuban question. But, evidently, the focal point of all contradictions is at present located in the territory of the peninsula of Indo-China and the adjacent areas. Laos and Viet Nam are torn by civil wars which have ceased being such by the entry into the conflict of U. S. imperialism with all its might, thus transforming the whole zone into a dangerous powder keg ready at any moment to explode.

In Viet Nam the confrontation has assumed extremely acute characteristics. It is not our intention, either, to chronicle this war. We shall simply remember and point out some milestones.

In 1954, after the annihilating defeat of Dien-Bien-Phu, the Geneva agreement was signed dividing the country into two separate zones; elections were to be held within a term of 18 months to determine who should govern Viet Nam and how the country should be reunified. The U. S. did not sign this document and started maneuvering to substitute the emperor, Bao Dai, who was a French puppet, for a man more amenable to its purposes. This happened to be Ngo Din Diem, whose tragic end—that of an orange squeezed dry by imperialism—is well known by all.

During the months following the agreement, optimism reigned supreme in the camp of the popular forces. The last redoubts of the anti-French resistance were dismantled in the south of the country, and they awaited the fulfillment of what had been agreed upon. But the patriots soon realized there would be no elections, unless the United States felt itself capable of imposing its will in the polls, which was practically impossible even resorting to all fraudulent methods known to them.

Once again, fighting broke out in the South and gradually acquired more intensity until the present, when the U. S. invading army numbers nearly half a million troops while the puppet forces decrease in number and, above all, have totally lost their combativeness.

Almost two years ago the United States started systematically bombing the Democratic Republic of Viet Nam, in yet another attempt to overcome the resistance of the South and impose, from a position of strength, a meeting at the conference table. At first, the bombardments were more or less isolated occurrences and were represented as reprisals for alleged provocations from the North. Later on, as they increased in intensity and regularity, they became one gigantic attack carried out by the air force of the United States, day after day, for the purpose of destroying all vestiges of civilization in the northern zone of the country. This is an episode of the infamously notorious "escalation."

The material aspirations of the Yankee world have been fulfilled to a great extent, despite the unflinching defense of the Vietnamese anti-aircraft artillery, of the numerous planes shot down (over 1,700) and of the socialist countries' aid in war supplies.

This is the sad reality: Viet Nam—a nation representing the aspirations, the hopes for victory of a whole world of forgotten peoples—is tragically alone. This nation must endure the furious attacks of U. S. technology, with practically no possibility of reprisals in the South and only some of defense in the North—but always alone.

The solidarity of all progressive forces of the world with the people of Viet Nam today is similar to the bitter irony of the plebeians urging on the gladiators in the Roman arena. It is not a matter of wishing success to the victim of aggression, but of sharing his fate; one must accompany him to his death or to victory.

When we analyze the lonely situation of the Vietnamese people, we are overcome by anguish at this illogical fix in which humanity finds itself.

U. S. imperialism is guilty of aggression—its crimes are enormous and cover the whole world. We already know all that, gentlemen! But this guilt also applies to those who, when the time came for a definition, hesitated to make Viet Nam an inviolable part of the socialist world; running, of course, the risks of a war on a global scale, but also forcing a decision upon imperialism. The guilt also applies to those who maintain a war of abuse and maneuvering, started quite some time ago by the representatives of the two greatest powers of the socialist camp.

We must ask ourselves, seeking an honest answer: Is Viet Nam isolated, or is it not? Is it not maintaining a dangerous equilibrium between the two quarrelling powers?

And what great people these are! What stoicism and courage! And what a lesson for the world is contained in this struggle! Not for a long time shall we be able to know if President Johnson ever seriously thought of bringing about some of the reforms needed by his people—to iron out the barbed class contradictions that grow more frequent each day with explosive power. The truth is that the improvements announced under the pompous title of the "Great Society" have been poured down the drain of Viet Nam.

The largest of all imperialist powers feels in its own guts the bleeding inflicted by a poor and backward country; its fabulous economy feels the strain of the war effort. Murder is ceasing to be the most convenient business for its monopolies. Defensive weapons, and never in adequate number, is all these extraordinary Vietnamese soldiers have—besides love for their homeland, their society, and unsurpassed courage. But imperialism is bogging down in Viet Nam, is unable to find a way out and desperately seeks one that will overcome with dignity this dangerous situation in which it now finds itself. Furthermore, the Four Points put forward by the North and the Five Points of the South now corner imperialism, making the confrontation even more decisive.

Everything indicates that peace, this unstable peace which bears the name for the sole reason that no world-wide conflagration has taken place, is again in danger of being destroyed by some irrevocable and unacceptable step taken by the United States.

What role shall we, the exploited people of the world, play? The peoples of the three continents focus their attention on Viet Nam and learn their lesson. Since imperialists blackmail humanity by threatening it with war, the wise reaction is not to fear war. The general tactics of the people should be to launch a constant and a firm attack on all fronts where the confrontation is taking place.

In those places where the meager peace we have has been violated, what is our duty? To liberate ourselves at any price.

The world panorama is of great complexity. The struggle for liberation has not yet been undertaken by some countries of ancient Europe, sufficiently developed to realize the contradictions of capitalism, but weak to such a degree that they are unable to either follow imperialism or to start on its road. Their contradictions will reach an explosive stage during the forthcoming years—but their problems and, consequently, their solutions are different from those of our dependent and economically backward countries.

The fundamental field of imperialist exploitation comprises the three underdeveloped continents: America, Asia, and Africa. Every country has its own characteristics, but each continent, as a whole, also presents its own characteristics. America constitutes a group of more or less homogeneous countries and in most parts of its territory U. S. monopoly capital maintains an absolute supremacy. Puppet governments or, in the best of cases, weak and fearful local rulers, are incapable of contradicting orders from their Yankee master. The United States has nearly reached the climax of its political and economic domination; it could hardly advance much; any change in the situation could bring about a setback. Its policy is to maintain that which has already been conquered. The line of action, at the present time, is limited to the brutal use of force with the purpose of thwarting the liberation movements, no matter of what type they might happen to be.

The slogan "we will not allow another Cuba" hides the possibility of perpetrating aggressions without fear of reprisal, such as the one carried out against the Dominican Republic, or before that, the massacre in Panama—and the clear warning stating that Yankee troops are ready to intervene anywhere in America where the established order may be altered, thus endangering their interests. This policy enjoys an almost absolute impunity: the OAS is a suitable mask, in spite of its unpopularity; the inefficiency of the UN is ridiculous as well as tragic; the armies of all American countries are ready to intervene in order to smash their peoples. The International of Crime and Treason has in fact been organized.

On the other hand, the national bourgeoisie have lost all their capacity to oppose imperialism—if they ever had it—and they have become the last card in the pack. There are no other alternatives: either a socialist revolution or a make-believe revolution.

Asia is a continent with different characteristics. The struggle for liberation waged against a series of European colonial powers resulted in the establishment of more or less progressive governments, whose ulterior evolution has brought about, in some cases, the reaffirming of the primary objectives of national liberation and in others, a setback towards the adoption of pro-imperialist positions.

From the economic point of view, the United States had very little to lose and much to gain in Asia. Changes benefit its interests; it struggles to displace other neocolonial powers and to penetrate new spheres of action in the economic field, sometimes directly, in other cases through Japan.

But there are special political conditions [in Asia], particularly in the Indo-China peninsula, which create certain characteristics of major importance and play a decisive role in the entire U. S. military strategy.

The imperialists encircle China through South Korea, Japan, Taiwan, South Viet Nam, and Thailand, at least.

This dual situation: a strategic interest as important as the military encirclement of the People's Republic of China and the capitalist ambition to penetrate these great markets—which they do not dominate yet—turns Asia into one of the most explosive points of the world today, in spite of its apparent stability outside of the Vietnamese war area.

The Middle East, though geographically a part of this continent, has its own contradictions and is actively in ferment; it is impossible to foretell how far the cold war between Israel, backed by the imperialists, and the progressive countries of that zone will go. This is just another of the world-threatening volcanoes.

Africa offers an almost virgin territory to the neocolonial invasion. There have been changes which, to some extent, forced neocolonial powers to give up their former absolute prerogatives. But when these changes are carried out without interruption, colonialism was succeeded, without violence, by a form of neocolonialism with similar effects as far as the economic situation is concerned.

The United States has no colonies in this region but is now struggling to penetrate its partners' fiefs. It can be said that following the strategic plans of U. S. imperialism, Africa constitutes its long-range reservoir; its present investments, though, are only important in the Union of South Africa and its penetration is beginning to be felt in the Congo, Nigeria, and other countries where a sharp rivalry with other imperialist powers is beginning to take place (nonviolent up to the present time).

So far it does not have great interests to defend there except its assumed right to intervene in every spot of the world where its monopolies detect the possibility of huge profits or the existence of large reserves of raw materials.

All this past history justifies our concern over the possibilities of liberating the peoples within a moderate or a short period of time.

If we stop to analyze Africa we observe that in the Portuguese colonies of Guinea, Mozambique, and Angola the struggle is waged with relative intensity, with particular success in the first and with variable success in the other two. We still witness in the Congo the dispute between Lumumba's successors and the old accomplices of Tshombe, a dispute which at the present time seems to favor the latter, those who have "pacified" a large area of the country for their own benefit—though the war is still latent.

In Rhodesia we have a different problem: British imperialism used every means within its reach to place power in the hands of the white minority, now in control. The conflict, from England's point of view, is absolutely unofficial; however, this power, with its habitual diplomatic cleverness—also called hypocrisy in plain language—presents a façade of displeasure before the measures adopted by the government of Ian Smith. Its crafty attitude is supported and followed by some Commonwealth countries, but is attacked by a large group of countries belonging to Black Africa, whether or not they are docile economic vassals of English imperialism.

Should the efforts of Rhodesia's black patriots to organize armed rebellion crystallize and should this movement be effectively supported by neighboring African nations, the situation in that country could become extremely explosive. But for the moment all these problems are being discussed in such innocuous organizations as the UN, the Commonwealth, and the OAU.

Nevertheless, the social and political evolution of Africa does not lead us to expect a continental revolution. The liberation struggle against the Portuguese should end victoriously, but Portugal means nothing in the imperialist field. The confrontations of revolutionary importance are those which place at bay all the imperialist apparatus, though this does not mean that we should stop fighting for the liberation of the three Portuguese colonies and for the deepening of their revolutions.

When the black masses of South Africa or Rhodesia start their authentic revolutionary struggle, a new era will dawn in Africa. Or when the impoverished masses of a nation rise up to rescue their right to a decent life from the hands of the ruling oligarchies.

Up to now, army putsches have followed one another; a group of officers succeeds one another or replaces rulers who no longer serve their caste interests and those of the powers who covertly manage them—but there are no great popular upheavals. In the Congo these characteristics appeared briefly, generated by the memory of Lumumba, but hey have been losing strength in the last few months.

In Asia, as we have seen, the situation is explosive. The points of friction are not only Viet Nam and Laos, where actual fighting is going on, but also Cambodia, where a direct U. S. aggression may start at any time, Thailand, Malaya, and, of course, Indonesia, where we cannot assume that the last word has been said, despite the annihilation of the Communist Party of that country carried out by the reactionaries when they took power. And also, naturally there is the Middle East.

In Latin America armed struggle is underway in Guatemala, Colombia, Venezuela, and Bolivia, and the first uprisings are appearing in Brazil. Other foci of resistance appear and are later extinguished. But almost every country of this continent is ripe for a type of struggle that, in order to achieve victory, cannot be content with anything less than establishing a government of a socialist nature.

On this continent, for all practical purposes, only one tongue is spoken (with the exception of Brazil, with whose people those who speak Spanish can easily make themselves understood, owing to the great similarity of both languages). There is also such a great similarity among the classes of the different countries, that an identification exists among them, as an "international American" type, much more complete than that of other continents. Language, customs, religion, a common foreign master, unite them. The degree and forms of exploitation are similar in their effects for both the exploiters and the exploited in many of the countries of our America. And rebellion is ripening swiftly here.

We may ask ourselves: how will this rebellion come to fruition? What type will it be? We have maintained for quite some time now that, owing to the similarity of characteristics, the struggle in America will achieve, in due course, continental proportions. It will be the scene of many great battles fought for the liberation of humanity.

Within the overall struggle on a continental scale, the battles which are now taking place are only episodes—but they have already furnished their martyrs, who will figure in the history of America as having given their necessary quota of blood in this last stage of the fight for the total freedom of man. These names will include Major Turcios Lima, the priest Camilo Torres, Major Fabricio Ojeda, Majors Lobatón and Luis de la Puente Uceda, all outstanding figures in the revolutionary movements of Guatemala, Colombia, Venezuela, and Peru.

But the active mobilization of the people creates new leaders; César Montes and Yon Sosa raise the flag of battle in Guatemala; Fabio Vázquez and Marulanda in Colombia; Douglas Bravo in the western half of the country and Américo Martín in El Bachiller direct their respective fronts in Venezuela.

New uprisings will take place in these and other countries of America, as has already happened in Bolivia; they will continue to grow in the midst of all the hardships inherent in this dangerous profession of the modern revolutionary. Many will perish, victims of their errors; others will fall in the hard battle ahead; new fighters and new leaders will appear in the heat of the revolutionary struggle. The people will produce their fighters and leaders in the selective process of the war itself—and Yankee agents of repression will increase. Today there are "advisers" in all the countries where armed struggle exists, and the Puruvian army, trained and advised by the Yankees, apparently carried out a successful action against the revolutionaries in that country. But if the foci of war are developed with sufficient political and military wisdom, they will become practically invincible, obliging the Yankees to send reinforcements. In Peru itself many new figures, practically unknown, are now tenaciously and firmly reorganizing the guerrilla movement. Little by little, the obsolete weapons which are sufficient for the repression of small armed bands will be exchanged for modern armaments and theU. S. military "advisers" will be replaced by U. S. soldiers until, at a given moment, they will be forced to send increasingly greater numbers of regular troops to ensure the relative stability of a government whose national puppet army is disintegrating before the attacks of the guerrillas. It is the road of Viet Nam; it is the road that should be followed by the peoples; it is the road that will be followed in America, with the special characteristic that the armed groups may create something like Coordinating Councils to make more difficult efforts of Yankee imperialism and contribute to the revolutionary cause.

America, forgotten continent in the world's more recent liberation struggles, now beginning to make itself heard through the Tricontinental in the voice of the vanguard of its peoples, the Cuban Revolution, will have a task of much greater relevance: to create a Second or a Third Viet Nam, or the Second and Third Viet Nam of the world.

In fact we must bear in mind that imperialism is a world system, the last stage of caiptalism—and it must be defeated in a great world confrontation. The strategic end of this struggle must be the destruction of imperialism. Our part, the responsibility of the exploited and underdeveloped of the world, is to eliminate the supply sources of imperialism: our oppressed nations, from which they extract capital, raw materials, cheap technicians and common labor, and to which they export new capital—instrument of domination—arms, and every kind of article, submerging us in absolute dependence.

The fundamental element of this strategic end is, then, the real liberation of all peoples, a liberation that will be brought about in most cases through armed struggle and will, in America, almost certainly have the characteristic of becoming a Socialist Revolution.

In envisaging the destruction of imperialism, it is necessary to identify its head, which is no other than the United States of America.

We must carry out a general task which has as its tactical purpose drawing the enemy out of his natural environment, forcing him to fight in places where his living habits clash with the existing reality. We must not underrate our adversary; the U. S. soldier has technical capacity and is backed by weapons and resources of such magnitude as to render him formidable. He lacks the essential ideological motivation which his bitterest enemies of today—the Vietnamese soldiers—have in the highest degree. We will only be able to triumph over such an army to the extent we can undermine its morale—and that is accomplished by causing it repeated defeats and repeated punishment.

But this brief scheme for victory implies immense sacrifice by the people, sacrifice that should be demanded beginning today, in plain words, and which perhaps may be less painful than what they would have to endure if we constantly avoided battle in an attempt to have others pull our chestnuts out of the fire.

It is probable, of course, that the last country to liberate itself will accomplish this without armed struggle and that people may be spared the sufferings of a long and cruel war against the imperialists. But perhaps it will be impossible to avoid this struggle or its effects in a global conflagration and the suffering may be the same, or even greater. We cannot foresee the future, but we should never give in to the defeatist temptation of being leaders of a nation that yearns for freedom but abhors the struggle it entails and awaits its freedom as a crumb of victory.

It is absolutely just to avoid all useless sacrifice. For that reason, it is necessary to study carefully the real possibilities that dependent America may have of liberating itself through peaceful means. For us, the answer to this question is quite clear: the present moment may or may not be the proper one for starting the struggle, but we cannot harbour any illusions, and we have no right to do so, that freedom can be obtained without fighting. And the battles will not be mere street fights with stones against tear-gas bombs, nor pacific general strikes; neither will they be those of a furious people destroying in two or three days the repressive superstructure of the ruling oligarchies. The struggle will be long, harsh, and its battle fronts will be the guerrilla's refuge, the cities, the homes of the fighters—where the repressive forces will go seeking easy victims among their families—among the massacred rural population, in the villages or cities destroyed by the bombardments of the enemy.

They themselves impel us to this struggle; there is no alternative other than to prepare it and decide to undertake it.

The beginnings will not be easy; they will be extremely difficult. All of the oligarchies' power of repression, all of their capacity for brutality and demagoguery will be placed at the service of their cause. Our mission, in the first hour, will be to survive; later, we will follow the perennial example of the guerrilla, carrying out armed propaganda (in the Vietnamese sense, that is, the propaganda of bullets, of battles won or lost—but fought—against the enemy). The great lesson of the invincibility of the guerrillas will take root in the dispossessed masses. The galvanizing of national spirit, preparation for harder tasks, for resisting even more violent repressions. Hatred as an element of struggle; relentless hatred of the enemy that impels us over and beyond the natural limitations of man and transforms us into effective, violent, selective and cold killing machines. Our soldiers must be thus; a people without hatred cannot vanquish a brutal enemy.

We must carry the war as far as the enemy carries it: to his home, to his centers of entertainment, make it a total war. It is necessary to prevent him from having a moment of peace, a quiet moment outside his barracks or even inside; we must attack him wherever he may be, make him feel like a cornered beast wherever he may move. Then his morale will begin to fall. He will become still more savage, but we shall see the signs of decadence begin to appear.

And let us develop a true proletarian internationalism, with international proletarian armies; let the flag under which we fight be the sacred cause of redeeming humanity, so that to die under the flag of Viet Nam, of Venezuela, of Guatemala, of Laos, of Guinea, of Colombia, of Bolivia, of Brazil—to name only the scenes of today's armed struggle—be equally glorious and desirable for an American, an Asian, an African, or even a European.

Each drop of blood spilled in a country under whose flag one has not been born is an experience for those who survive to apply later in the liberation struggle of their own countries. And each nation liberated is a step toward victory in the battle for the liberation of one's own country.

The time has come to settle our discrepancies and place everything we have at the service of the struggle.

We all know that great controversies agitate the world now fighting for freedom; no one can hide it. We also know that these controversies have reached such intensity and such bitterness that the possibility of dialogue and reconciliation seems extremely difficult, if not impossible. It is useless to search for means and ways to propitiate a dialogue which the hostile parties avoid. But the enemy is there; it strikes every day, and threatens us with new blows and these blows will unite us, today, tomorrow, or the day after. Whoever understands this first, and prepares for this necessary union, will earn the people's gratitude.

Because of the virulence and the intransigence with which each cause is defended, we, the dispossessed, cannot take sides with one or the other form of manifestation of these discrepancies, even if we at times coincide with the contentions of one party or the other, or in greater measure with those of one part than with those of the other. In time of war the expression of current differences constitutes a weakness; but as things stand at this moment, it is an illusion to hope to settle these differences by means of words. Time will erase them or give them their true explanation.

In our struggling world, all discrepancies regarding tactics and methods of action for the attainment of limited objectives should be analyzed with the respect that the opinions of others deserve. Regarding our great strategic objective, the total destruction of imperialism via armed struggle, we should be uncompromising.

Our aspirations to victory may be summed us thus: total destruction of imperialism by eliminating its firmest bulwark: imperialist domination by the United States of America. To carry out, as a tactical method, the gradual liberation of the peoples, one by one or in groups; forcing the enemy into a difficult fight far from its own territory; liquidation of all of its sustaining bases, that is, its dependent territories.

This means a long war. And, we repeat once more, a cruel war. Let no one fool himself at the outstart and let no one hesitate to begin in fear of the consequences it may bring to his people. It is almost our sole hope for victory. We cannot elude the call of this hour. Viet Nam is pointing it out with its endless lesson of heroism, its tragic and everyday lesson of struggle and death for the attainment of final victory.

There, the imperialist soldiers encounter the discomforts of those who, accustomed to the vaunted U. S. standard of living, must face a hostile land, the insecurity of those who are unable to move without being aware of walking on enemy territory, death to those who advance beyond their fortified encampments, the permanent hostility of an entire population. All this provokes internal repercussions in the United States and propitiates the resurgence of a factor which was attenuated in the full vigor of imperialism: class struggle even within its own territory.

What a luminous, near future would be visible to us if two, three or many Viet Nams flourished throughout the world with their share of death and their immense tragedies, their everyday heroism and their repeated blows against imperialism obliging it to disperse its forces under the attack of the increasing hatred of all the peoples of the earth!

And if we were all capable of uniting to make our blows more solid and more infallible so that the effectiveness of every kind of support given to the struggling peoples were increased—how great and how near that future would be!

If we—those of us who, on a small point of the world may fulfill the duty that we advocated and place at the disposal of this struggle whatever little we are able to give: our lives, our sacrifice—must some day breathe our last breath in any land, already ours, sprinkled with our blood, let it be known that we have measured the scope of our actions and that we consider ourselves no more than elements in the great army of the proletariat, but that we are proud to have learned from the Cuban Revolution, and from its great maximum leader, the great lesson emanating from Cuba's attitude in this part of the world: "What do the dangers or the sacrifices of a man or of a nation matter, when the destiny of humanity is at stake?" Our very action is a battle cry against imperialism, and a call for the peoples' unity against the great enemy of mankind: the United States of America. Wherever death may surprise us, it will be welcome, provided that this, our battle cry, has reached a receptive ear and that another hand be extended to take up our weapons, and that other men come forward to intone the funeral dirge with the staccato of machine guns and new cries of battle and victory.

GUEVARA'S BOLIVIAN DIARY 10

The diary that Guevara kept daily in Bolivia for eleven months had an existence almost as adventurous as its author. Written in a German calendar notebook, the dairy was captured by the Bolivian army. Because of the intense interest in the document, book, magazine, and newspaper publishers from the United States, Europe, and elsewhere sought to obtain copies of it, offering bids to the Bolivians which ranged over $100,000. The matter was settled, however, when Cuba announced that it had obtained and was publishing the diary (it lacked a few pages) and had made arrangements with foreign publishers for publication in their respective countries. Subsequently it was learned that Premier Castro had obtained the diary from Bolivian Interior Minister Antonio Arguedas, who acted through motives which have never been fully clarified. The diary is a human document, recording in a highly personal manner Guevara's victories, mishaps, and discomforts as he attempted to build a guerrilla movement in Bolivia. At the end of each month he wrote a summary of that month's activities, and these summaries contained Guevara's analysis of what had gone right—and what had gone wrong. As the months went by, and the first successful ambushes gave way to increased difficulties, Guevara clearly indicated in his writings that he knew he was in trouble. He apparently never gave up hope, however. A photographic copy of the diary was supplied to the editor by Cuban Foreign Minister Raúl Roa. In the following pages are photographic reproductions of the summaries, together with translations prepared at the Research Institute for Cuba and the Caribbean.

... en el terso llegamos al campamento por la noche, luego de hacer la medición del río. Aquí sin novedad; Coco salió a Santa Cruz para esperar al Chino.

30

Marcos, Pacho, Miguel y Pombo salieron en plan instrucción de explorar un arroyo más lejano, deben estar dos días fuera. Llovió bastante. En la casa, sin novedad

Análisis del mes

Todo ha salido bastante bien: mi llegada sin inconvenientes; la mitad de la gente está aquí también sin inconvenientes, aunque se demoraron algo; los principales colaboradores de Ricardo se alzan contra viento y marea. El panorama se perfila bueno en esta región apartada donde todo indica que podremos pasarnos prácticamente el tiempo que estimemos conveniente. Los planes son: esperar al resto de la gente, aumentar el número de bolivianos por lo menos hasta 20 y comenzar a operar. Falta averiguar la reacción de Monje y cómo se comporta la gente de Guevara.

Guevara's Diary: November summary

de la revolución.

Fidel me envió el mensaje adjunto.

Análisis del mes

Se ha completado el equipo de cubanos con todo éxito y la moral de la gente es buena y solo hay pequeños problemitas. Los bolivianos están bien aunque son pocos; la actitud de Monje puede retardar el desarrollo de un lado pero contribuir por otro, al liberarme de compromisos políticos. Los próximos pasos, fuera de esperar más bolivianos, constan en hablar con Guevara y con los argentinos Mauricio y Jozami (Moretti y el partido de Kolle, la...).

GUEVARA'S BOLIVIAN DIARY

November

Everything has turned out rather well: My arrival [was] without difficulty; half of the men are also here without trouble, although they were somewhat delayed; Ricardo's main collaborators rise up against winds and tides. The panorama looks good in this isolated region where everything indicates that we shall be able to stay practically as long as we deem necessary. The plans are: to wait for the rest of the men, to increase the number of Bolivians to at least 20 and to begin operations. We still have to find out Monje's reaction and how [Moisés] Guevara's people behave.

December

The team of Cubans has been completed successfully; the morale of the men is good and there are only little problems. The Bolivians are fine, although they are few in number. Monje's attitude can hold back the development on one side but contribute on the other, by releasing me of political entanglements. The next steps, besides waiting for more Bolivians, consist in talking with Guevara and with the Argentineans, Mauricio and Jozami (Massetti and the dissident party).

January

As was to be expected, Monje's attitude was evasive at first and later on treacherous. The party is now taking up arms against us and I do not know how far this will reach, but that will not stop us, and it may in the long run prove beneficial (I am almost certain of this). The most honest and combative men are with us, although they may go through more or less serious conflicts with their consciences.

Up until now, Guevara has responded well. We shall see how he and his men behave in the future.

Tania has departed but there have been no signs of life from the Argentineans nor from her. Now we begin the actual guerrilla stage and we shall test the troops; time will tell the results and what the perspectives of the Bolivian revolution are.

Out of all that was foreseen, the incorporation of Bolivian combatants was the one going slowest.

February

Although I have no news about what happened in the camp, everything goes fairly well, with due exceptions, fatal in this case.

FEBRUAR 1967

TERMIN-ÜBERSICHT

FEBRUAR

1 Mi

2 Do

3 Fr

4 Sa

5 So

6 Mo

7 Di

8 Mi

9 Do

10 Fr

11 Sa

12 So

13 Mo

14 Di

Mittwoch

1

FEBRUAR

Guevara's Diary: January summary

Resumen del mes

Aunque no tengo noticias de lo ocurrido en el campamento, todo marcha aproximadamente bien, con las debidas excepciones, fatales en estos casos.

En lo externo; no hay noticias de los dos hombres que debían mandarme para completar el conjunto; el francés ya debe estar en La Paz y cualquier día en el campamento; no tengo noticias de los argentinos ni del Chileno; los mensajes se reciben bien en ambas direcciones; la actitud del Partido sigue siendo vacilante y doble, lo menos que se puede decir de ella, aunque queda una aclaración, que puede ser definitiva, cuando hable con la nueva delegación.

La marcha se cumplió bastante bien, pero fue empañada por el accidente que costó la vida a Benjamín; la gente está débil todavía y no todos los bolivianos resistirán. Los últimos días de hambre han mostrado una debilitación del entusiasmo, caída que se hace más patente al quedar divididos. De los cubanos, dos de los de poca experiencia, Pacho y el Rubio no han respondido todavía, Alejandro lo ha hecho a plenitud; de los viejos, Marcos da continuos dolores de cabeza y Ricardo no está cumpliendo cabalmente. Los demás bien.

La próxima etapa será la del combate y decisiva.

Guevara's Diary: February

From the outside, there is no news of the two men that should be sent to me to complete the group; the Frenchman should be in La Paz already and in the camp any day now; I have no news from the Argentineans nor from Chino; the messages are received well in both directions; the attitude of the party continues to be vacillating and double, the least that can be said concerning it, although there is another explanation, which could be decisive, when I talk with the new delegation.

The march was carried out quite well but was tarnished by the accident which cost Benjamin's life; the people are still weak and not all of the Bolivians will endure. The last days of hunger have shown a lessening of enthusiasm which becomes more evident when they are divided.

Of the Cubans, two of the ones with little experience, Pacho and Rubio, have yet to respond; Alejandro has done so to the fullest; of the old ones, Marcos continuously causes headaches and Ricardo is not performing properly. The rest are doing well.

The next stage will be combative and decisive.

March

This month is full of events but the general outlook has the following characteristics: a period of consolidation and purification for the guerrillas, strictly fulfilled; a period of slow progress with the incorporation of those who came from Cuba who do not appear bad, and those of Guevara who in general are of low grade (two deserters, one "talkative" prisoner, three quitters and two weaklings); a period of beginning the fight, characterized with a spectacular and precise attack but sprinkled with glaring indecisions before and after the feat (Marcos' withdrawal, Braulio's action), a period of the beginning of the enemy counteroffensive, which has been characterized up until now by: a. a tendency to establish controls that would isolate us, b. a clamoring on a national and international level, c. total ineffectiveness until now, d. mobilization of the campesinos.

Evidently, we shall have to start the march before I had thought, leaving behind a group in reserve and with the handicap of four possible informers. The situation is not good, but another period of trials is beginning now for the guerrillas which will be good for them once they overcome it.

Composition: Vanguard: Chief: Miguel; Benigno, Pacho, Loro, Aniceto, Camba, Coco, Darío, Julio, Pablo, Raúl.

Rearguard: Chief: Joaquín; Second in command: Braulio; Rubio, Marcos, Pedro, Médico, Polo, Walter, Víctor (Pepe, Paco, Eusebio, Chingolo).

Freitag

31

MÄRZ

Sin mayores novedades. Guevara anunció para mañana la terminación de la cueva. Inti y Ricardo reportaron
que los guardias habían vuelto a tomar nuestra pequeñita,
previa una preparación artillera (morteros) aviación, etc. Ésto
obstaculiza nuestros planes de ir a Pirirenda a abastecernos,
no obstante, le di instrucciones a Manuel de avanzar con la gente hasta la costa. Si esta está vacía, tomarla y cuando los
bravos a avisarme para que nosotros nos movilicemos en el
paso de mañana; si está tomada y no se puede hacer un
toque por sorpresa, retornar y explorar la posibilidad de
flanquear Arpajosz para hacerles una emboscada entre
Cal y Lagunillas.   11

La radio sigue con su alharaca y los partes se suceden a
ciencia oficiosa de combate. Hoy fijado nuestra posición con absoluta precisión entre el Yaki y el Ñacahuazú y
temo que traten de hacer algún movimiento envolvente.

Hablé con Benigno sobre su error en no irnos a buscar y le expliqué la situación de Moisés; reaccionó bien.

Por la noche hablé con Toro y Aniceto. La conversación fue
muy mala. Toro llegó a decir que estábamos podridos tú
cuando lo planteó, dejó eso para Moisés; Benigno; Aniceto se
solidarizó a medias con él pero luego le confesó a Lo-
co que habían sido cómplices en un robo de latas y Le-   16
Inti que no se solidarizaba con las expresiones de Toro sobre
Benigno y otra sobre Pombo y sobre la "disciplina
general de la guerrilla", aproximadamente.   18

Resumen del mes.   19

Éste está pletórico de acontecimientos pero el panorama general se presenta con los siguientes carac-
terísticos: etapa de consolidación y depuración para
la guerrilla, cumplida a cabalidad; lenta etapa

(Dates in right margin: 16, 17, 18, 19, 20)

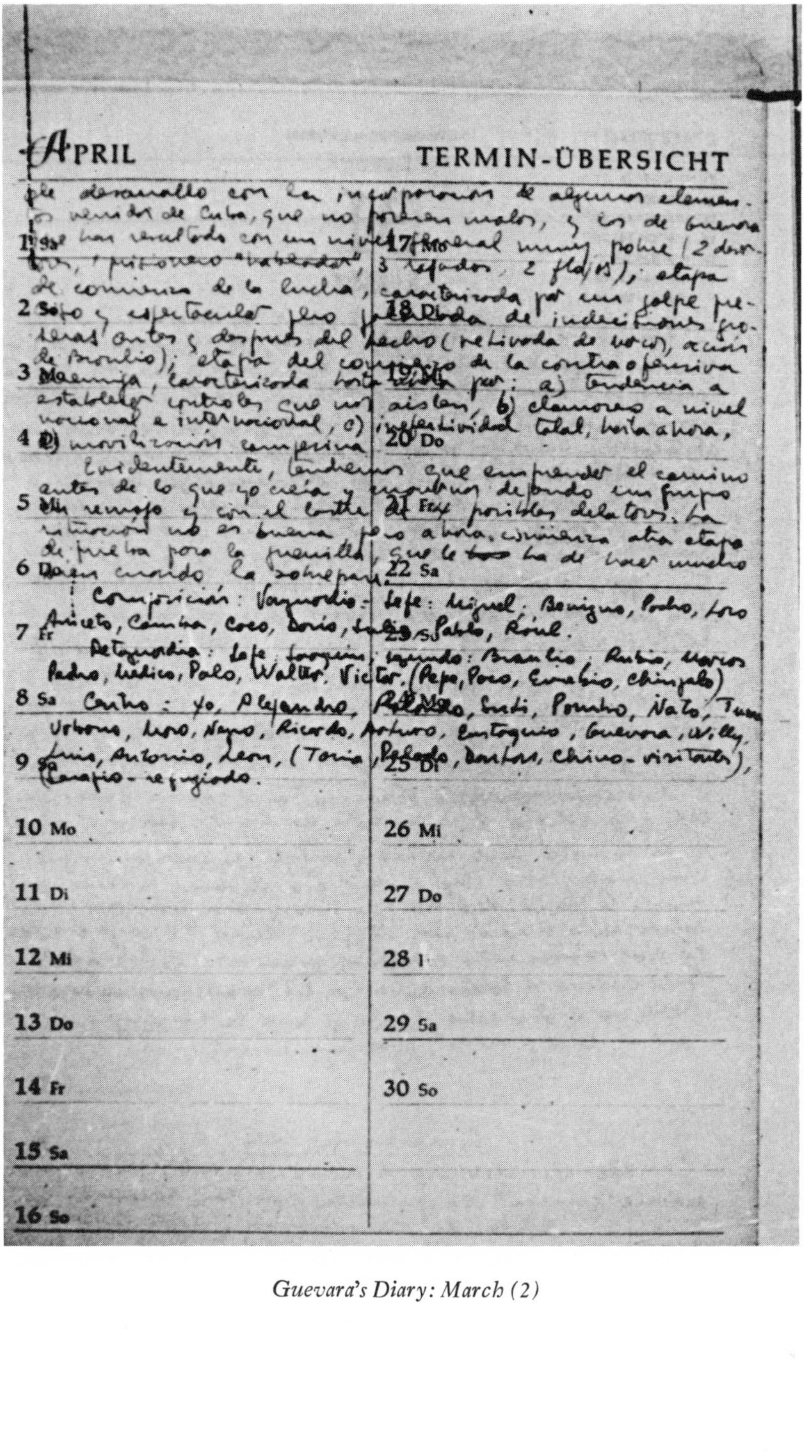

1

2

3

4

5

6

7 Fr

8 Sa

9

10 Mo

11 Di

12 Mi

13 Do

14 Fr

15 Sa

16 So

17

18

19

20 Do

22 Sa

25 Do

26 Mi

27 Do

28 I

29 Sa

30 So

Guevara's Diary: March (2)

Center: Myself, Alejandro, Rolando, Inti, Pombo, Ñato, Tuma, Urbano, Moro, Negro, Ricardo, Arturo, Eustaquio, Guevara, Willy, Luis, Antonio, León (Tania, Pelado, Danton, Chino—visitors), (Serapio—refugee).

April

Things are within normal limits, although we have to regret two great losses: Rubio and Rolando; the death of the latter is a severe blow, as I had intended leaving him in charge of an eventual second front. We had four more actions; all of them were positive in general and one was very good: the ambush in which Rubio died.

In another aspect, the isolation continues to be complete; sickness has undermined the health of some of the campañeros, compelling us to divide forces, which has diminished our effectiveness. We still have not been able to make contact with Joaquín. The peasant base has not yet been developed, although it seems that through planned terror we can neutralize most of them; support will come later. Not one person has joined up with us, and in addition to the deaths, we have lost Loro, who disappeared after the action in Taperillas.

From the notes on military strategy, the following can be emphasized: a. The controls have not been effective up until now, they disturb us but they allow us to move around because of their slight mobility and their weakness. Besides, after the last ambush against the dogs and the instructor, it is to be presumed that they will be more careful on entering the woods. b. The clamor continues, but now on both sides, and after the publication of my article in Havana, there can be no doubt about my presence here. It seems certain that the North Americans will intervene strongly here and are already sending helicopters and, apparently, Green Berets, although they have not been seen here. c. The army (at least one or two companies) has improved its technique: they surprised us in Taperillas and they were not demoralized at El Meson. d. The campesino mobilization does not exist, except for informative tasks which annoy somewhat. They are neither very rapid nor very efficient; they can be neutralized.

Chino's status has changed, and he will be a combatant until the second or third front is formed. Danton and Carlos fell victims of their own haste, their near desperation to leave, and of my lack of energy to stop them, so that communication with Cuba has been cut off (Danton) and the plan of action in Argentina (Carlos) has been lost.

In short: it's been a month in which everything has been resolved normally, taking into consideration the necessary eventualities of the guer-

Los cosas se presentan dentro de lo normal, aunque debemos lamentar dos reveses perdidos: Rubio y Rolando; la muerte de este último en un revés golpe, pues lo privaba después a cargo del eventual segundo frente. Tenemos cuatro acciones más, todas ellas con resultado positivo en general, y una muy buena; la emboscada en que murió el Rubio.

En otro plano; el aislamiento sigue siendo total. Las enfermedades han minado la salud de algunos compañeros, obligándonos a dividir fuerzas, lo que nos ha quitado mucha efectividad; todavía no hemos podido hacer contacto con Joaquín; la base campesina sigue sin desarrollarse, aunque parece que, mediante el terror planificado, lograremos la neutralidad de los unos, el apoyo vendrá después. No se ha producido una sola incorporación y, a parte de los muertos, hemos tenido la baja del Loro, desaparecido luego de la acción de Tañerillas.

De los puntos anotados sobre la estrategia militar, se puede recalcar: a) los controles no han podido ser eficaces hasta ahora y nos causan molestias pero nos permiten movernos, dada su poca movilidad y su debilidad; además, luego de la última emboscada contra los perros y el instructor, es de presumir que se cuidarán mucho de entrar en el monte; b) el clamoreo sigue pero ahora por muchas partes y luego de la publicación en La Habana de mi artículo, no debe haber duda de mi presencia aquí. Parece seguro que los norteamericanos intervendrán fuerte aquí y ya están mandando helicópteros y, parece, boinas verdes, aunque no se han visto por aquí; c) el ejército (por lo menos una compañía o dos) ha mejorado su técnica; nos sorprendieron en Tañerillas y no se desmoralizaron en el Mesón; d) la movilización campesina es inexistente, salvo en las tareas de información que molestan algo, pero no son muy rápidos ni eficientes; los podemos anular.

El estatus del Chino ha cambiado y será combatiente hasta la próxima de una segunda o tercer frente.

Dantón y Carlos cayeron víctimas de su afán, casi exasperación, por salir y de mi falta de energía para impedírselos, de modo que también se cortan las comunicaciones con Cuba (Dantón) y se pierde el esquema de acción en la Argentina (Carlos).

En resumen: un mes en que todo se ha resuelto

MAI

dentro de lo normal, considerando los eventualidades
nerviosas de la guerrilla. La moral es buena en lo

1 Mo ~~No~~ .... ha tenido que .... **17 Mi** ..... aprobado su examen
preliminar de guerrilleros.

2 Di

3 Mi

4 Do Christi Himmelfahrt

5 Fr

6 Sa

7 So

8 Mo

9 Di

10 Mi

11 Do

12 Fr

13 Sa

14 So Pfingsten · Muttertag

15 Mo Pfingstmontag

16 Di

18 Do

19 Fr

20 Sa

21 So Dreieinigkeitsfest

22 Mo

23 Di

24 Mi

25 Do Fronleichnam

26 Fr

27 Sa

28 So

29 Mo

30 Di

31 Mi

Guevara's Diary: April (2)

rilla groups. The morale is good among all those combatants that have passed their preliminary test as guerrilla fighters.

May

The negative point is the impossibility of making contact with Joaquín notwithstanding our wandering through the mountain ridges. There are indications that he has moved to the north.

From the military point of view the three new combats, causing losses to the army without suffering any ourselves and the penetrations into Pirirenda and Caraguatarenda, indicate success. The dogs have been declared incompetent and have been withdrawn from circulation.

The most important characteristics are:

1. Total lack of contact with Manila, La Paz, and Joaquín, which reduces us to the 25 men who comprise the group.

2. Complete lack of incorporation of the campesinos, although they are losing their fear of us, and we are succeeding in winning their admiration. It's a slow and patient task.

3. The party, through Kolle, offers its collaboration, apparently without reservations.

4. The clamor about the Debray case has given more belligerency to our movement than ten victorious combats.

5. The guerrilla group is acquiring a powerful and secure morale, which, well managed, is a warranty of success.

6: The army still has not organized itself and its technique does not improve substantially.

The news of the month is the apprehension and escape of Loro, who should now rejoin us or go to La Paz to make contact.

The army issued a communiqué about the detention of all the campesinos who collaborated with us in the zone of Masicurí. Now comes a period when both sides will use terror against the campesinos, but in different ways; our triumph will mean the qualitative change necessary for a leap in development.

June

The negative points are: the impossibility of making contact with Joaquín and the gradual loss of men, each of which constitutes a serious defeat, although the army does not know it. We have had two small combats during the month, causing the army four deaths and three wounded, according to their own information.

The most important characteristics are:

1. The total lack of contacts continues, which reduces us now to 24 men, with Pombo wounded and our mobility reduced.

El punto negativo es la imposibilidad de hacer contacto con Joaquín, pese a nuestro empeño por los extremos. Hay indicios de que **17** se han marchado a la zona del norte.

Desde el punto de vista militar, tres nuevos combates, causándole bajas al Ejército y sin sufrir ninguna, además de las penetraciones en Pirirenda y Caraguatarenda, indican el buen éxito. Los perros se han declarado incompetentes y son retirados de la circulación.

Las características más importantes son:

4 So   1º Falta total de contacto con Manila, La Paz y Joaquín, lo que nos reduce a los 25 hombres que **5** constituyen el grupo.   **21 Mi**

2º Falta completa de incorporación campesina, aunque **6** nos van perdiendo el miedo y se logra **22 Do** la admiración de los campesinos. Es una tarea lenta y paciente.

7 Mi   3º El partido, a través de **23 Fr** ofrece su colaboración, al parecer, sin reservas.

4º El clamoreo del caso **24 Sa** le da a todo más beligerancia **8 Do** nuestro movimiento que los combates victoriosos.

5º La guerrilla va adquiriendo una moral prepotente, **9** segura que, bien administrada, es una garantía de éxito.

10 6º El Ejército sigue sin organizarse y su técnica no mejora sustancialmente.

11 So Noticia del mes es el apresamiento y fuga del Loyola, **27 Di** ahora debe de incorporarse o dirigirse a La Paz a hacer contacto. **12 Mi** El Ejército dio el parte de la **28** detención de todos los campesinos que colaboraron con nosotros en la zona de Masicurí. **13** Ahora viene una etapa en la **29 Do** que el terror sobre los campesinos se ejercerá desde ambas partes, aunque con ca- **14** racteres diferentes, nuestro triunfo significará el cambio cualitativo necesario para un salto en su desarrollo.

15 Do

16 Fr

Guevara's Diary: May

Guevara's Diary: June

2. We continue to feel the lack of incorporation of campesinos. It is a vicious circle: to obtain this incorporation we need to carry out permanent action in populated territory, and to do this we need more men.

3. The guerrilla legend grows as foam; we are now the invincible supermen.

4. The lack of contacts extends to the party, although we have made an attempt through Paulino which may be successful.

5. Debray continues being news, but now as related to my case, in which I appear as leader of this movement. We shall see the result of this step taken by the government and find out whether it is positive or negative for us.

6. The morale of the guerrillas continues to be solid, and the decision to fight is increasing. All the Cubans are examples in combat and there are only two or three weak Bolivians.

7. The army continues to be nil with respect to military tasks, but they are working on the campesinos in a way that must not be underestimated, as they transform all the members of the community into informers, whether by fear or by deceiving them with respect to our objectives.

8. The massacre in the mines greatly clarifies the panorama for us and, if the proclamation can be spread, it will be an important factor of clarification.

Our most urgent task is to reestablish contact with La Paz, to be resupplied with military equipment and medicine and to obtain the incorporation of some 50-100 men from the city, although the number of combatants in action will be reduced to some 10-25.

July

The negative points, the same as the previous month, continue to be the impossibility of making contact with Joaquín or the outside and the loss of men; now there are 22 of us, three being crippled, including myself, and this decreases our mobility. We have had three clashes, including the taking of Samaipata, causing the army seven dead and ten wounded, which are approximate figures according to confused dispatches.

We lost two men and one was wounded.

The most important characteristics are:

1. The total lack of contact continues.

2. The lack of incorporation of the campesinos continues to be felt, although there are some encouraging signs in the reception given to us by old campesino acquaintances.

17

18

19

20 Sa

21 So

22

23

24

25 Mo

26 Sa

10 Do

11

12 Sa   28 Mo

13 So   29 Di

14 Mo   30 Mi

15 Di   Mariä Himmelfahrt   31 Do

16 M

Guevara's Diary: July (1)

que lo da a conocer. Calculamos unos 2 muertos y en la
exposición de ellos por... y unos... noticias contradictorias.
... especie ... de Chile habla de 6 heridos y 5 muertos del 30

Dienstag 1

de... después otra parte en su armamento la toma de
... y que un subteniente está fuera de peligro.
... muertos... Abril no puede ser considerado,
... era un introspección ... pero combativo y poco tra-
... pero ... y constantemente interesado en los
problemas políticos, aunque no hacía nunca pregunta.
Ricardo era el más indisciplinado del grupo interno y
menos decisión tenía frente al sacrificio cotidiano
pero era un extraordinario combatiente y un viejo
... de aventuras en el primer fracaso de Segundo...
el Congo y ahora aquí. Es otra pérdida sensible por su...
Somos 22, entre ellos, dos heridos, Pacho y Pablito
y yo, con el asma a todo vapor.

9

Día tranquilo. Miguel y Camba iniciaron
la senda pero avanzaron poco más de un kiló-
metro debido a las dificultades del terreno esta
vegetación. Matamos un potro helado que nos
debe dar carne para 5-6 días. Se hicieron las
trincheritas para tender una emboscada al
ejército si viniera por aquí. La idea es dejar-
pasar si vinieran mañana o pasado y no descu-
brirán el campamento y meterles bala después.

h = 650 m.

15

16

17

18

19

20

Guevara's Diary: July (2)

3. The legend of the guerrilla group is acquiring continental dimensions: Onganía closes the border and Peru takes precautions.

4. The attempt to make contacts through Paulino fails.

5. The morale and the fighting experience of the guerrillas increase with each combat; Camba and Chapaco remain weak.

6. The army keeps on missing the mark, but there are units which seem to be more combative.

7. The political crisis in the government increases, but the U.S.A. is giving small credits which are a great help on the Bolivian level and contribute to ease the discontent.

The most urgent tasks are: to reestablish the contacts, incorporate fighters, and obtain medicine.

August

It was, without any doubt, the worst month we have had since the war started. The loss of all the caves containing the documents and medicine was a hard blow, above all psychologically. The loss of two men at the end of the month and the subsequent march on a horsemeat diet demoralized the men and provoked the first case of giving up, Camba, which would constitute a net gain except under these circumstances. The lack of contact with the outside and with Joaquín and the fact that prisoners taken from him have talked, also demoralized the troops a little. My illness caused uncertainty in several others and all this was reflected in our only clash, in which we should have caused several enemy losses but only wounded one. On the other hand, the difficult march through the hills without water brought out some negative aspects of the men.

The most important characteristics:

1. We continue without contacts of any kind and without reasonable hope of establishing them in the near future.

2. We continue without any incorporation on the part of the campesinos, logical to understand if we take into account the little contact we have had with them in recent times.

3. There is a lowering, I hope temporary, of the fighting morale.

4. The army does not increase its effectiveness nor its combativeness.

We are in a downward period in our morale and in our revolutionary legend. The most urgent tasks continue to be the same as those of last month, i.e., to reestablish contacts, to incorporate fighters, to supply ourselves with medicine and equipment.

It should be taken into account that Inti and Coco excel ever more firmly as revolutionary and military cadres.

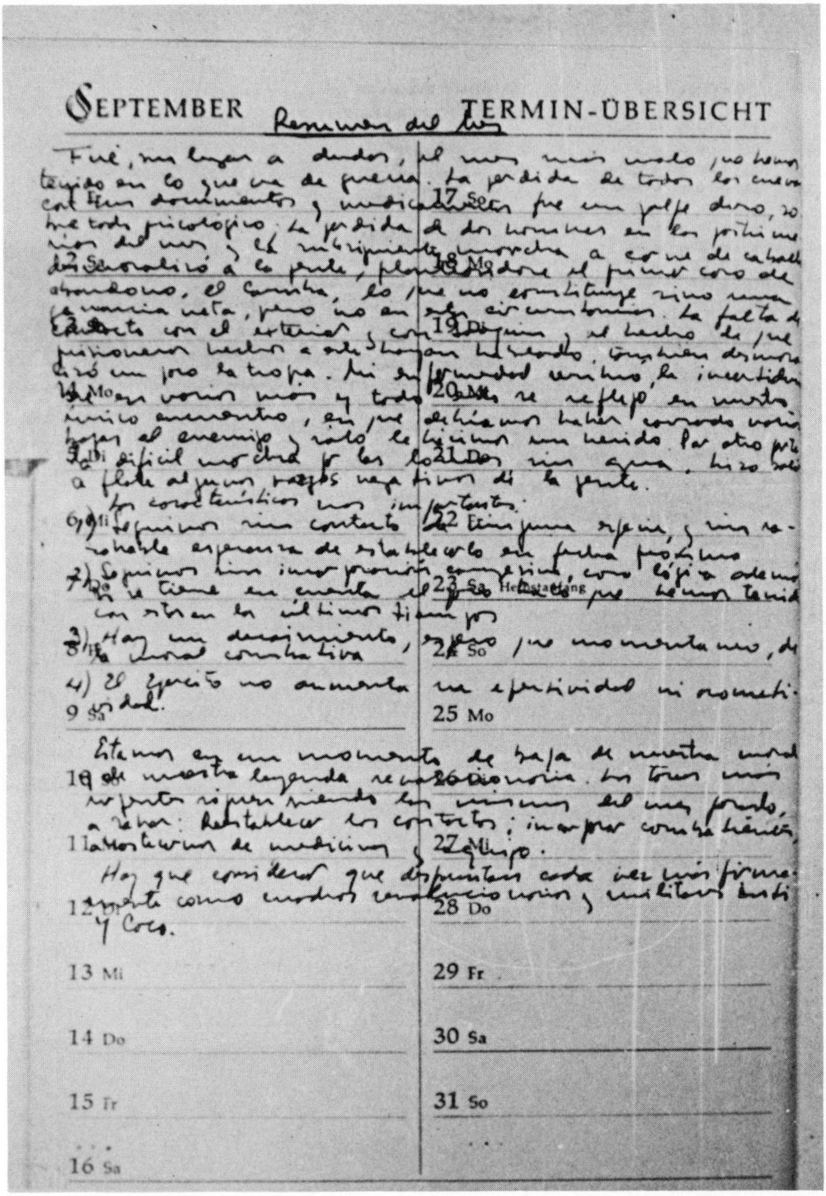
SEPTEMBER TERMIN-ÜBERSICHT

Resumen del mes

Fue, sin lugar a dudas, el mes más malo que hemos tenido en lo que va de guerra. La pérdida de todas las cuevas con sus documentos y medicamentos fue un golpe duro, sobre todo psicológico. La pérdida de dos hombres en las postrimerías del mes y la subsiguiente marcha a carne de caballo desmoralizó a la gente, planteándose el primer caso de abandono, el Camba, lo que no constituye sino una ganancia neta, pero no en estas circunstancias. La falta de contacto con el exterior y con Joaquín, y el hecho de que prisioneros hechos a éste hayan hablado, también desmoralizó un poco la tropa. Mi enfermedad sembró la incertidumbre en varios más y todo esto se reflejó en nuestro único encuentro, en que debíamos haber causado varias bajas al enemigo y sólo le hicimos un herido. Por otra parte la difícil marcha por las lomas sin agua, hizo salir a flote algunos rasgos negativos de la gente.

Las características más importantes:

1) Seguimos sin contacto de ninguna especie, y sin razonable esperanza de establecerlo en fecha próxima.

2) Seguimos sin incorporación campesina, cosa lógica además si se tiene en cuenta el poco trato que hemos tenido con éstos en los últimos tiempos.

3) Hay un decaimiento, espero que momentáneo, de la moral combatiente.

4) El ejército no aumenta su efectividad ni acometividad.

Estamos en un momento de baja de nuestra moral y de nuestra leyenda revolucionaria. Las tareas más urgentes siguen siendo las mismas del mes pasado, a saber: Restablecer los contactos, incorporar combatientes, abastecernos de medicinas y equipo.

Hay que considerar que despuntan cada vez más firmemente como cuadros revolucionarios y militares Inti y Coco.

Guevara's Diary: August

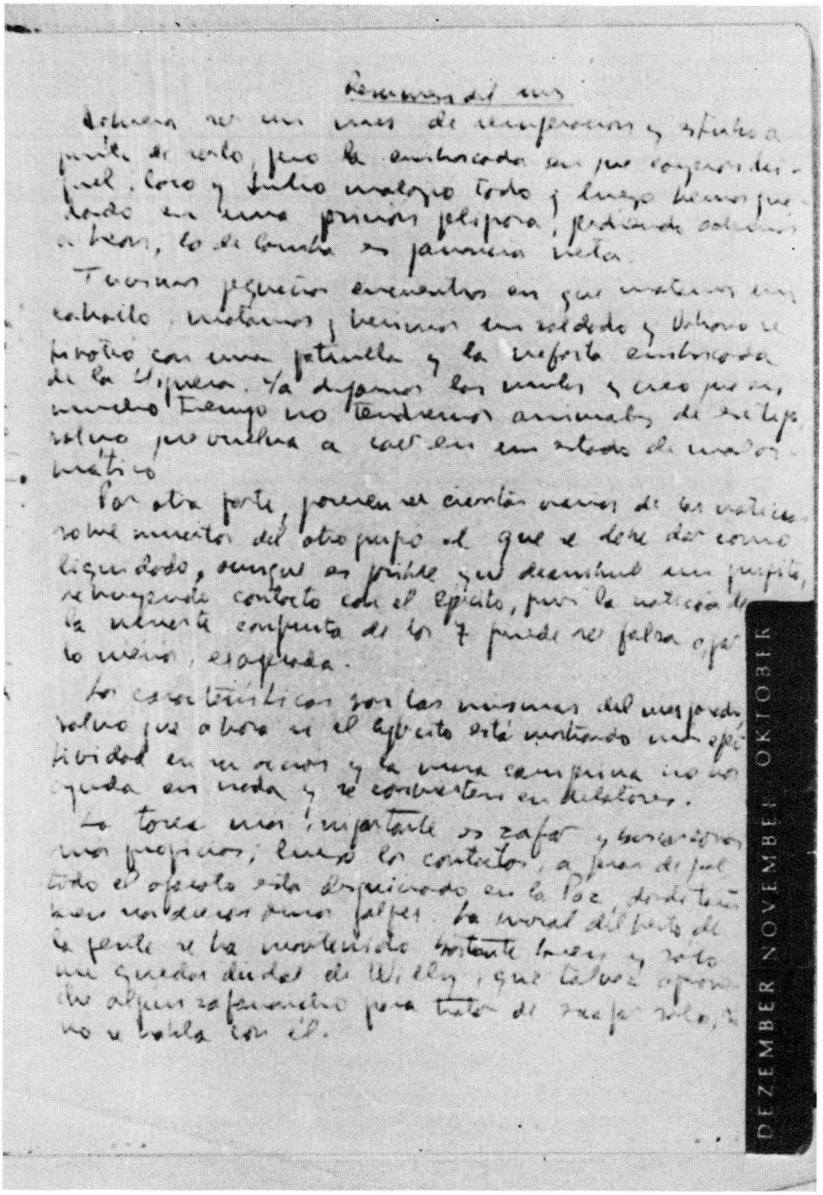

Resumen del mes

Debiera ser un mes de recuperación y estuvo a punto de serlo, pero la emboscada en que cayeron Miguel, Coco y Julio malogró todo y luego hemos quedado en una posición peligrosa, perdiendo además a León; lo de Camba es ganancia neta.

Tuvimos pequeños encuentros en que matamos un caballo, matamos y herimos un soldado y Urbano se tiroteó con una patrulla y la nefasta emboscada de La Higuera. Ya dejamos las mulas y creo que en mucho tiempo no tendremos animales de ese tipo, salvo que vuelva a caer en un estado de mal asmático.

Por otra parte, parecen ser ciertas varias de las noticias sobre muertos del otro grupo al que se debe dar como liquidado, aunque es posible que deambule un grupito, rehuyendo contacto con el Ejército, pues la noticia de la muerte conjunta de los 7 puede ser falsa o, por lo menos, exagerada.

Las características son las mismas del mes pasado, salvo que ahora sí el Ejército está mostrando más efectividad en su acción y la masa campesina no nos ayuda en nada y se convierten en delatores.

La tarea más importante es zafar y buscar zonas más propicias; luego los contactos, a pesar de que todo el aparato está desquiciado en La Paz donde también nos dieron duros golpes. La moral del resto de la gente se ha mantenido bastante bien, y sólo me quedan dudas de Willy, que tal vez aproveche algún zafarrancho para tratar de escapar solo, si no se habla con él.

Guevara's Diary: September summary

September

It should have been a month of recuperation and it was on the point of being so. But the ambush in which Miguel, Coco, and Julio fell spoiled everything, and then we have remained in a dangerous position, besides losing Leon. As to Camba it is a net gain.

We had small clashes in which we killed a horse, killed and wounded a soldier, and Urbano exchanged shots with a patrol, also there was the ominous ambush in La Higuera. We already have left the mules, and I believe that for a long time we shall have no more animals of that type, unless I should relapse into an asthmatic condition.

On the other hand, some of the news about the dead in the other group seems to be true, and that group should be considered liquidated, although it is possible that a little group is roaming, avoiding contact with the army, because the news of the joint death of the seven may be false, or at least exaggerated.

The characteristics are the same as those of last month, except that now the army is showing more effectiveness in its action, and the mass of campesinos does not help us at all and they have become informers.

The most important tasks are to escape and look for more propitious zones; later [reestablish] the contacts, despite the fact that the whole apparatus is badly disjointed in La Paz, where they have also given us hard blows. The morale of the rest of the men has been sustained fairly well. My only doubts are about Willy, who may take advantgae of some clash to try to escape by himself unless I have a talk with him.

ACCOUNT BY CIRO ROBERTO BUSTOS 11

Early in 1964 a Castroite guerrilla movement was launched in the province of Salta in northwest Argentina. The guerrillas were, however, within a short time decisively crushed by the Argentine armed forces. Linked with the revolutionaries, either at the time of their uprising or subsequently during the imprisonment of the survivors, was a commercial artist named Ciro Roberto Bustos. Later, when Guevara set in motion his Bolivian venture, intending to extend the guerrilla movement to Argentina and other countries, Bustos was summoned to Bolivia. Whether Bustos knew he would be seeing Guevara is not clear—he claims in the following account that he was aware only that he would be attending a secret "political meeting" in Bolivia. At any rate, Bustos did confer with Guevara and was informed of Guevara's continental plan. He was provided with funds and given detailed instructions on the role he was to play in furthering this plan in Argentina. Bustos, together with the French writer Regis Debray and the Englishman George Andrew Roth, then left the guerrillas and attempted to make his way through the Bolivian army lines. They were captured, however, and although Roth was later released, Bustos and Debray were brought to trial and each sentenced to 30 years in prison. The following is an account Bustos gave Bolivian intelligence authorities of his stay with the guerrillas. It is a firsthand view of Guevara and his men, and it provides insight into why Guevara was in Bolivia and what he hoped and planned to accomplish.

ACCOUNT BY CIRO ROBERTO BUSTOS OF HIS STAY
WITH GUEVARA'S GUERRILLAS IN BOLIVIA

Contact in Buenos Aires (Argentina)

URING THE EARLY PART of February, 1967, and after having made some contacts in Buenos Aires about which I know nothing (except the meeting with Isaac Rutman), Elma or Tania came to my house in Cordoba and asked me to attend a clandestine political meeting that was to be held in Bolivia. Her invitation was prompted by the fact that I was the only person tied in with the group arrested in Salta, because of the help I had given in the collection of funds, etc. She stressed the need to discuss a similar plan with a group or front that had been recently formed in La Paz.

Her attitude was reserved, secretive, yet revealing of important expectations on a high level. She insisted that she could not reveal much more but that I had nothing to lose; that my expenses would be covered and that there was a possibility of collecting firsthand information that would result in a substantial newspaper story on my return. I argued the difficulties involved because of my work and the amount of time that the trip would take. I requested a concrete reply as to how long the venture would take and she replied that certainly the meeting would not take longer than two days and the whole trip would take around a week, ten days at the most.

I made it clear that I had the responsibility of a family which included small children and that I could not possibly spare more time. She indicated that the trip would not take longer than the end of February at the latest and that if something different came up she would let me know. She gave me U.S. $150.00 for the trip and explained how I would be contacted in case she were absent from La Paz at that time. At the door of the hotel at 6:00 P.M., holding the latest issue of *Life* in my hands, I would be asked by someone, holding *Life* also, if I was touring in order to see the sun of Bolivia.

She recommended discretion and said that the trip should be kept a secret. She also said that if by any chance I were unable to go on the trip that I should deliver the money to Rutman who, incidentally, would be the one to help me leave Buenos Aires by plane. Nobody knew about my trip except Rutman. I told my wife and my friends that I was going to Montevideo for a job possibility and that I would be back within a week.

Tania told me of the interest in my supplying a general view of the political situation in Argentina, of the possibilities of leftist parties and groups, of what was to be expected from the government in the future and, finally, of information about rather well-known people with pro or con positions as to insurrection. Since all of the above was publicly known, I did not prepare any specific material but simply bought some magazines and that's all.

I left for Buenos Aires on February 25 and telephoned Rutman at a number that Tania had given me and where I was to ask for an appointment with a TV spare-parts salesman by the name of Ignacio Márquez. I asked for an appointment in the afternoon and I met with Rutman at a coffee shop which had been selected. Rutman told me that I needed a passport to go to Bolivia, and I thought this would be the excuse I was looking for to avoid taking the trip. I was wrong, because Rutman told me this would present no difficulties; that this was just routine. He asked me for photographs, which I didn't have, and I had to have them made. I gave him the photographs on Sunday and on Monday afternoon he gave me my passport with no more fuss.

From that time on till 8:00 P.M. I hesitated whether to go ahead with the trip or back down, now that I was aware I might be getting myself in a jam with false documents, etc. It was only my stupid pride in not wanting to look like a coward, and the fact that my family was already compromised, added to the expectations, in all honesty, of getting some good stories for the newspapers, that directed my steps to buy the ticket just before closing time at Bolivian Airlines.

The Trip

On February 28 I took the Bolivian Airlines plane, which landed at La Paz at approximately 4:00 P.M. (the route was via Santa Cruz-Cochabamba). I stayed at the Hotel Sucre and at 6:00 P.M., while standing at the door of the hotel, a dark young man, approximately 30 years old, holding the latest issue of *Life* in his hands (just like I was), came towards me and asked me "if I was touring, and had come to see the sun of Bolivia." I answered yes, since I had heard a lot about it. He told me that his name was Andrés and that Elma was waiting for us and that we should walk over to her. Nevertheless, after we had walked a few blocks we took a taxi and stopped across from the Universo movie house.

Tania (Elma) was in the coffee shop next to the movie house. My companion said goodbye to Elma and she stayed with me and asked me about my luggage and told me that on the following day we had to leave for Cochabamba. The weather was quite cold and she advised me to buy a wool poncho and a jacket to take along instead of my suit. She regretted that I had bought a round-trip ticket since she said it would be more feasible to leave through the southern part of the country by train. She made an appointment to meet me at the bus terminal at 6:00 P.M. on the following day. We had walked to the terminal and she had bought a ticket and had handed it to me, saying goodbye.

On the following day—Wednesday, March 1—I did all my shopping. I even bought some wrought silver pins and bracelets which I was planning to take for my wife and girls back home and a devil's head which I thought might go well in my office.

I was at the bus station of the Galgo company at 6:00 P.M. and it was raining, but there was no sign of Elma. When the departure of the bus was announced I hardly knew what to do but I got on board. The bus was about to leave when she arrived and after arguing with the conductor the luggage was brought on and she got into the bus. Then we left.

She hardly looked at me except when the bus stopped at a place to eat and then she signaled me to sit at her table. She also signaled to a blonde man who was just as much a stranger in the bus as I was. We ate without any further comments in a very mysterious atmosphere, and then we continued the trip. We arrived at Cochabamba at dawn and after staying there for a couple of hours we took another bus for Sucre. Meanwhile, it had become evident that the blonde man—presumably French—was traveling with us and although we talked, our conversation was brief and only on general matters.

After an exhausting trip which lasted more than 24 hours, we arrived in Sucre. We had an argument there because at 8:00 P.M. Tania wanted us to take another bus to a place unknown to me (Camiri), which was leaving at 2:00 A.M. I was very tired and refused to go on and the Frenchman also refused. She had no other alternative but to accept our decision and she took us to a hotel (Gran Hotel, I believe). The Frenchman and I were lodged there but she went somewhere else. She told us that she would not be with us in that town. That same evening she hired a taxi that would take us at dawn on Saturday. We should be ready to leave and waiting at the door of the hotel at 2:20 A.M.

We spent the whole day Friday touring the city and we left at 4:00 A.M. after Tania had had an argument with the taxi driver because of the delay. She had had made arrangements with the taxi driver to take us to Monteagudo—evidently trying to hide our actual destination—but in a town called Padilla, where we stopped for lunch, we were told that we would never make it to Monteagudo by car. Therefore, after a terrific argument with the taxi driver, we changed to a jeep which she rented and left around 4:00 P.M. We stopped at a town just before Camiri because it was raining very hard.

On Sunday morning we left town around 8:00 A.M. and we arrived in Camiri before noon. Leaving the baggage in a jeep which Tania said belonged to her, she took us to a restaurant. After we had lunch she took us to a house which looked like a hotel and told us we could rest in her room. We didn't see her at all in the afternoon, but at dinner time she took us to the same restaurant where we had had lunch. She told us to be at the park at 10:00 P.M. Here we got on a jeep that was being driven by a man named Coco. I asked about my bag and she told me there was no need to carry the bag for just a couple of days, that she had left it in the other jeep where it would be safe and that she would give it to me when we came back.

At the time I didn't even know where we were. I hadn't the slightest idea of where Camiri was so I didn't know where the jeep was going. Tania and the driver were the only ones who talked during the whole trip, while we two, in the back, were more concerned about cushioning the bumps on the road.

Around 2:00 or 3:00 A.M. we reached a small, tin-roofed house where there were two other persons. (Later I found out that they were called León or Antonio and Serapio, or, to make it more clear, León was called Antonio then, but after we left the finca he was called León to avoid confusion with another Antonio.) Some flour, two or three boxes full of cans, and so forth were unloaded from the jeep. The man who was driving ordered some coffee to be made and said that we would leave at dawn.

I asked where the hell we were going and he answered that we should have patience, that Ramón and the other persons in charge had left for some errands but that they would be back in one or two days, and that for security reasons we were being transferred to another camp where we would be more comfortable; that this other camp was further inside the finca. He said there were some security hazards because of too much running around with the jeep and of people during those days. It seems that they had been accused of being involved in the production and traffic of cocaine, and the police had searched the finca twice already (he told this to Tania during the trip) and that for this reason he could not let us remain.

We slept a few hours and at daybreak we started our journey. We crossed a cornfield, and after going over a trail in the woods, we came to a clearing where we waited until 9:00 A.M. A group of bearded men in uniform and carrying arms showed up. Suddenly it dawned on me what this was all about. They affectionately welcomed Tania and we were introduced respectively as "a French compañero and an Argentinean visiting us," and the others were introduced as Antonio, who had a foreign accent (Cuban), and Moisés, Julio, Pablo, and Víctor—these last four were Bolivians. We drank coffee and ate bread which León had brought from the house.

After unloading what we had brought in the jeep all of us left, save León and Serapio. We started walking and we crossed a river, then went through a wood and finally came to the river again. Antonio instructed us then to wade until he signaled. We walked for about 500 meters with water up to our waists at times, then along the banks of the river, moving in and out of the water.

The Camp

The trip was arduous, at least for me. The river had risen and there were sections where we couldn't get into it and had to climb up the embankments. After walking for approximately five hours we reached a rocky section and Antonio warned us again to avoid leaving any footprints by walking on the rocks. A little farther along we met some men bathing in the river. On the righthand side, past the rocks, there was a trail cut on the side of the hill that led into the woods. The trail travelled alongside a brook for about 500 meters and led us right into the encampment. The encampment was divided into three parts. The first part was the Rearguard camp, the second part was the Center camp, and the farthest back was the Vanguard camp. Between the Vanguard and the Center was the bread oven.

When we arrived the following persons were in the Center camp: Arturo, a foreigner. El Ñato, an important person who was assistant supply officer and the holder of the secret of the caves. He was also an experienced hunter (he was from Beni). Camba, a very tall, reserved man who seemed to be one of the trusted ones. Willy, a reserved and hardworking miner and Moisés' man, who was the Center's cook. El Chino, a smiling man of true Chinese ancestry, who was apparently a leader of Peruvian nationality and who had been waiting for Ramón since the early part of February. El Médico or El Negro, also Peruvian, as was Eustaquio. El Médico was a big man, at least 1.85 meters tall, of mixed African-Peruvian bloods, who was a cardiologist. Eustaquio was a radio and television technician. Also there was Luis, from Tarija, an engineer who was a specialist in hydraulic works and was unofficially in charge of the armory. Also there, of course, were the ones who brought us, like Antonio, who was in charge of the camp and of the assignment of duties and organization of guards, etc. Moisés, who was some kind of *caudillo* and had his own people and was waiting for others. Two men who later deserted, Salustio (also a deserter), Willy, Pablo, and Víctor—all of these were Moisés' men. Víctor was a baker. Julio, a doctor from Beni, without doubt seemed to be the most humanitarian.

Antonio ordered food for all the travellers and clothing and equipment for the three of us (the Frenchman, Tania, and myself). El Ñato gave us each a blanket, a hammock, a raincoat, clothes, boots, and a plate, a spoon, and a mug. Later he also gave us an empty flour sack to use as a knapsack, and food rations which included two big cans of milk, one can of meat, one big can of sardines, one can of beef hash, one package of coffee, three packages of salt, and one carton of cigarettes. We were instructed to make up the knapsacks right away and to keep them handy at all times with the supplies that were given to us. This was a forewarning so that in the event of a quick withdrawal we'd be sure to take along with us supplies that would keep us going for a while. Not even in the most critical periods were we allowed to get our hands on the reserve supplies.

That same afternoon Antonio took us for a tour of the camp. And, obviously in order to compromise us, he disclosed to us positions that had been built in the camp. The defensive positions were a series of trenches, strategically built so as to have full coverage of the curve of the river over the largest area possible. There was also an observation post placed on a rocky hill to the right of the brook and there was communication from this post to a little house of the Rearguard. The communication was by means of a U.S.-manufactured, military-type telephone, battery-charged and linked by a long cable.

That same night, while we talked at dinner time, it became clear that the Frenchman was none other than the philosopher and sociologist, Regis Debray, writer and author of theoretical works which they were studying just then. No explanation was given at the time as to the purpose of his visit although some mention was made that he could witness how his theories were being applied.

On the following day, to avoid our remaining longer at the camp since Ramón would arrive any afternoon, Antonio told me that Ramón was Che. He added, "The wily one is hidden here." Then Antonio suggested that we should go with the hunting squad. We did go hunting— El Ñato and Julio, the Frenchman, Tania, and myself—to a plain that was close to the upper part of the river, and after two or three hours El Ñato shot a *urina* (a young deer).

When we returned I spent some time observing camp life. The fundamental tasks of camp life were four: The "gondola"—the daily, or almost daily, expedition to the finca, which consisted of four or five men who went to get provisions. They left in the morning with empty knapsacks and came back in the afternoon loaded with grains, cans, flour, batteries, etc. The guards—at the observation post and at the telephone below, men were on a 24-hour basis, in one-hour shifts. The hunting—which very rarely was successful. The "food"—which included the cook and the kitchen help shifts. The latter were in charge of collecting wood and preparing the meals. Breakfast was either coffee and bread with butter sometimes or *api*, which was some kind of purplish corn flour that the Bolivians liked very much but not the others. For lunch we had grains and rice and canned or fresh meat. In the afternoon we had coffee, and we had a hearty dinner and more coffee late at night. All this changed afterwards, but we will come to that later.

On the third day Antonio told us that we were going to meet Ramón, who was coming from the north, that is from behind the brook. In the evening he distributed the chores: a group for the "gondola," the two future deserters for the hunting, while he, Moisés, Pablo, the Frenchman, and I would head north. We left at 7:00 A.M. and walked along the brook for about 40 meters, crossing a place which they called El Elevador. This was a dried-up cascade that was extremely difficult to climb, but they had placed handrails made of vines attached to trees in order to go up and finally reach the bed of a dried stream to the right. After that a trail opened in the wood. The trail rose almost vertically until it left behind the small hills, and we were in barren land. Up there we could see an enormous panorama of bare hilltops amidst wooded canyons. We waited there all the afternoon.

It took us thirty minutes to climb down the hill and another thirty minutes to reach the camp. It was quite late then, but there was no sign of the hunters. Moisés was worried and went to the Rearguard camp to see what had happened. He went to the hammock of one of the hunters and found a note stuck to the end of a rifle. The note stated that they were deserting and that it was hopeless to go after them. This shocked everybody at the camp, especially those in charge of security. (I was especially shocked because I felt something terrible was trapping me.) A messenger was sent to the finca with instructions that someone should go to Camiri and tell Coco to see if he could do something about this. This might be called the beginning of the development of future events.

In honest truth, all suspicions aroused about the steps that would be taken by the deserters turned out to be right. It was figured that they would try to sell the rifle (the .22 they took with them) and that they would be caught. And that was exactly what happened. The messenger sent to Camiri met with Coco and informed him of events. He had found out in Lagunillas that the two deserters had passed through and sold the rifle for 400 Bolivian pesos. Later, Coco talked with the deserters in Camiri and warned them about the probable consequences of their actions, but he also took the opportunity to use them to identify four of Moisés' men whom Coco had gone to pick up but didn't know personally. These four men were already in Camiri and got in touch with the deserters, who explained to them the situation, but the new men didn't change their minds about joining the guerrillas.

Coco felt that there was no immediate danger and returned to the finca with the four new recruits three days after the desertions. The four were Paquito, a carpenter from Aruro, Pepe, Darío and Chingolo, a youth of about 18. Antonio was not as confident as Coco and placed a guard post for protection in the woods close to the small house at the finca. The guard was composed of four men who would be stationed there, fully equipped, until further notice.

Meanwhile, it was already the tenth and Ramón had not arrived. This should have been a source of concern since he said that he would be coming by the fifth and there should have been some kind of explanation for the delay, if only for self-discipline in the carrying out of the plans. On the eleventh the point men of the Vanguard of the expedition showed up. They came by way of an unexpected route that brought them directly to the finca. The man in charge of the Vanguard, Marcos, was careless and was seen by some laborers working for a neighbor by the name of Algarañaz, who, according to Coco, was responsible for the accusations to the police. This increased our worries and when Marcos and his people arrived at camp a meeting was called. Marcos had arrived with Benigno, Pocho, Loro, and a fifth man whose name I can't recall.

Meanwhile, Víctor arrived unexpectedly. Exhausted, he told about the arrival of army units at the finca. (Later, Serapio clarified that these were police units.) El Negro, who was on guard duty with Víctor, told Víctor to take down the hammocks while he went to investigate, but Víctor, believing that they were surrounded, did not take down the hammocks, but, abandoning everything, fled to camp with the news. He arrived at noon.

The meeting was held after dinner with the participation of Antonio, Arturo, Marcos, Benigno, Pocho, Ñato, Loro, and Camba. El Negro arrived almost at dawn; he had become lost taking a roundabout route to avoid running into any men in uniform. He believed these men to be Rangers and was very excited and sweating. In his rush he had even abandoned his gun clips. Because of the news, the final outcome of the meeting was a decision for "total mobilization," with the participation of everybody. They reported the situation to Debray, El Chino, and myself, and we were told that we would be moved somewhere else because they were responsible for our security. They also discussed the advisability of moving the food deposits toward the rear, of setting up a guard group, and of reinforcing the guards. Marcos would be in command. We also learned that, on top of everything, the news brought by the Vanguard was not good, either. Ramón apparently had been blocked because the Grande River had risen, and since he had been unable to cross the river he had probably spent days on end with nothing to eat except roots, etc. Marcos had brought orders to send food immediately to Ramón's group.

The departure was organized in this way: Debray, El Chino, Tania, Julio, and I would withdraw to El Oso camp to wait for Ramón. Benigno, El Negro, and Eustaquio would take the food. El Ñato (with an assistant) would be in charge of moving everything without haste. The rest would be in charge of the defense of the camp in order to insure that the area would be safe when Ramón arrived. That evening El Ñato gave us a week's supply of food, and next morning all of us left since we were all going in the same direction. Benigno lagged behind because Eustaquio and El Negro were delayed, and they slept at El Oso and continued their journey on the following morning.

We remained at El Oso for three days, and the only break in the monotony was the arrival of Rolando, who had managed to cross the river and had been sent to urge that food be dispatched. It was a good thing that Tania was there because no one else knew him. Rolando looked very thin and totally exhausted. He had a bite to eat and continued on his journey to the camp. As I mentioned before, we had been there three days when Arturo arrived with orders that we should turn back to the brook at the foot of the barren hill and should camp there. They wanted us to be closer to facilitate contact. In addition, tension had decreased because, according to Serapio, the affair at the finca seemed just another police search.

We had lunch and started on our way back. We arrived at the foot of the hill at sundown and camped close to the brook. Julio and Debray were to go on to the camp. Tania, El Chino, and I were the only ones who remained. After we had set our camp, had dinner and coffee, and were just passing time before turning in for the night, El Ñato showed up with the news that the army had come back, this time with trucks, and the finca had been occupied. The two men who had been stationed there (León and Serapio) had left, therefore, and had joined the guerrillas. The guards in the post were withdrawn towards the river to avoid encirclement. All the decisions taken revealed a great lack of organization and faltering command. This whole thing amounted to a disorganized withdrawal of forces.

Julio and Debray returned, bringing with them a man sick with malaria, Luis, who moaned as though he was about to die. Orders were given to dismantle camp and to return to El Oso immediately. It was almost impossible to carry out the orders because it was nighttime, we had just arrived, and we had someone who seemed to be seriously ill. We decided to leave at dawn. El Ñato spent the whole night bringing things over to transfer them later to El Oso. All the new men and those who had been stationed at the finca helped him. We left at dawn. Luis, the sick man, was assigned to our group. El Ñato was in charge of all the new men and León and Serapio carried the load. We arrived in the afternoon, completely exhausted because of the heat and the load. Much to the regret of his group, El Ñato had to go back to get the rest of the things. We got settled once again and began to wait. This happened around the fifteenth or sixteenth.

Two days later Pocho turned up with orders to take Debray with him and to go look for Ramón. They left that same day but they returned in the evening because Pocho had lost his way. There was a change in plans that evening and Pocho told us that Debray and myself and two other men (Serapio and León) would go ahead to meet Ramón. This meant at least one hour of walking. We would leave every morning at 6:00 A.M. and return at 6:00 P.M. We would leave camp with Pocho and he would continue after leaving us stationed on a hill.

The Arrival of Ramón

Nothing happened during the first day, but on the second day—March 20—at around 8:00 in the morning Benigno showed up. He was coming from the north and told us that the previous day he had met with Ramón, who had camped to eat and had sent orders dealing with the situation. El Negro and Eustaquio passed by one hour later and, like Benigno, were carrying the knapsacks of those who were more ill. The rest of the Vanguard group (Miguel and I don't remember who else) passed by around 2:00 P.M. León went to meet all of them because he had been longest at the finca and, therefore, knew them all. Urbano, who was always the point of the Center, arrived at 3:00, and immediately afterwards we saw the arrival of the column which included Ramón. As

"Che" Guevara in the jungles of Bolivia in complete guerrilla array

in the case of the arrival of the Vanguard group the impression we got was that they were completely exhausted, with their clothes torn, some of their trousers barely covering their knees and the rest ripped, their shirts without sleeves, etc., and all of them extremely thin.

Then and there, on the top of the hill, Pocho, who had come with them, and León introduced each of the members of the column. Ramón was very cordial and apologized for his delay and with no more ado sat down to rest a few minutes before continuing his journey to El Oso. He ordered that food be served continuously until the following day. The Rearguard arrived one hour later and it was an even more pitiful sight. As soon as Ramón arrived he began learning how things stood. El Ñato arrived from camp with a load of things and news. The news was more concrete now and it concerned a first encounter; I'm not very sure between whom, although I believe it had to do with Coco who was either at his post at the finca or on his way there when he ran across an army patrol and opened fire and killed a soldier. Following this encounter there was a lot of commotion and Salustio's absence was discovered. The question was whether he had been arrested or had become lost or had deserted. In view of this—Ñato reported—Marcos and Antonio decided to withdraw the advance post and begin to dismantle the camp. The area was mined and all the supplies transferred to El Oso, after a halt at the foot of the hill and the setting up of an ambush at El Elevador.

Ramón reacted to the news. He began to shout and to question, asking whether he was surrounded by cowards or by traitors. He turned to El Ñato and shouted: "No one is allowed to come this far. Go back and tell everyone they're strictly forbidden to come here or to leave camp. I want everybody to remain in the camp and further on than the camp itself." He argued about the withdrawal and some of the decisions that had been taken. El Ñato got on the road back and made all those who had come with him carrying the load to return, too. Immediately afterwards Ramón also ordered the Rearguard to leave and placed Joaquín in command.

On the following day the rest of the group left except Tuma, Pombo, Urbano, and Ramón and the "refugee" group, including myself, who had been staying at El Oso. I said that upon his arrival Ramón had ordered food to be served, and it was. We first had coffee with a lot of sugar, and as soon as food was ready it was distributed every two or three hours, from sunset on through the night, without sleep. The conversation was general, but with special emphasis on the journey of the column. It became clear that the trip had been toward the north, farther off than El Oso and always along the tops of the hills until they reached the intersection of the Ñancahuazu and Grande Rivers. The column crossed the Grande at the time of the year when it reaches its highest level. They had to swim across and build barges to carry the equipment. During the first part of the trip one of the Bolivians—I don't remember his name— was carried away by the waters and nobody was able to do anything. Later they cut their way through places that Ramón never thought they would get through until they arrived near Vallegrande. (I was never able to find this place on a map.)

Then came the return trip. They had no problems establishing contacts with the peasants around that area. The return trip was more of an ordeal because in their first crossing of the river they had lost part of the food, and their provisions were exhausted before schedule. In spite of the fact that they had been able to buy some port and chicken and corn, etc., they had no food by the time they got back to the river. And to top this, they realized they couldn't cross because conditions were worse than before, so they had to remain there for a whole month without anything to eat except strange fruits, bugs, roots, and some occasional game they were able to hunt. The point of the Vanguard was finally able to cross over and continued the trip, as I related previously.

Later on Rolando crossed over alone, and after a tremendous effort the Center and the Rearguard also crossed. Another Bolivian died and the Rearguard lost practically all its equipment, the men being left with no clothing, no shoes, and some with no weapons. (When the Rearguard arrived the men were wearing pants and undershirts that had been loaned to them by the Center group.) The Bolivian who drowned was named Carlos. Ramón thought a lot of him; in discussing him with us he said that he was the best of the Bolivian cadres. I don't know who he was.

After crossing the river they killed a horse. All the time they had been on the other side of the river they had been watching horses romping around. Afterwards they met Benigno, who had food, and now at last they could think of eating without stopping. Sanitary conditions had also been very poor, and two of the men, Joaquín and Alejandro, were in bad health and would get worse during the following days.

Without there being any discussion other than about the events of the trip, nevertheless a good view of the group itself emerged. There were sixteen Cubans in Ramón's group. All of them, except Antonio and Arturo, went along on the journey. The Bolivians included the two drowned men and Inti, Pedro, Loro, Raúl, Aniceto, and Eusebio. There was no argument about the fact that Ramón was in full command. The duties he had delegated, saying, "Well, I have not given anyone any rank or position, but . . . ," were: Joaquín, commander of the Rearguard, and second in command in case of the absence or disability of Ramón; Marcos, commander of the Vanguard (succeeded later by Miguel); Alejandro, chief of operations; Rolando, political commissar; Inti, political commissar and formal Bolivian chief; Ricardo, as the person responsible for communications; Antonio, responsible for information; Moro, responsible for sanitation; Pombo, responsible for supplies. Out of this roster, the only persons with actual functions were the men in charge of the Vanguard and the Rearguard, and Pombo and Arturo, the latter being the radio technician (radio operator). The rest of the appointments, in my opinion, were for the future. Discipline was very strict, and I believe their morale was very high, otherwise there is no explanation for the unbelievable efforts they had to make, as for example going back the next day, as in the case of Benigno and Pocho, or walking barefoot from the Río Grande to El Oso.

Next morning, after the people of the Center had left, Ramón turned his attention to each one of us individually, that is one by one and far from the camp. Respecting the length of time El Chino had been there, he began with him and they talked until noon. Afterwards he talked with Debray, and late in the afternoon he talked with me. He spoke with Tania last. In my particular case, he took me to an isolated spot, we sat down on the ground, and he began his talk. In the first place he briefly stated his plan which in résumé was this: The strategic objective was the seizure of power in one or more countries of South America upon the development of the armed insurrectional struggle, serving as detonator for this the present guerrilla group. This unit must develop, consolidate and extend itself through its own actions, serving at the same time as the mother and guiding nucleus of other groups that would be created and would break away in order to operate where conditions would best permit them to do so. Doctrinaire political support would be based on the common factor of the Latin-American peoples, that is, the anti-imperialist struggle. Imperialism was the real enemy. It acted above and despite the local (national) oligarchies, reducing to secondary level and causing the failure of the struggle, always partial, of the peoples against these oligarchies, which were enemies in form, not depth. The main enemy is one and common to all, and therefore there is a need for a new strategy which, favoring the possibilities of triumph (not only militarily, but also economically once in power), should be based on this premise: In Latin America, no country alone, separate from the others, can carry out revolution. Not even a ruling regime sustained by the army itself and originally supported by the people can do this. It would achieve palliatives, remedies of transformation, but it would not make a revolution. One country alone would be rapidly encircled, strangled and subdued by imperialism because revolution is an economic-social deed, not a romantic, patriotic event. The under-developed Latin American economy is a result of the imperialist economy, and this is possible as long as the whole is controlled. Change will be possible when the whole is in opposition.

This was the main thesis of a work that he left for publication in Cuba and which, according to broadcast information, has already been published. This work was entitled, *One, Two, Three or More Viet Nams in Latin America, That is the Goal.* I believe this was the title of his work where he maintained the thesis of uniting the Latin American peoples in a common front against the United States. With regard to my being there, he said that he intended to speak with different individuals of the neighboring countries, mainly from Argentina, Brazil, Peru, and Chile at the moment. He explained that these were countries where more active political participation was possible and, therefore, where it might be easier to develop a movement of public opinion in favor of his thesis. This was the crux of the problem; it is worthwhile to set forth his exposition.

He believed that his thesis could be applied in two continents: Africa and South America, with the advantage in favor of Africa because of its greater distance from the United States and its greater logistic possibilities (Soviet Union, China, United Arab Republic, Algeria). During his extensive voyage through Africa and Asia before disappearing from Cuba, Guevara arranged for his voluntary incorporation in the struggle in the Congo, that is, he chose Africa. But the experience turned out to be negative, because, he said, the human element failed. There is no will to fight, the leaders are corrupt; in a word, there was nothing to do. After six months he abandoned that.

But meanwhile, he had prepared nothing for the second choice, South America, and difficulties began to arise. In Venezuela there was a confrontation between the Communist Party and the guerrilla groups not belonging to it. It was impossible for him to be there under such political conditions. The rest of the Latin American countries did not offer favorable conditions of support. The Communist parties were not accompanying Cuba. The pro-Castro movements had either been destroyed everywhere or had not done a thing.

There remained only a strategic choice. Within this context Bolivia seemed to be best because of its closeness to the best political bases (Argentina, Brazil, Chile, Peru), even though it lay between two countries where experiences failed (Argentina, and above all Peru). Bolivia had a military government and an acute social situation, with imperialist economic pressures added. One of Ramón's men, Ricardo, who had been with him in the Congo, went to Bolivia (I think at the beginning of last year). He was in charge of the work of organization, establishment of contacts and recruitment of the working team. The team, it seems, was not numerous: someone by the name of Pablo, who was in charge, two or three other persons, and Tania. The preliminary work included renting of houses, purchase of the jeep, the finca, etc.

But the fundamental factor, the political basis, was destined to failure. The pro-Moscow Communist Party did not agree with the plan and insisted on further discussion. The pro-Chinese Communist Party refused completely. The only support left was from individual members of those parties, as for example Moisés Guevara, who led his own group, and Inti, El Ñato, etc., although I do not know what their role has been.

Another problem that came up and speeded his arrival was that the Communist Party did not give any guarantees of keeping his presence in Bolivia secret—at least not in the inner circles of the Communist parties in South America. It seems that during a trip that Ricardo made to Cuba he said that Ramón would have to enter Bolivia then or never. Thus, in order to assure his entry into Bolivia, although preparations had not been completed, he decided to come. This happened in October of last year, I think.

There was a meeting with the Communist Party (I don't know when or where, but it took place around the last part of the year). During this meeting, the Communist Party definitely refused to participate, to the point of expelling the members who had joined the guerrilla group. (This news was given by Ramón when he returned from his journey; it was probably heard in a radio report.) Thus, the objective of Ramón's meetings with invited guests was mainly to create or give impetus to political support of efforts outside the country, since this was not possible inside the country.

He said that he was not at all interested in political parties; furthermore, that they should not know about this. What he wished was to talk to individual persons or representatives of small, or large, groups who, either in theory or in practice, were in favor of armed struggle. One of these groups, although destroyed, were the people of Salta. Of course, being as they were in prison, someone connected with them had to come, but not someone who was already "burned," as was the case of their lawyers and relatives.

He said that two Argentineans had already come, but had failed to make contact with him because Tania's stupidity and failure to understand his instructions had disrupted everything. Tania had set the appointments, as in my case, for February, the end of February being the last possible date, when actually that was the date perviously set for the march. These Argentineans came during the middle of February and refused to wait until the fifth of March (actually the twentieth) and returned to Buenos Aires with no further ado. (If I had come immediately, instead of hesitating, I would be at home right now.) El Chino, who came at the beginning of February, was the only one who remained. Ramón did not wish to tell me who the persons were who came, saying only that they were from Buenos Aires. There were other persons who had also come before (I do not know from where). Tania, defending herself from my anger, said: "Some of them hardly stayed for a day and left."

As for me, I explained that the political situation in Argentina was not favorable for an insurrectional approach after the armed forces took power, with large sectors of the country complacent and the Peronista leadership hoping to get into the government. I made it clear that the leftist groups had realized this and discarded any possibility of insurrection for the next four years, at least. This period of time might be postponed indefinitely if the government succeeded in its economic development objectives. I especially stressed the fact that the left, and the opposition groups in general, rejected the guerrilla concept.

The Salta experience was more or less analyzed by us and the conclusion reached that the adventurousness of this method had been demonstrated upon no consideration being given to the national situation: political, economic and, above all, geographic factors, and what was implied socially in a country where 75 percent of the population—the bourgeoisie and the proletariat—was concentrated in large cities. The remaining 25 percent lived in rural areas and were made up of farm owners, small owners, and renters in the main, and a minimum of exploited peasants scattered over an area of 2,700,000 square kilometers. With this situation it would be crazy to dream of setting up guerrilla activities in Argentina. On the other hand, the working class was mostly Peronista, and there was no doubt that the only fight they would make would be for *peronismo*, not for a Castroite socialist revolution. Only the fanatics of revolutionary sectarism, who neither represent nor can mobilize anybody, speculate theoretically on these positions (e.g., Communist Vanguard, a pro-Chinese group).

My answer to his request was that the Peruvian experience proved that in Argentina, when an event of this kind occurs in a brother country, the only thing that happens is a state of expectation. Politically, a current of support begins to emerge in proportion to the degree of success and of popular participation in the struggle (as in the case of Santo Domingo).

If there is no such participation and success, and the struggle does not last, does not endure, soon the expectation is lost and ends up in political and journalistic archives.

I told him that I thought I could obtain immediate success in mobilizing political support. News of his personal leadership, of his physical presence becoming known after there had been so much speculation about him would undoubtedly bring a lot of publicity which undoubtedly would turn into a support movement.

But that was precisely what he did not wish: his presence could not be revealed until the struggle was fully developed. Then his participation and that of the Cubans who were with him would be just a simple matter of proletariat-revolutionary international support. Before this happened the struggle should emerge as a Bolivian effort in which the people would join little by little. I spoke my doubts: I could not understand how, beginning with a large Cuban group, this reverse process could be developed. This was the answer: The Bolivians who had already joined must carry out the task of establishing contacts with the population and profit from the results of continuous and widespread publicity, beginning with a call to arms included in a political manifesto that would be distributed simultaneously in Bolivia and in the neighboring countries.

He said that we would discuss this point further in a conversation that would take place later on, before I left. First, he said, we had to see how the present situation was developing. He said that on the following day we would go on to the Center camp to study the problem and my subsequent departure. He ordered a fire for a good dinner and went to talk to Tania until dinner was served. He had been with me for about three hours. We ate at leisure, had a good night's sleep and left for the camp.

The Events

We arrived at the Center camp at noon of the twenty-second. The atmosphere was tense, but nothing happened at first. Each one of us looked around for a good place to set up our hammocks. Then Joaquín arrived and made a report. First, an ambush had been set higher up the river. Then a three-man post was also placed more than one kilometer up the river, and patrols were scheduled to move out in other directions. Some of the things that had been transferred, especially food, had been brought back, since the number of people had increased. All the people were busy, although when we arrived the camp had seemed deserted. Noticeable was the generally poor sanitation. All the men had diarrhea and most of them had swollen feet and arms, especially Joaquín, Alejandro, and Miguel. Ramón ordered a medical staff meeting immediately, and the resulting diagnosis was extreme weakness and lack of vitamins. The medics prescribed that the patients remain in bed and be well fed. Ramón relieved Joaquín of command of the Rearguard, placing Rolando as his substitute. He ordered the three sick people to bed, and in addition ordered that all the men should get three double-ration meals a day.

The troubles started later. Marcos and Antonio tried to explain the reasons for their decisions, and Ramón raised his voice and increased his criticisms. He said that what had happened had been negative and that morale was low because of so much escaping and hiding (this was true: before his arrival there was a feeling of retreat). Ramón kept on raising his voice until he shouted at Marcos and ordered him to retire to his camp (the Vanguard, 100 meters away). The argument with Antonio continued and he was asked to make a full report the next day on everything that had happened. Ramón seemed ready to release all his ire, and he turned on Tania, making her cry, telling her that she shouldn't have come and that her lack of discipline had left the guerrillas without contacts. Then he picked on Arturo, and I remember him saying, "You wanted to come because you were a technician and now you can't make a radio work."

After that we listened to radio broadcasts (news, Radio Havana, and the Voice of the Americas). This custom of listening to the radio, starting at 7:00 P.M., was always followed. He ordered reveille and breakfast to be at five in the morning and at that hour the guards were relieved. The day went by uneventfully. Ramón didn't speak with anyone except Antonio, who submitted his report. The blame for the presence of the army was not clear. It seems that after crossing the Río Grande, Marcos changed his route and visited peasants—I don't know where. Then, while carrying all his equipment, knapsacks and weapons, etc., he let himself be seen on the finca by Algarañaz's laborers, and he must have been an impressive sight. On the other hand, Marcos had criticized the fact that the orders for the withdrawal from the camp had been opposed by Ramón who said that the camp should have been defended. (I should point out that others, including Debray and myself, shared this critical point of view, based on Che's own premise, expressed in his books, that guerrillas should be constantly on the move and there should be no defense of fixed positions.) Ramón viewed this critical attitude of Marcos as an act of insubordination.

The Ambushes

In mid-morning Coco arrived completely wet and' agitated. He went directly to Ramón and told him that there had been an encounter at the ambush site. I remember his words: "Well, now, it has started. Five dead, six wounded, ten prisoners." Ramón said: "Well, the war has started. People are needed to carry all that [captured material]." He asked about his own losses. He said, "Now I am going to smoke a pipe with the best tobacco."

Coco said they had captured a lot of arms, ammunition, mortars, etc., but that there were not enough people to carry it all. They went to one side, and Pombo, Ricardo, Inti, etc., joined them. Ramón ordered Moro to get his first-aid equipment and surgical instruments ready and to go and care for the wounded. He told Inti to take as many people as were available in the camp and in the posts, etc., and to bring back the weapons, leaving nothing behind, not even one bullet. He also asked him to do the interrogating. Even so, he later sent Alejandro, who could hardly stand on his feet, to participate in the questioning, too. He ordered that the ambush remain in place and that the prisoners be moved closer to the camp. He also set up a relay team to keep in touch with those in charge of the questioning. This was what I could hear of orders given in a loud voice. Everybody started to leave immediately. The first liaison came at noon and reported that one of the prisoners (a captain, I believe) said that an intensive bombing of the camp was scheduled for 2:00 P.M. and that we should leave immediately. Nobody paid any attention to this. Nevertheless, at the time indicated, aircraft began flying over the area, but they did not fire. By mid-afternoon all the equipment, having been brought back little by little, was at the entrance to the camp. Ramón sent all of us (including himself and Urbano [Negro]) to bring it up.

El Moro (the physician) and Alejandro had returned, so we received a clear picture of the whole situation. The ambush had been carried out by seven men. They were led (due to the change in command) by Rolando. Involved in the action were Benigno, Moisés, Julio, and Coco. I don't remember the rest. Benigno was emplaced facing the river, that is, at the end of the ambush, and he had a BZ-30 machine gun. The rest of the men were along the sides of the ambush. Ricardo was the first to open fire. Then the others followed, defeating an army column of some 25 men. According to Julio it was a hunt and a butchery. The soldiers couldn't tell where the fire was coming from and they didn't know what to do. It appears that some of them just dropped their guns and ran back. They were the only ones who were able to get away from the trap.

The combat—if you could call it that—didn't last long, not more than five minutes. The soldiers were quickly ordered to surrender, and in view of the large number of casualties, they did surrender. There were five dead, six wounded and eight prisoners. A lot of arms were captured, I can't remember exactly how many, but I think there were 19 Garand rifles with their clips, one .30 caliber machine gun (more welcome even than the mortars) with its boxes of bullets, two BZ-30 machine guns like those they already had, three Belgian submachine guns and three mortars with six boxes of projectiles. There was an enormous quantity of ammunition and supplies. According to information supplied by the prisoners some mules loaded with food were at the rear of the army patrol. Naturally, these mules were not captured, although Rolando said he had sent someone after them.

The prisoners were transferred to the back of the camp, along with the wounded, to whom Julio had given first-aid treatment. Later El Moro reported that he had given them surgical treatment, just like in a hospital. Inti and Alejandro questioned them there at the camp, and the gaps were filled in to complete the picture. It became clear that after the arrest of the two deserters, and of Salustio later, the existence of a guerrilla camp was learned. The Fourth Division had been assigned to look for the camp and destroy it.

From what Ramón said, nothing spectacular was learned from the questioning. The prisoners were given coffee that night and food the following day, and in the afternoon Ramón ordered their release, giving the army a 24-hour truce to pick up their dead. The prisoners' uniforms were taken from them and they were given some civilian clothes and old shoes in exchange.

A group from the Vanguard accompanied the prisoners almost to the finca and at the same time, following orders from Ramón, moved the ambush forward to the thicket of the finca. Since the prisoners had indicated that the army would be coming from both ends of the river, Ramón also ordered an ambush to be set upriver at a distance of about one kilometer. He also ordered the Rearguard to take over the defensive positions at the camp. Thus, everyone had specific assignments, and that is why Ramón ordered that we should be utilized, that is Debray, El Chino, Tania, and I, to carry all the weapons and equipment to a place selected by El Ñato, who was the head of these operations. The spot was near the brook to the north, beyond El Elevador. There was another steep climb, so, to help, they set up a sort of ladder and a handrail of vines. Some 50 meters beyond this point, El Ñato asked us to leave the goods by the brook, and for a couple of days afterwards he was busy carrying everything up to a cave or a hideout that he had previously prepared.

All our expectations centered on what Ramón would do next. We all

The girl with three other unidentified guerrillas is Loyola Guzmán. She served with Guevara and is now a prisoner of the Bolivian army

Guevara rides a mule somewhere in the jungles of Bolivia

thought—including myself—that he would give orders to abandon the camp and move to a different area in order to avoid any further encounters. What a mistake! For eleven full days he remained stationary, under strafing from planes and with army advances all around (although our scouts more or less had them under close observation). There was another encounter although it did not involve any shooting. This occurred at the finca, where they barred passage of the Red Cross to pick up the corpses because, with the truce period over, they came in two trucks with troops. The Red Cross ordered a withdrawal and nothing happened. It was during those days that some horses were captured. We ate part of the meat and the rest was salted.

Ramón didn't speak to anyone except to give orders. After three or four days he announced that there was to be a general meeting in the evening. At 7:20 P.M. the members of the Vanguard and of the Rearguard, who had been asked to leave their positions like everyone else, arrived at the camp and the meeting started. The only one who did not attend was Joaquín, who was in bed very sick. Ramón said that now that hostilities had started he wanted to discuss the positive and negative factors up to then. He went back to the march they had taken, which had its good points and its painful ones—he said it was only fair to mention the good things and the bad things as well. Among the good things, he wanted to commend the good behavior and the high morale of five comrades: Miguel, Pombo, Inti, Rolando, and Carlos (the latter was one of those drowned in the river), who had been exemplary in every way. Ramón said he did not include Joaquín, because he had become nervous, nor Benigno, because he had not gone to find them with the food but rather had waited for them at a spot on the way. He said that he had to mention sad events and he talked about the death of the two Bolivians who had drowned in the river. He also mentioned the problem of Marcos, who had disobeyed his orders and taken a different route, and who, together with Loro, had established contact with peasants pretending to be a geologist. They had been followed by an employee of the YPFR,* who reported their presence to the army and served as a scout for it. (This was learned through the questioning of the captured officers.) Later Marcos had shown himself at the finca, and his withdrawal had been bad for the morale of the group. Because of all of this, Ramón relieved Marcos of command of the Vanguard and of all his duties, which were transferred to Miguel. Marcos was given the alternative of remaining as a private or returning to Cuba.

* *Yacimientos Petrolíferos Fiscales Bolivianos*, the Bolivian national agency that deals with the exploration and development of petroleum resources.

The fourth issue that Ramón brought up was Moisés' carelessness in recruiting. He said that he had had to expel four men because they were not fit for the job. One of them had a heart ailment, another was handicapped, another was a thief, and the fourth was lazy. All of them (Paquito, Pepe, Eusebio, and Chingolo) were scared, and they were expelled from the guerrillas, but under the strict rule, "No work, no food," they remained until it was feasible to send them away with enough money to get back home. But this, Ramón said, should serve as an example. This was the first and last time there was an expulsion. This ended the meeting.

Days went by and the atmosphere was tense because of the continued bombing and the emplaced ambush. Our position did not offer any future to anyone. Ramón was very aloof; he didn't speak with anyone or discuss his plans with anyone. We had generous servings of food but the supplies were running low rapidly. El Ñato had to begin going on trips to El Oso to bring food. The sick people remained the same or were worse.

The only ones who seemed to be getting something done were the scouts who made trips in all directions until they encountered the military, only to come back and find angry looks on Ramón's face because of their findings. Miguel carried out the same reconnaissance three times until Ramón was satisfied. I learned later that these trips scouted the way to Gutiérrez, a route by which Ramón believed that Debray and I could get out.

One day Ramón started the private meetings in the same order as before, that is, first El Chino, then Debray, and after that myself. He told me that he thought the way out was very difficult and that he was sure that we would be captured. He stated his opinion that I should wait until he could overcome the sanitary and food problems and then he would be ready to start a long march towards the north. Then, if at all possible, he would leave me on the road to Cochabamba. All this meant from one to two months longer. I refused and asked him to give me a scout to get me to some road, and from then on I would be on my own. He said that he couldn't let people leave under those circumstances and that any movement would include all of us. Finally, because of my pressure he promised to think of something so that Debray and I would leave, at any rate, but he was not willing to risk El Chino until the way had been tested. Debray wouldn't have any problems and they would make a credential for me. For this purpose he asked me to give Tania a photograph, if I had one. I did, and Tania prepared for me a credential from the Press Department (Bolivia). I didn't know how or from where she had obtained them, but she had official papers, signed and everything. It

seemed to me that this was another mess I was getting into but a necessary one, since we had already heard over the radio that the whole area
was now a military zone and that passes were required. This meant that
nobody could come in or leave without a pass, but the paper I was given
appeared to be what was needed.

Ramón told me that under the circumstances there would be no call
to arms but that he would issue military communiqués to be given publicity by the newspapers and to be distributed inside leftist parties and
groups. He would hand these to me before I left. I mentioned the ambush
to him and the reaction this would arouse not only in the population
because of the massacre, but also inside the guerrilla group because this
had been practically carried out by the Cubans. He admitted that this
posed a problem, but said that this could not be overcome until the
Bolivian comrades gained experience in combat. Nevertheless, he said,
the ideal thing would be if Bolivia would ask for military help and
Yankee, Argentine, Brazilian, etc., military forces would get involved.
I told him that I had no idea what the Bolivian government would do
but that I was positive the Argentine Army would not participate because at that time it was building up its image among the Argentine
people.

He said that I was a dreamer and that whenever the Department of
State or the Pentagon made a decision all those armies went along. I
assured him that at least in the case of Argentina this was not so, that I
believed this was more his wishful thinking than an objective possibility.
He said that my attitude was typical of the analysts and theorists of
Argentina who refuse to acknowledge realities until they see that events
have taken place and then they have to throw all their blueprints in the
wastepaper basket. I reminded him that the only real and serious confrontation between the Argentine people and Perón (a popular government) occurred when the attempt was made to send Argentine troops to
Korea. The government had to give up the idea in 24 hours. The aver-
age Argentinean rejects any type of intervention. Any Argentinean
would think that sending Argentine troops to fight here in Bolivia or in
Chile because of internal strife was a crazy idea. Proof of this lies in the
fact that the Inter-American Force has not been approved by any conference so far.

In short, we did not reach any agreement although it was evident that
the matter of the Cuban group, which represented a majority, was a
real problem. I should point out that there was always ambiguity in
regard to the number of guerrillas and/or groups in the area. But now,
calmly going over everything, I realize that all contacts came from this

group. I never saw any new people, nor did anything new arrive at the camp. Yet the Frenchman said that he had seen something; therefore, were there more? Were they Cubans? Were they Bolivians ready to join? Or was there nothing more?

Going over my conversation with Ramón, I realize that nothing was added to the topics that we had discussed the first time, except the matter of the neighboring armies. I discussed the financial problem that Tania had said I should tell him about. He stated that he would give me money for us (the Salta group), and that I was to take my expenses from there.

The Problems

My second meeting with Ramón ended with this discussion of finances. Actually, this was to be my last meeting, too. Future talks would be brief and in passing. The days of waiting and doubts continued in an atmosphere that grew tenser as new problems arose. The people were tired of the continuous guard duties, reconnaissance, ambushes, moving of loads, etc. To top it all we just had one meal a day (in the evening) and the supplies were rapidly becoming depleted. After the capture of the horses we had real banquets but the results were bad because the meat of the horses had so much lard that everybody had liver trouble afterwards. Everybody had diarrhea and our supply of pills to cure this became exhausted. The people with swelling members did not improve and had to remain in bed. We lacked even the most vital things. There came an evening when we had our last coffee with sugar. The next morning we had bread for the last time. Another day we had our last pot of beans. Days earlier we had run out of rice. It all culminated when we didn't have any more coffee. Soon all we had to eat was corn with boiled brined meat. The brined horse meat was rotten and had a loathsome taste. Diarrhea increased. Salt had to be rationed. In addition, almost all the batteries for the flashlights ran out, the last ones being used for the radio receiver. Most of the boots were worn out or about to wear out. (The boots captured from the army were, with few exceptions, too small and were stored away.) The same thing was happening with the knapsacks and clothes. When things were brought out of the caves for use, it was discovered that many of them (clothes, weapons, books, supplies, etc.) were in bad condition because of the humidity. There was not enough oil or grease to clean the arms and keep them in good condition. In short, the situation was on the verge of being disastrous.

Ramón, however, remained unconcerned. He didn't speak at all. All he did was spend the day reading in his hammock. (He devoured all the magazines that the Frenchman, El Chino, and myself had brought along. Also books.) Life at camp was only a constant rotation of tasks, with a few of the men just lying around waiting for food time. We listened to the radio together at dinner, and Arturo and Ricardo listened at night by themselves. The work was so scattered that it was impossible to get a good idea of the morale of the people. But discipline was still strong.

One day, at the end of the month, Miguel finished his third reconnaissance and then had a long talk with Ramón. A meeting was called that evening and Ramón announced the beginning of operations aimed at solving two problems: the visitors' departure and the purchase of food. This was to be done before the guerrillas left the area completely. He said that all his plans had been delayed because of the sick people. Since they could not be abandoned he would leave them in the charge of the chief physician (Moro) and some other comrade in a place that would be a hospital where they would remain until they got well (the camp hospital). For this purpose Moro and El Ñato would leave and look for a place that would be safe from any incursion by the army. Later we would transfer the provisions that we could (one horse). The rest of the people were to make preparations for a trip that would last fifteen days, and the camp would be dismantled and everything hidden in the caves toward the rear (Elevador, Hospital, Poza and Oso). In better spirits, the next days were spent carrying out all these tasks. The planes still flew over us, but less frequently. At times we heard sporadic shooting in different directions. The army was seen for the last time on the upper part of the river some one to two hours' walk from where we were. An advance was feared, but nothing happened.

At last, on the fourth or the fifth, I can't remember very well, the Vanguard left at 2:00 in the morning. An hour later the Center left, and an hour after the Center the Rearguard left. Those who remained in order to go to the hospital were Moro, Joaquín, Alejandro, Serapio, and I can't recall who else. Those in the Vanguard were (more or less) Miguel, Coco, Loro, Julio, Braulio, Pocho, Marcos, Benigno, and Aniceto. The Center included Urbano, Ramón, Tuma, Pombo, Ricardo, Arturo, Inti, Ñato, Moisés, Willy, León, Luis, Eustaquio, Médico (Negro), and Antonio. Tania, El Chino, Debray, and myself joined them. The Rearguard was under the command of Rolando and included Rubio, Camba, Médico (Chinese), Pablo, Víctor, Darío, and Raúl, and the useless Paquito, Pepe, Chingolo, and Eusebio.

The weapons were the usual ones, the individual weapons that each of them carried. The most impressive weapons were the two BZ-30 (I think) machine guns that Benigno and Rolando were carrying. The load was impressive. In my particular case I had to carry my sleeping things and reserve supplies, like everybody else, and in addition, my bag with clothes for my departure and, since I wasn't carrying any weapon, I was given food for the group (corn and brined meat) to carry. The march along the river—in order to avoid leaving footprints—was arduous but silent. By six we had reached the thicket just before the little house on the finca. Suddenly an airplane was flying over us. Ramón ordered a halt until we saw one of the Vanguard liaison men, and then we continued our march. The airplane was still over us. We crossed the cornfield to the left of the house and came to a brook with filthy water. We climbed a small hill and again halted. We remained there, close to the house, until one o'clock. At that time two scouting parties arrived. One of these had proceeded ahead, and the other, headed by El Ñato, had gone along the river. We resumed marching for about an hour, more or less, and then we were ordered to halt and set up camp.

It seems that the army was everywhere and Ramón wanted new reconnaissance. We camped and started a fire for our food early, around five. We heard distant shooting. The shooting came closer and we even heard some farther down from our position during the night. We were crossing right through an encirclement. Using an astonishing technique, they communicated with each other along the line by shots fired approximately every hour. Ramón, as usual, was unconcerned. He ordered breakfast (*mote** and *api*). The night guard duties were few because we left at three. We fell into a brook but kept on marching until daylight. Ramón ordered our knapsacks to be hidden on a hill which had been reconnoitered (we took out our bags). After some hours we continued our march, now with a lighter load. In the afternoon we reached the fence of the finca. We stopped there and waited for the liaison. Debray and I prepared to leave. We would try to do this by getting transportation that would be able to go on those roads and for which we would have to pay an exhorbitant price (around 2,000 or 3,000 pesos) so that it would take us close to the Santa Cruz-Cochabamba road.

We resumed marching and later, after sunset, we reached a house where some of the Vanguard group were (they were also in more distant houses). The whole plan went to pieces there in a way that I was never able to understand very well. The men spent their time buying and preparing food, and they killed a hog and made coffee, which they also bought. Time went by. The Vanguard point reported that a man had defected. Information that was gathered indicated that a few days ago 150 soldiers had been stationed there but that all of them had left already. We

---

* Stewed corn (*api*, corn flour).

ate so much food that soon there was nothing left of the pork, cheese, eggs, flour, etc. At 10:00 in the evening Ramón announced that we were going back without completing the operation aimed at getting us out and buying things in Gutiérrez. I argued with him, first from the point of view of the whole plan, to no avail, and then from the point of view of my own involvement. I asked him for some money (he had not yet given me either the money or the communiqué). I also asked him to provide me with a scout to take me to a road (it must be borne in mind that I hadn't the slightest idea where I was), and to allow me to take the supply of food cans. I would then walk to Santa Cruz. He refused. I insisted. He said that he could not dispense with anyone and that, besides, he was sure we would have a bad time—I should wait for a better opportunity. He said his responsibility was to refuse my request. I argued that each day things would become more difficult, that every time we reached a town we would run into the army. We could no longer try in that way. Very soon we wouldn't be able to turn in any direction, and I hadn't the slightest intention of remaining with them because I hadn't gone there for that. He said that his main concern was to get us out, but at this time his mind was made up and that was that. I didn't say anything else and I think we didn't speak again until the day following the second ambush, when I questioned him as to whether, according to his criteria, the situation had improved.

The return trip had all the characteristics of a tragic march (at least I saw it as such). Everybody had expected to return with large amounts of various foods (sugar, for the Cubans, is a dream). Pombo had made a list of things and now his belly had just enough for that day, but what about the following day? And the day after? We walked in silence until sunrise. We picked up our knapsacks once more and, still in silence, continued on until we reached the Center Camp. We stayed overnight there. The army was still in the environs, and Ramón ordered us to leave at 2:00 in the morning. We followed a brook which flowed into the river. We had barely crossed the river when a large army patrol appeared. As luck would have it, they stopped right were we were hiding in a canefield and we couldn't move or the sugar canes would crackle like shots. There we were, they and us, until it became light and we were able to leave the place little by little by taking advantage of their talking.

We climbed the hill on the lefthand side of the river and continued our march north over hilltops. We were almost at the river again in the late afternoon when we ran into some cowhands with cows. Ramón gave orders to capture some of the cows, and they grabbed three or four cows and two calves. Later we continued walking inside the river for another hour until we came to a small brook, choked with weeds, which flowed towards the left. We followed it without leaving footprints. The Rearguard left a guard post at the mouth of the brook and the rest of us kept on walking for about an hour until finally Ramón gave orders to camp. The plan was to eat the cows and to brine meat to carry with us. This would take days, so provision had to be made for the defense of the camp. Rolando was placed in charge and his first measure was to set an ambush at the entrance to the brook and to place an observation post on top of a hill which would provide, he said, a view of the river in both directions into the distance.

Ramón had made an evaluation of the overall morale of the people and he decided to resume the classes that had been discontinued since the march to the north. The next day Aniceto started his Quechua classes and on the following day Ramón started his class in political economy. Classes were always in the evening at 7:00, and all those with responsibilities (future officers, I presume) had to take these classes. The rest of the men were allowed to audit them or not attend at all. During those days they killed some of the cows, and we ate so much that the consequences were very unfortunate. Antonio suffered bad liver trouble and everyone had acute diarrhea and stomach cramps.

Time went by until on the 10th at mid-morning we heard shooting coming from the area of the ambush. It didn't last long, and almost immediately Médico (Negro) arrived to warn us that troops were coming. The first messenger arrived one hour later. He reported that fifteen soldiers had been ambushed and all of them had surrendered except two or three who escaped. The total casualties were one soldier dead and others wounded, two of them seriously. But one of the guerrillas had been seriously wounded, too: El Rubio had a bullet in his head. Ramón ordered Médico (Negro) to do all that was possible for him. He also ordered him to take along Julio (the physician in the Vanguard) and at the same time to care for all the wounded. But the chief surgeon (Moro) was far away in the hospital with the surgical equipment. There was nothing that could be done for El Rubio, and very little for the soldiers, one of whom died shortly afterwards.

This ambush was just as bloody as the previous one. The only difference was that this time one of the soldiers spotted El Rubio and shouted or fired first, giving the alarm. The guerrilla response was thunderous and instantaneous. Fortunately the soldiers surrendered quickly and there were less dead. Rifles were captured and a light machine gun of the FAL type, but they did not know the make. This weapon pleased Benigno because it was given to him. The operation this time, too, was under

Rolando, with participation by men of the Rearguard and Vanguard—
about eight men, including Marcos, Braulio, Pablo, Rubio. Coco and
Inti were in charge of the questioning and they found out that a 100-man
force was due to leave the finca to reconnoiter that part of the river. As
usual Ramón ordered that everything that had been captured be moved,
including the clothes. The latter, however, would be taken from the
soldiers just before they were set free. He also ordered the ambush to
be moved ahead one kilometer. Soon afterwards the weapons started
arriving at the camp and El Ñato left to find a good hiding place for
them. The body of El Rubio was also brought closer to the camp and
he was buried. At mid-afternoon there was more shooting, longer than
in the morning, with sporadic shots half an hour after the heavy firing.
About one and a half hours later Pombo arrived with news. This time it
was more tragic, seven or eight dead, a number of wounded and prisoners, and an arsenal of arms, equipment, and a mortar captured. The
guerrillas did not suffer any casualties. According to the prisoners there
were around 80 soldiers but not all of them were in the area of the ambush, because they came scattered. According to Pombo, Rolando was
trying to capture a .30 calibre machine gun that had been set up by the
soldiers who were able to get away from the ambush. Miguel and
Benigno had ordered a cleanup along the sides of the river where many
of the soldiers were hiding. They were captured one by one.

Ramón ordered a march to the brook for the following day, taking
with us the cows and everything to the last strip of paper. The intention
was to camouflage this camp and conceal the direction we were taking.
The prisoners were freed in the afternoon and they were advised of a
truce until the following afternoon so that the dead soldiers could be
retrieved. We walked for an hour the following morning along the
reed-filled brook until we came to a place where the reeds ended and the
stream widened. There were large rocks in the water, and we set up
camp on both sides of the stream.

I forgot to mention something. When Ramón had heard about El
Rubio's wound, he sent Urbano to the Hospital Camp to bring Moro
(physician) and also the other men if they were well enough. Upon our
arrival, we met all the people from the hospital, who were looking for us.
Moro reported that the army had come into the Central Camp. He was
there at the time, with Serapio, looking for milk in the caves when the
troops entered the Center after firing some mortar shots.

After a good diet of food, vitamins, and antibiotics the sick men had
recovered. Joaquín again took over command of the Rearguard, and
Ramón ordered him to set up an ambush at the place where the camp

had been the previous day, but to return to join the Vanguard after two days. We were very busy transferring large amounts of arms and ammunition, boots, clothing, cartridge belts, canteens, etc. El Ñato had found a brook with filthy water which, fifteen meters from the camp, turned left and rose between two hills. Toward the end of the brook, on the lefthand side, Ñato and Moisés dug a cave, where all the material was stored. We remained there that day.

After we finished the cows, we left, heading for the Central Camp. This journey took us two days of incredibly superhuman efforts since we had to climb embankments one after the other. The first night we slept in the last water clearing right on the bare ground. At sunset on the following day we reached the camp more dead than alive. (At least that's how I felt.) The Vanguard had already taken all possible security measures to detect any mines or traps. There were none, and one of the caves, the only one that was full, was still untouched. It seemed as though no one had been there; everything was in its place. Even the oven, which they thought had been destroyed, was intact. Unfortunately there was nothing to put in it. Toward night, the men who had lagged behind arrived.

The Rearguard came a day later. Ramón had a meeting with those "responsible," and Miguel went on a two-day reconnaissance. The classes continued with fair enthusiasm in the evenings. Trips were made to all storage bases (Hospital, Poza, Oso, and Elevador) to get our last food reserves. Pombo distributed the load, and finally Ramón announced that we would leave at dawn on the sixteenth. He told me that he would try to take us out through the south and that he needed to get supplies for at least one month; that he wanted to get himself "lost," without contacts with either the army or the population. I warned him that this time I was determined to leave, even at the risk of getting caught. We agreed on that. At 5:00 A.M. we began our march behind the Vanguard, heading up the river toward the south.

The Departure

We walked until midday, when we reached a point where there was a stream to our right and where the army had had a camp on a small island in the river. After drinking tea, we continued until we reached a small, abandoned school (to the right of the river). There we took a path to the left through a dense thicket. Toward nightfall we again reached the river and were now—according to Coco of the Vanguard—very close to the first houses. Ramón ordered the purchase and preparation of a hog, and in order not to tire the men further, we settled down to await the food. Ramón sent for several people who, because of illness, had been delayed in leaving the camp. He had left orders, in the former army camp on the small island, for them to set themselves by the stream that began there, remaining until the column returned. Among them was Tania, her incredible strength now depleting, and Alejandro, Serapio, and El Médico (Negro), who was in charge of them. If they had not been sent for, however, food would have had to be dispatched to them. I tell of this to emphasize the confusion in orders and counterorders, which meant difficult hikes for the messengers.

At night the food that had been purchased began to arrive: melons, watermelons, potatoes, yucca, cauliflowers and corn cobs. The group ate throughout the night, almost without sleep. In the morning the part of a hog arrived that was for the Center and the Rearguard. They continued cooking until nightfall. The time set for the departure was six in the evening, but indigestion prevented their moving. At exactly ten we left. We knew that we were passing several houses because of the barking dogs, and that explained the night march, almost without flashlights. The march lasted all night. We would walk an hour and stop for fifteen minutes, with two rests of three-quarters of an hour in all the night.

At dawn a halt was ordered. We were before another town in the Yacumba gorge. The Vanguard sent word about the hamlet and advised that the distance remaining to reach the road was five leagues (25 kilometers). Ramón decided to spend the day there because he did not want to march in daylight. He ordered that a house be taken and food prepared. Another hog was purchased, and the day went by. People on horseback arrived from both directions and were detained by the Vanguard and the Rearguard and sent to the house around which the Center was staying.

Among these detainees, all of them local people, appeared at midday the Englishman, with two children who served as his guides. News of the presence of the guerrillas in the zone had been carried to Lagunillas by a boy who, further back, had evaded the guerrilla vigilance the previous day. This was related by the Englishman to Inti, who naturally interrogated him. In view of the news, the Englishman had obtained a guide in Lagunillas who took him across the hills and into the ravine. There, according to the Englishman, he switched to the boys, and finding tracks of the passage of many people, he continued until stopped by the sentries. In the beginning the story was not believed by Ramón, nor by anyone. It was, in truth, very suspicious. He had an alteration in his passport and a powerful camera with a telescopic sight. Ramón concluded that he was a spy for the army who was to verify his—Che's—

presence there. Ramón decided after several hours, in the face of the news that their presence was already known in Lagunillas, to continue to the road anyway and take advantage of the Englishman in order to get us out, since he had the famous pass. For the moment he said nothing more, and we continued the march.

I believe it would be of interest to tell something of the guerrilla relations with the population. The first thing that comes to mind is the fear of the people. Because of this fear they try to avoid having guerrilla visits. To achieve this they deny having everything the guerrillas seek to buy —even though the hogs walk between them. Thus the negotiations are lengthy. Despite all the convincing arguments, however, finally the purchase is completed. That is to say, the guerrillas announce that they will take as a purchase such and such a thing. The same method is used in regard to the right to use a grill and necessary utensils. As the hours go by, and the doctors or doctor work, taking care of children, treating wounds, giving injections and so on, the tension eases and there is a new exchange in the relationship, although the people do not lose all their fear.

That day, to top it all, just when we were leaving there appeared a plane flying low over the center of the ravine. There was a panic that caused a general scattering of women, children, and men. Others tried to stop the running, and later Ramón personally explained to the women that when there were planes, they should remain standing and not run. He said, "If the pilot sees you run, he thinks we are here and he fires." The departure was cordial and without pressures. That day a horse was confiscated. It belonged to the brother of a man who had gone to Lagunillas to inform on us. The owner of the horse had been detained in this house by the guerrillas. Other things were paid for.

Soon night fell and the hike was once again in the most absolute darkness. At eleven o'clock we met a messenger from the Vanguard who was waiting to speak with Ramón and who told us the road was near. Ramón, after giving some orders, summoned Debray and myself to tell us that he had thought of only one plan: We would go with the guerrillas to the town of Muyupampa, where he would find a jeep that would take us to Sucre, or, in the confusion, we would go around the town by ourselves and beyond it take a vehicle the following day. The contract for the jeep would be made utilizing the Englishman's documents. The Englishman, in addition, agreed to front for us until we were out of the Military Zone. In reward, Ramón returned his camera to him and promised him an exclusive story with photos and all the details. I accepted the plan without further ado, stating that for no reason would I fail to leave; Debray also accepted. Ramón told us to get ready quickly because the ones who were going to carry out "Operation Purchase" were already leaving in the darkness with the help of those who could provide boots, pants, nylon shirts, and so on. (I did not know the details of the "Purchase" plan.)

I changed clothes and approached Ramón. He told me that Inti would give me Bolivian money, that I was to use it to pay taxis or whatever was necessary, and that I was to be careful not to fall prisoner. If this did happen, I would have to care for myself, since no one would be able to help me. I was to remember not to speak of him and of the Cubans, and I was to deny their presence at all times and at all costs. This was a serious recommendation which I was to carry out at the risk of my life.

We were bidding farewell when Ramón called Pombo and told him, "Give him some dollars." "How many, Ramón?" "Give him 2,000." He turned back to me and said that possibly I had lost my job, that it had not been his desire that I remain so long, and that I was to take out of the money enough to straighten my affairs. Three hundred or more dollars I was to use to leave the country—although I did not value my life so expensively. The remainder was to be given to the lawyers of the detainees in Salta to help pay the costs of the trial and their future release. He also asked me to transmit to them the salutations of the National Liberation Army of Bolivia, and to say that he proposed to battle like them for the fate of our fatherlands.

Surprised by the money, I took the bills which Pombo hurriedly counted and gave me. They were all $20 bills, which I didn't know where to put. In his rush, Pombo counted $20 less, because I had $280 in my passport, and when my things were confiscated, there were only $2,260. We very quietly said goodbye and I ran to catch up with the group that was moving away. Upon reaching the road Inti stopped and introduced the Englishman. Inti gave me 2,000 bolivianos separately and told us that we should follow in back of the others.

We left the road and hiked 20 kilometers. We spoke with the Englishman about our departure; he had absolute confidence in his pass. He said he was already known in Camiri and that all the military knew that he wanted to do a report on the guerrillas—in his opinion we should head toward Camiri and not Muyupampa. He thought we were also newspapermen.

Suddenly people were seen on the path. We were told to wait, and later we were placed alongside the path. Finally we were told to leave there, to turn back and go into the hills, hide and be silent. We were told that at any moment there might be shooting. It was about 12:30 at night, and we stayed there until three in the morning.

Later they took us to the path, and Inti came to tell us that the operation would not be carried out, that Ramón said we could go back with the retreat or remain with the Englishman, whom they would leave on the path. Automatically I said, "I'll remain!" Debray also wished to remain. They bid simple farewells and left. Inti had told us that they had a number of prisoners from the village who had informed them that that afternoon three trucks had arrived with army troops, that all the entrances were guarded. That is why, to avoid an encounter, Ramón ordered the retreat. The prisoners were taken with them, to be released further away. The spirits of those who were going back were gloomy. Another failure after the most exhausting march!

After they left, we discussed the situation. To hike at that hour meant to expose ourselves to being killed, riddled by the army. We went back into the woods and, dying of cold, waited until six in the morning. At that hour we discussed our situation again: I held that we would without doubt be taken prisoners, and the Englishman said this was not so. I proposed going around the village and coming out on the path further on, but I was defeated by the majority. We began, then, to walk, and we were entering the village.

Soon the army appeared, deploying on the street and ordering us to halt. They told us to take off our coats and put on the ground all the documents we were carrying. We did this. Meanwhile, more soldiers arrived and men in civilian clothing (of the D.I.C.).* They made us march down the center of the street to a building on the plaza, where we were lodged in the patio. In was April 19, one month and some days after my arrival in La Paz.

There was a great commotion. Many people wanted to see; a woman secretly took photos from a nearby roof. A priest and a newspaperman spoke briefly with us. There were two interrogations, without much order. They took our things away from us, including the valises with changes of clothes that the Frenchman and I had brought with us, my medications, the photographs of my daughters.

There was a continuous mass meeting in the patio; the women and men of the town brought breakfast to the troops, who gladly received coffee, bread, sweets. An army lieutenant asked that they invite us, also. This they did, with no animosity toward us, and we were able to breakfast. With this the cold began to leave us. Later they took us to a house next door, where we remained seated in a room until an army helicopter arrived with the Commander of the Fourth Division, who carried out a brief interrogation. Afterwards, at midday, they brought us food, and

* *Departamento de Investigaciones Criminales.*

in the afternoon they took first the Frenchman, and, later on, separately, the Englishman. I was not able to leave that day. Early in the afternoon of the following day they moved me to Camiri.

Until I was alone the night before, I had not remembered the money I had in my pocket. In the quiet of the night I thought over what I should do with it, and I knew I could not get rid of it or try to give it to anyone. I decided to push some of it through a hole in the pocket of my coat. Messing of the coat, its use as a pillow or mattress, made the money spread around inside the lining as though this had been done on purpose.

The first thing that happened when we reached Camiri was what was to be expected, something they hadn't done yet; that is, I was searched. An officer took the coat and felt around the edges. He put his fingers through the hole and started digging out dollars. That was a riot. The Colonel ordered me to take off all my clothes, while dollars were still popping out of my coat, and I naively handed over the remaining half that was in the back pocket of my trousers. A Captain found the 2,000 Bolivian pesos in another pocket. Finally I was handcuffed and placed on the floor of a room until a group of interrogators arrived the following day.

My situation before them was extremely difficult from the start. I had been carrying with me dollars and a forged passport, and there was a grave threat hanging over me if I talked. Another thing was that I was utterly alone—nobody, either relatives or friends, knew where I was. I thought that perhaps if the name in the passport had already been disclosed publicly or was to be disclosed, then Rutman would get in touch with the lawyers, but I would be running the risk of relaying information if I were to let them know about by double personality. I decided to gain some time by sticking to the passport. I knew, however, that very soon they would realize that I was lying, since I didn't know any of the personal data, address, etc., in the passport. With regard to withholding facts about Ramón, I had the intention of contacting my family first so as to prepare them for anything. I thought that I would not remain incommunicado very long, as is the case in Argentina. In all the rest of my statements I conformed with these two lies. But the story was fundamentally inconsistent because my role in this game was like that of a pawn of another chess set, and I did not fit into the actual picture.

The rest is already known. There is only one thing left, and that is to mention the treatment I have received from the army, which was correct at all times. I was naturally warned about the seriousness of my situation, which would be worse if I adopted a negative attitude. Nevertheless, I was never badly treated, not even in words. With reference to my food and lodging, I received the same as the members of the army, and as the interrogations have continued and my situation has clarified, the conditions of my detention have improved reasonably. I have no complaints; on the contrary, when the money I had been given was exhausted, the Captain in charge of this place purchased with his own money the medications that I required for my illness. Considering the number of dead persons, perhaps comrades, friends, or relatives of our custodians—tragic deaths without any warning, the persons who were assassinated innocent victims of the political and war schemes of a group isolated from the people who have no right to bear arms and, to top it all, taking orders from foreigners who have set up a mechanism foreign to the country—harsher and more implacable treatment of me could have been expected. Such cases have happened before in America. The Bolivian Army has shown in this its high moral and humanitarian standards, reflecting the best traditions of a country that has never been an aggressor even when attacked. I am not complaining but I do resent being held incommunicado because I want to know about my family, about my wife and daughters, whom I left for ten days without any warning, and it's been three months now.

The Assignments

Evidently, I wasn't the main guest from Argentina, just as I wasn't the only one. The invitation was not for me personally but as the representative of a group that had acted in like fashion. What they wanted to know was the thinking of the group following their experience. Of course, I mean nothing politically in my country, or anywhere else. There was not much, therefore, that Ramón could assign to me. If he expected, or still expects, to converse with those who truly represent a party or a movement or at least with a group which is active and strong and is not destroyed and its members not in prison, it is logical that he would not have made his most important requests to me. Least of all would he have done so when it became clear during our talks that I was not in agreement either personally or as the representative of any group, and that anyway I was not a spokesman for anyone, not even for those who were in prison, although I could convey their views. Anyhow, circumstances changed my role a little, that is, the role that I could have played in the event that future contacts were not possible for a long time. But just a little.

To be exact, during our meetings Ramón had entrusted me with several things that I should do, and others that, theoretically, I was to do when I was so advised later on. The first assignment was to try to contact separately the leaders of those groups which theoretically were in revolutionary positions. Which ones? I wasn't told this; I would have to find out by myself, feel my way around, because of the security risks involved on both sides. If I succeeded, then I would hold a meeting and establish a committee for support of, and solidarity with, the struggle in Bolivia which would be able to further this position with reports of the ambushes and an account of his political-strategic plan. In addition, news published in the newspapers would give veracity to the matter, and after that everything would move by itself. Thus, there was nothing concrete or direct.

All of this is a bit abstract simply because I was not the main contact for him, nor was I a guarantee of anything, not even solidarity. Just as it is clear and certain that I was not in agreement before coming, I did not agree with him when I was face to face with him, and I disagree more than ever now.

My future assignments were to be of a journalistic publicity type. I would be getting at my house, through I don't know what means, information, communiqués, denials of official reports, etc. By means of connections with the press media that this Committee of Support might have, these would be released or published. Among the intellectual circles with means of divulgence through magazines and other publications, articles, analyses, disputes, etc., would be encouraged.

That was all, except for the problem of the money for the prisoners. Perhaps this had a twofold intent. If I did not bend every effort to develop political support through that means, those who were in prison, but have more political weight than I do, would do so, even though only out of gratitude. They can, from where they are, move people, influence groups, agitate. Why not? Attention centers on them.

Santa Cruz, June 7, 1967

THE GUEVARA AND BUSTOS ACCOUNTS COMPARED 12

Ciro Roberto Bustos' account of his contacts with, and life within, the guerrilla movement operating in Bolivia under "Che" Guevara's command is not only interesting, but enlightening as well. This account brings out the domestic and international questions the guerrillas had to face.

Much more detailed in many aspects than Guevara's own diary, Bustos' story is probably also more objective in judging the situation that existed and the possibilities of success of the movement. Although Bustos' account was made when he was already in a Bolivian jail, his narration of events is entirely accurate if compared with Guevara's diary. Only minor differences as to the timing of some of these events have been found, and this is to be expected in a statement made weeks afterwards. This similarity in the Bustos and Guevara accounts eliminates any suspicion that Bustos' narration might have been forced or previously prepared.

There is only one important point of disagreement between Guevara's diary and Bustos' account, although this does not necessarily affect the re liability of the rest of the information given by Bustos. This point refers to Bustos' attitude and answer to Guevara's request for support, as well as to Bustos' planned role in this support. Being tried by the Bolivian military on charges of having participated in the guerrilla movement, Bustos underplays his own role in the affair, presenting himself as a journalist who went to Bolivia without really knowing the purpose of the trip nor whom he was going to meet, nor under what circumstances. He emphasizes in his account that he tried to discourage Guevara from his plans and refused to carry on the most important tasks assigned to him.

If the reader compares Bustos' statements with the references in Guevara's diary to "Mauricio," "Pelao," and "Carlos" (war names of Bustos), a different conclusion is reached. Although Guevara's diary indicates that Bustos was never a member of the guerrilla forces, it does show that he came to the camp, after being contacted by "Tania," in order to plan with Guevara material and moral support for the movement from various Argentine sources.

According to Guevara's notations in his diary on March 21, 1967:

> El Pelao, of course, is willing to be under my command, and I made the proposal to him to be at present a sort of coordinator of the groups [led by] . . . Jozamy, Belman, and Stamponi, and to send five men to begin training. He was to give my regards to María Rosa Oliver and the old man. He will be given 500 pesos [probably U.S. dollars] to send and 1,000 pesos for traveling. If they accept, they should begin reconnaissance in the north of Argentina and send me a report.

This clearly implies an agreement between Bustos and Guevara that the former would start recruiting people to be trained as guerrillas, followed by the eventual opening of a guerrilla front in the north of Argentina. This notation also does not agree exactly with Bustos' statement about the purpose of the money given to him.

Only those parts related to Bustos' eventual role in Argentina as a supporter of the guerrilla movement have to be taken with reservation. The rest of his story completely coincides with Guevara's diary, and being more detailed and objective, it offers a valuable source of information about Guevara's activities in Bolivia.

Guevara's body strapped to a stretcher for transportation in helicopter

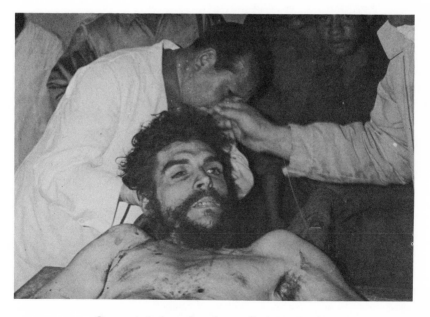

Guevara's body undergoing medical examination

A rest after a march in the campaign. Left to right: Alejandro (Ricardo Gustavo Machín), Inti (Guido Pereda), Pombo, Acana Campero, "Che," "Tuma" (Guevara's double), Camba (Orlando Jiménez), Joaquín (Juan V. Acuña Núñez)

Another view of the above group

LIST OF 13
GUERRILLAS

LIST OF PERSONS APPEARING IN BUSTOS' ACCOUNT OF GUEVARA'S GUERRILLAS IN BOLIVIA OR OTHERWISE IDENTIFIED AS BEING WITH THE GUERRILLAS

War name*	Real Name	Position with Guerrillas†	Fate	Previous Occupation
Ramón	Ernesto "Che" Guevara de la Serna	Commander in Chief	Died Oct. 9, '67, in La Higuera	Maj., Cuban Army; Min. of Industries; member PCC Central Committee
CUBANS				
Alejandro	Gustavo R. Machín Hoed de Beche (Tavo)	Member of Center; Chief of Operations; because of illness remained with Rear on Apr. 17, '67	Died Aug. 31, '67, in Vado del Yeso	Maj., Cuban Army; Military Chief of Matanzas
Antonio	Orlando Pantoja Tamayo (Olo)	Member of Center; Chief of Information	Died Oct. 8, '67, in Vallegrande	Chief, Cuba's Border Forces
Arturo	Nelson Aspuru	Member of Center; radio operator	Died Oct. 8, '67, in Vallegrande	Chief, Fidel Castro, Jr.'s bodyguards

* War names are those either used in Bustos' account or in Guevara's Diary.
† Positions given are those held until the original large group split up on April 17, 1967. Later the Rearguard was unable to rejoin the rest of the guerrilla forces.

War name	Real Name	Position with Guerrillas	Fate	Previous Occupation
Benigno	Daniel Alarcón Ramírez	Member of Vanguard	Returned to Cuba	Not known
Braulio	Israel Reyes Zayas	Member of Rearguard	Died Aug. 31, '67, in Vado del Yeso	Lt., Cuban Army
Joaquín	Juan Vitalio Acuña Núñez (Vilo)	Chief of Rearguard; second in command to Guevara	Died Aug. 31, '67, in Vado del Yeso	Maj., Cuban Army; member PCC Central Committee
Marcos	Antonio Sánchez Díaz	Chief of Vanguard replaced by Miguel Mar. 25, '67; became member of Rearguard	Died June 2, '67, in Iquira	Maj., Cuban Army; member PCC Central Committee
Miguel	Not known	Chief of Vanguard as of Mar. 25, '67	Died Sep. 26, '67, in Abra de Picacho	Not known
Moro, Mugamba, Morogoro, Médico	Octavio de la Concepción de la Pedraja	Member of Center; Chief Surgeon	Died Oct. 14, '61, in Vallegrande	Lt., Cuban Army; Physician in Havana hospital
Pacho, Pocho, Pachungo	Alberto Fernández Montes de Oca	Member of Vanguard	Died Oct. 8, '67, in Vallegrande	Cap., Cuban Army; Director of Mines
Pombo	Harry Villegas	Member of Center; Chief of Supplies	Returned to Cuba	Cap., Cuban Army
Ricardo, Papi, Chincho	Roberto (?) Aspuru	Preliminary contacts in Bolivia, Chief of Communications; Member of Center	Died July 30, '67, in Moroco	Was with Guevara in the Congo
Rolando	Eliseo Reyes Rodríguez	Member of Center; Political Commissar; acted temporarily as Chief, Rearguard, Mar., '67	Died Apr. 25, '67, in El Mesón	Cap., Cuban Army; member PCC, Central Committee
Rubio, Félix	Jesús Suárez Gayol	Member of Rearguard	Died Apr. 10, '67, in Iripiti	Cap., Cuban Army; Vice-Minister, Ministry of Sugar Industry

War name	Real Name	Position with Guerrillas	Fate	Previous Occupation
Tuma, Tumaini	Not known	Member of Center	Died June 26, '67, in Piray de la Florida	Was with Guevara in the Congo
Urbano	Leonardo Tamayo Núñez	Member of Center	Returned to Cuba	Cap., Cuban Army; Secretary, Cuban Delegation to Punta del Eeste, '61

BOLIVIANS

War name	Real Name	Position with Guerrillas	Fate	Previous Occupation
(deserter)	Pastor Barrera Quintana	Arrived in camp while Guevara was on exploratory march with most of his men	Deserted in early Mar. '67; arrested	Recruited by Moisés Guevara
(deserter)	Vicente Rocabado Terrazas	Same as above	Same as above	Same as above
Aniceto	Ancito Reynaga Gordillo	Member of Vanguard	Died Oct. 9, '67, in La Higuera	Member, National Executive Committee, Bolivian Communist Youth
Camba	Orlando Jiménez Bazán	Member of Vanguard	Deserted Sep. 26, '67; arrested	Not known
Carlos	Lorgio Vaca	Participant, exploratory march	Drowned Mar. 17, '67, during march	Received guerrilla training in Havana
Coco	Roberto Peredo Leigue	Member of Vanguard	Died Sep. 26, '67, in Abra de Picacho	Member, Bolivian Communist Party (pro-Moscow)
Chingolo	Hugo Choque Silva	Not accepted as guerrilla; was in Rearguard	Deserted July 23, '67; arrested	Recruited by Moisés Guevara
Darío	David Adriazola	Member of Vanguard	Not known	Farmer from Huanuni
Eusebio	Eusebio Tapia Aruni	Not accepted as guerrilla; was in Rearguard	Deserted July 23, '67; arrested	Not known
Inti	Guido Peredo Leigue	Member of Center; Political Commissar; Bolivian Chief	Not known	Member, Bolivian Communist Party (pro-Moscow)

War name	Real Name	Position with Guerrillas	Fate	Previous Occupation
Julio, Médico	Mario Gutié-rrez Ardaya	Member of Vanguard; physician	Died Sep. 26, '67, in Abra de Picacho	Physician from El Beni
León	Antonio Rodrí-guez Flores	Member of Center	Deserted Sep. 26, '67; arrested	Not known
Loro, Jorge, Bigotes	Jorge Vázquez	Member of Vanguard	Captured in late Mar., '67; shot while trying to escape	Member, Bolivian Communist Party (pro-Moscow); trained in Cuba
Luis, Chapaco	Jaime Arana Campero	Member of Center	Died Oct. 14, '67, in Valle-grande	Engineer, former student leader
Médico chino, Ernesto	Fredi Ernesto Maimura Hur-tado	Member of Rearguard	Died Aug. 31, '67, in Vado del Yeso	Received medical training in Cuba
Moisés	Moisés Guevara Rodríguez	Member of Center; later joined the Rear-guard; recruiter	Died Aug. 31, '67, in Vado del Yeso	Union leader; member Bolivian Communist Party (pro-Peking)
Ñato	Julio Méndez Cano	Member of Center	Not known	Not known
Pablo	Francisco Huanca Flores	Member of Vanguard	Died Oct. 14, '67, in Valle-grande	Recruited by Moisés, lived in Oruro
Paquito	José Castillo Chávez	Not accepted as guerrilla; was in Rearguard	Captured Aug. 31, '67, in Vado del Yeso	Recruited by Moisés
Pedro, Pan Divino	Antonio Jimé-nez Tardío	Member of Rearguard	Died, Aug. 9, '67, in Monte Dorado	Member, National Executive Committee, Bolivian Communist Youth
Pepe	Julio Velasco Montaño	Not accepted as guerrilla; was in Rearguard	Deserted in late May; arrested, was killed May 23, '67, while trying to escape	Member, Bolivian Communist Party (pro-Peking)
Polo, Apolinar	Apolinar Aqui-no Quispe	Member of Rearguard	Died Aug. 31, '67, in Vado del Yeso	Member, Bolivian Communist Party (pro-Peking)
Raúl	Raúl Quispaya	Member of Vanguard	Died July 30, '67, in Moroco	Not known

War name	Real Name	Position with Guerrillas	Fate	Previous Occupation
Salustio	Salustio Choque	Arrived in camp while Guevara was on exploratory march	Arrested by police when the farm was raided in Mar. '67	Not known
Serafín	Benjamín Coronado	Participant, exploratory march	Drowned Feb. 26, '67, during march	Not known
Serapio	Not known	Called a refugee in Guevara's diary; was in Rearguard	Died July 9, '67	Not known
Víctor	Casildo Vargas Condori	Member of Rearguard	Died June 2, '67, in Iquira	Carpenter
Walter	Walter Arencibia Ayala	Member of Rearguard	Died Aug. 31, '67, in Vado del Yeso	Not known
Willy, Ulises	Simón Cuba	Member of Center	Died Oct. 9, '67, in La Higuera	Union leader

PERUVIANS

War name	Real Name	Position with Guerrillas	Fate	Previous Occupation
Chino	Juan Pablo Chang Navarro	Came as visitor, later member of Center	Died Oct. 8, '67, in Vallegrande	Peruvian Communist leader; trained in Cuba
Eustaquio	Lucio Edelberto Salván Hidalgo	Member of Center, radio technician	Died Oct. 14, '67, in Vallegrande	Radio technician
Médico negro	Gustavo Rodríguez Murillo	Member of Rearguard, physician	Died Sep. 3, '67, in Cañón Palmarito	Cardiologist

ARGENTINEANS

War name	Real Name	Position with Guerrillas	Fate	Previous Occupation
Pelao, Carlos, Mauricio	Ciro Roberto Bustos	Came to organize support for guerrillas in Argentina	Left and was arrested; tried and sentenced to 30 years	Commercial artist; active in leftist causes in Salta, Argentina.
Tania, Elma	Haydée Tamara Bunke Bider alias Laura Gutiérrez Bauer de Martínez	In charge of external contacts; remained with Reargaurd	Died Aug. 31, '67, in Vado del Yeso	Born in Argentina, went to East Germany, then to Cuba; has been identified as a Soviet spy planted in Guevara's group

War name	Real Name	Position with Guerrillas	Fate	Previous Occupation
FRENCH				
Francés, Dantón	Jules Regis Debray	Came to organize support for guerrillas in Europe; allegedly a courier between guerrillas and Havana	Left and was arrested; tried and sentenced to 30 years	Writer, theoretician on the Cuban revolution
BRITISH				
Inglés	George Andrew Roth	Came to obtain information for publications	Left with Debray and Bustos; arrested and released	Freelance journalist

CAPTURED GUERRILLA DOCUMENTS 14

In addition to the diaries of Guevara and several of his lieutenants, other guerrilla documents were found by the Bolivian military. Most of them consisted of messages received by Guevara, some containing brief news items, others detailing the movements of individuals. Also captured, however, were a series of "communiqués" the guerrillas planned to issue on the progress of their movement. One of these was a call to Bolivia's miners, a potent force in that country, asking them to join the rebel cause. Another document contained instructions on the setting up of clandestine organizations in cities. It was, in effect, a primer on subversion. The texts of this latter document and the call to the miners follows. It is not clear whether Guevara himself wrote both of these, but it is safe to assume that he, being of literary bent, had a hand in their preparation. The captured documents, together with Guevara's diary, were published by the Cuban government, and the following translations were made from photographic copies obtained from Cuba.

GUERRILLA DOCUMENTS CAPTURED IN BOLIVIA

INSTRUCTIONS FOR CADRES TO WORK IN URBAN AREAS

THE FORMATION of a supporting network of the kind that we want to establish should be guided by a series of norms, a generalization of which follows.

Action will be fundamentally underground, but it will alternate with certain kinds of work in which contact with individuals or organizations will be necessary, thus forcing certain cadres to come out into the open. This demands strict sectioning off, isolating every front engaged in this work.

The cadres should be strictly governed by the general line of conduct laid down by the army command through the levels of authority, but they will have complete liberty in the practical form this line will take.

In order to carry out the difficult tasks assigned him and survive, the underground cadre should have highly developed the following characteristics: discipline, complete secrecy, guile, self-control, and cold blood, and should use work methods which will keep him from becoming entangled in unforeseen contingencies.

All the compañeros who work partially in the open will be governed by higher echelons—also clandestine—which will issue orders and control their work.

Whenever possible, both the leader of the network and the various persons in charge will have only one function, and horizontal contacts will be made through the leader. Every organized network will have at least the following officials:

The chief and a person in charge of each of the following:
1. supplies,
2. transportation,
3. information,
4. finances,
5. urban action, and
6. contacts with sympathizers.

On its being developed, the network will need a person in charge of communications, who will take his general orders from the leader.

The leader will receive his instructions from the Army Command and will put them in practice through the various persons in charge. He should be known only to this small directing nucleus so as to avoid endangering the whole network if he should be captured. If those persons responsible for certain functions know each other, in any case each one's work should be concealed from the others, and any change will not be communicated.

Measures will be taken so that, if an important member of the network should be arrested, the Leader and all those who knew the one arrested will change their places of residence and/or methods of contact.

The person in charge of supplies will have the job of providing supplies for the army, but his task is organizational: starting at the center, he will create smaller supporting networks which will extend up to the E.L.N.,* whether they be purely rural organizations or receive the support of businessmen or other individuals or organizations.

The person in charge of transportation will see to the transporting of supplies from receiving points to the points where the smaller networks will take them or directly to liberated territory, as the case may be.

These compañeros should do their work under good cover; for example, organizing small businesses which will allay the suspicions of the repressive authorities when the magnitude and goals of the movement are made public.

The person in charge of information will gather all military and political information received through the proper contacts. He will work partially in the open, gathering information from sympathizers in the army or government. This makes his post a particularly dangerous one. All the information gathered will be sent to the person in charge of information in our army. The former must obey two commanders: the network leader and the chief of our Intelligence Service.

The person in charge of finances will control the organization's expenses. This comrade must be fully aware of the importance of his post. Despite being in great danger, exposed to an obscure death, he is to live in the city, will not suffer the physical hardship of the guerrilla, and may grow careless in handling the funds and supplies, thus running the risk of lowering his revolutionary standards as a result of constant exposure to temptation. This comrade should check how every peso is spent and see to it that not a single cent is spent without justification. He will also be in charge of the money from collections and taxes and will organize the collection of the latter.

The person in charge of finances will be under the direct orders of the network leader, but he will also act as his inspector in financial matters. It is thus to be understood that the person in charge of finances must have unshakable ideological convictions. The work of the person in charge of urban action covers all types of armed action in the city: the

* Ejército de Liberación Nacional (National Liberation Army).

execution of informers, notorious torturers, and high officials of the regime; the kidnapping of some persons with the aim of obtaining ransom; the sabotage of centers of economic activity; etc. All action will be ordered by the network leader; the person in charge of urban action is not allowed to act on his own except in cases of extreme urgency.

The person in charge of contacts with sympathizers will be the one within the network to work most in the open and will be in contact with weaker elements, those who clear their consciences by giving certain sums of money or other aid without committing themselves. These are people you can work with only as long as you keep in mind that their support is conditional on their not running any risks. Taking this into account, an effort must be made to transform them gradually into active militants, urging them to make substantial contributions to the movement not only in the form of money but also in the form of medicines, hideouts, information, etc.

In this type of network there must be some people who work very closely together; for example, the person in charge of transportation should be closely united with the person in charge of supplies, who will also be his immediate chief; the person in charge of contacts with sympathizers will take orders from the person in charge of finances; action and information will work in direct contact with the leader of the network.

The networks will be subject to inspection by cadres sent directly by the army. These have no executive function, but will simply check that instructions are carried out and norms observed.

The networks should "move" toward the army as follows: the high command issues orders to the network leader; he, in turn, will organize the network in the important cities, from which branches will extend toward the towns and from there to hamlets or individual houses occupied by peasants who will make contact with our army and where the actual delivery of supplies, money or information will take place.

As our army's sphere of influence extends, our contact points will advance toward the city, and the area under direct control of the army will grow proportionately. This is a long process, with its ups and downs, and whose development, as that of this war, must be measured in years.

The network headquarters will be established in the capital; branches will be organized in the cities which at the moment are more important to us: Cochabamba, Santa Cruz, Sucre, and Camiri—that is, the rectangle encompassing our zone of operations. The men in charge of these four cities should be tested cadres insofar as is possible; they will be in charge of similar but simplified organizations. Supplies and transportation will be under one leadership, and finance and sympathizers under another leadership; the third will be urban action—we can do away with information, leaving the local leader in charge of that. Urban action will be tied in with the army as army territory reaches the cities, and finally its members will become suburban guerrillas, acting under the orders of the military commander.

The network already described will branch out from these cities.

We must not overlook the development of the network in cities which today are far from our field of action. We should ask for the support of the population and get ready in time for future action in these cities. Oruro and Potosi are the most important of these cities.

Special attention should be given to the border spots of Villazón and Tarija for contact and supplies from Argentina; Santa Cruz, for Brazil; Huaqui or some other place on the Peruvian border; and some place on the Chilean border.

For the organization of a supply network it would be convenient to have staunch members who have formerly engaged in some activity similar to that which is needed now. For example, the owner of a warehouse could organize the matter of supplies or participate in some other way in this section of the network; the owner of a transportation enterprise would be in charge of organizing this branch, etc.

If this cannot be done, an effort must be made to set up the organization patiently, without forcing events, thus avoiding the pitfall of installing an advance post without taking sufficient precautions, only to lose it and place others in jeopardy.

The following shops or businesses should be organized: grocery stores (in La Paz, Cochabamba, Santa Cruz, and Camiri), transportation services (La Paz-Santa Cruz, Santa Cruz-Camiri, La Paz-Sucre and Sucre-Camiri), shoe factories (in La Paz, Santa Cruz, Camiri, and Cochabamba), clothing factories (in La Paz, Santa Cruz, Camiri, and Cochabamba) and machine shops (in La Paz and Santa Cruz). Lands (in Chapare and Caranavi).

The first two will take care of the receiving of supplies and the transportation of same—which will include war material—without causing suspicion. The shoe and clothing factories will meet two needs. They could buy material and manufacture shoes and clothing for us without raising suspicion. The machine shop could do the same with the war material and the lands will serve as a base of support for future transfers and also for propaganda by settlers among the peasants.

Once again we must emphasize that the cadres must have unshakable ideological conviction, since the revolutionary movement gives them what is strictly necessary for meeting their basic needs, while they give all their time and, if necessary, their freedom and/or their lives. Only thus will we achieve the formation of the effective network needed for the success of our ambitious plans: the total liberation of Bolivia.

TO THE MINERS OF BOLIVIA

Compañeros:

Once more the blood of the proletariat has been shed in our mines. This age-old exploitation—alternating the bleeding of the enslaved miner with the spilling of his blood whenever great injustice causes violent outbursts of protest—has been repeated without variation in cycles covering hundreds of years.

In recent times this pattern was temporarily broken, and workers in rebellion played a major role in the April 9 victory. This event gave rise to hopes that new horizons were opening up and that finally the workers would become masters of their own destiny. But the machinery of the imperialist world shows to those who wish to see it that in the matter of social revolution there are no halfway solutions; either seize complete power or lose advances gained through so much sacrifice and bloodshed.

The armed militia of the miner proletariat—the only strong factor in the initial stage—was joined by militia from other sectors of the working class, by the destitute and the farmers, whose members were not able to see the essential overall interests involved and entered into conflict among themselves, manipulated as they were by demagogy aimed against the people. And, in the end, the professional army came on the scene, a true wolf in sheep's clothing. And that army, small and insignificant at the beginning, was transformed into the armed instrument against the proletariat, into the most reliable accomplice of imperialism. That is why imperialism approved of a military coup d'etat.

We are now recovering from a defeat brought about by repeated tactical errors on the part of the working class, and patiently preparing the country for a deep revolution to change the system completely.

We should not insist on false tactics, heroic in themselves but useless, which plunge the proletariat in a bloodbath and decimate its ranks, thus depriving us of its best fighting elements.

In long months of struggle the guerrillas have caused an upheaval in the country, have killed a large number of soldiers and have demoralized the army almost without suffering any losses. On the other hand, in a battle lasting only a few hours that same army scored a complete victory, and like peacocks the soldiers strut in front of the workers' bodies. The thin line between correct and erroneous tactics accounts for the difference between victory and defeat.

Compañero miner: don't listen again to the false apostles of the mass struggle who interpret this struggle as a compact frontal attack of the people against the weapons of the oppressors. Let us learn from experience! Heroic chests are useless against machine guns, and barricades, no matter how strong, are useless against modern demolition methods. The mass struggle in the underdeveloped countries, with a large rural population and extensive land area, must be undertaken by a small mobile vanguard, the guerrillas, established within the people. This organization will grow stronger at the cost of the enemy army and will serve as the catalyzing agent for the revolutionary fervor of the masses until a revolutionary situation is created in which state power will crumble under a single effective blow, dealt at the right moment.

Understand this well: this is not a call to total inactivity, but rather a recommendation not to risk forces in any action where success is not guaranteed. But the working masses must, at all times, exert pressure on the government, because this is a class struggle without limited fronts. Wherever there is a proletarian, he is under the obligation to struggle within the limit of his power against the common enemy.

Compañero miner: the guerrillas of the E.L.N. await you with open arms and invite you to join the workers of the subsoil now fighting at our side. Here we will rebuild the worker-campesino alliance destroyed by demagogy aimed against the people. Here we will turn defeat into victory and the lament of the workers' widows into a paean of victory. We await you.

E.L.N.

NOTES TO THE
INTRODUCTION

1. *Granma* (Havana), October 22, 1967. This and future references are to the English-language edition. Parallel material appeared in the Spanish-language edition on slightly different dates. (The newspaper *Granma* was named after the vessel that carried the Castro expedition to Cuba in 1956.)
2. *Ibid.*
3. *Ibid.*
4. The precise origins of Guevara's anti-Americanism are not clear. It may have stemmed from his leftist mother, from his reported man-handling by an American sailor (*Time*, August 8, 1960), or from the general anti-American attitudes engendered in Argentina during the era of President Juan Perón. Ironically, one of Guevara's grandparents—his father's mother—was a United States citizen.
5. *Granma, op cit.*
6. Details of this period in Guevara's life were published in *Time, op. cit.* Extensive research in Cuba and elsewhere in Latin America was carried out by *Time* correspondents in preparing this cover story.
7. *Granma,* October 29, 1967.
8. *Ibid.*
9. It is generally believed that the guerrilla movement started with only 12 survivors but the fact is that 15 men, including Fidel and Raúl Castro and Guevara, signed a note thanking a citizen who sheltered them after the expedition's debacle. *Rotograbado de Revolución,* December 2, 1963.
10. For additional accounts of the guerrilla campaign, see Robert Taber, *M-26, The Biography of a Revolution,* New York: Lyle Stuart, 1961; Jay Mallin, *Fortress Cuba,* Chicago: Henry Regnery Co., 1965; *idem,* "Castro's Guerrilla Campaign," *Marine Corps Gazette,* January, 1967.
11. Guevara's father was quoted as saying facetiously, "Any business we Guevaras put money into has always been a failure" (*Time, op. cit.*).
12. *Current Digest of the Soviet Press,* Vol. XIII, No. 4, February 22, 1961.

13. *Mao Tse-tung on Guerrilla Warfare*. Translated and with an introduction by Brigadier General Samuel B. Griffith, New York: 1961.

14. Fidel Castro is not usually included in this group. Although he came to power through a guerrilla campaign, and although he subsequently used guerrilla warfare as a major means of subversion in other countries, his own military leadership in the Cuban revolution consisted primarily in surviving as a symbol of resistance. More aggressive maneuvers and decisive campaigns were conducted by his brother Raúl, Guevara, and other rebel officers. Castro has been a vociferous exponent of guerrilla warfare, but he has written virtually nothing on the subject and done little to add to or define this concept of combat. The concepts of European Communist theoreticians beginning with Marx and Engels and continuing on through the twentieth century leaders, including Lenin, Stalin, and the modern-day Russians, were rooted in the experiences of the French Revolution of 1789, the revolution of 1848, and the French Commune of 1871, with their urban upheavals, street barricades, defections of regular armed forces, etc. Lenin and Stalin placed some emphasis on guerrilla operations, but only in terms of assistance to a main revolutionary effort on the part of urban masses.

15. Griffith, *op. cit.*

16. *Ibid.*

17. *Ibid.*

18. Robert S. Elegant, *China's Red Masters—Political Biographies of the Chinese Communist Leaders*, New York: Twayne Publishers, 1951.

19. Edward L. Katzenbach, Jr. and Gene Z. Hanrahan, "The Revolutionary Strategy of Mao Tse-tung," *Political Science Quarterly*, September, 1955.

20. Mao Tse-tung, "On Protracted War," *Selected Military Writings of Mao Tse-tung*, Peking, 1963.

21. Vo Nguyen Giap, *People's War, People's Army*, Hanoi, 1961.

22. Mao, *ibid.*

23. Giap, *ibid.*

24. Mao, *ibid.*

25. Giap, *ibid.*

26. Giap, *ibid.*

27. Giap, *The South Vietnam People Will Win*, Hanoi, 1965.

28. *Guerra del pueblo, ejército del pueblo*, Havana, 1964.

29. William E. Ratliff, "A New Old Che Guevara Interview," *The Hispanic American Review*, August, 1966.

30. Ernesto Guevara, *La guerra de guerrillas*, Havana, 1960.

31. *Ibid.*

32. *Ibid.*

33. September, 1963.

34. This and the following quotes are from Guevara, "Guerrilla Warfare: A Method," *Cuba Socialista*, September, 1963.

35. *Ibid.*

36. Part of the material on Guevara in Bolivia that follows in this Introduction appeared in an article by the author, "Che Guevara: Some Documentary

Puzzles at the End of a Long Journey," in the *Journal of Inter-American Studies*, Vol. X, No. 1, January, 1968, pp. 74-84.

37. *Granma*, April 23, 1967.
38. Although this phrase—"two, three or many Viet Nams"—is generally credited to Guevara, Castro in a speech delivered on December 18, 1966, had declared, "[imperialism] will be defeated when instead of one Viet Nam there will be in the world two Viet Nams, three Viet Nams, four Viet Nams, five Viet Nams . . ." (*Bohemia*, December 23, 1966). It is possible that at this time Castro already had the Guevara message which was to be released later.
39. *Granma*, April 23, 1967.
40. See "Man and Socialism in Cuba" in this volume.
41. *The Complete Bolivian Diaries of Che Guevara and Other Captured Documents*, ed. Daniel James, New York: Stein & Day, 1968.
42. "Guerrilla Warfare: A Method," *op. cit.*
43. *Comandante*, technically the equivalent to the rank of Major in other armies, is the highest rank in Castro's army.
44. A photographic copy of the dairy is in the possession of the editor.
45. *Ibid*, was read at the trial of Regis Debray.
46. These quotes are from "Guerrilla Warfare: A Method," *op. cit.*
47. Karl Marx, *The Eighteenth Brumaire of Louis Bonaparte*, New York, 1963.
48. Press wire service reports, October 16, 1967.
49. This radio exchange was reported by *El Diario*, La Paz, October 23, 1967.
50. *Ibid.*
51. Speech, October 15, 1967.

SOURCES

Guevara's Account of Cuban Campaign: *Granma* (English-language edition), October 22, 1967.

"Social Projections of the Cuban Army": Gregorio Selser (ed.). *Fidel Castro —La revolución cubana.* Buenos Aires, 1960. Translated by Jay Mallin.

"The Cadre, Spinal Column of the Revolution": *Cuba Socialista*, September, 1962. Translated by Jay Mallin.

"Guerrilla Warfare: A Method": *Cuba Socialista*, September, 1962. Translated by Roberto Hernández.

Prologue to Book by General Vo Nguyen Giap, *People's War, People's Army*, Havana, 1964. Translated by Jay Mallin.

Speech Before the United Nations: *Colonialism Is Doomed*, Havana, probably 1965.

"Socialism and Man in Cuba": published as a small book, Havana, 1967.

Guevara's Farewell Letter: *Bohemia*, October 8, 1965. Translated by Margarita M. Pelleyá.

Message to *Tricontinental* Magazine: *Granma* (English-language edition), April 23, 1967.

Monthly Summaries, Guevara's Bolivian Diary: Photostats of these were obtained from the Cuban government. Translated by Roberto Hernández.

Account by Ciro Roberto Bustos: Translated by Margarita M. Pelleyá.

Captured Guerrilla Documents: Photostats provided by the Cuban government. Translated by Roberto Hernández.

BIBLIOGRAPHY OF
GUEVARA'S WORKS

Ernesto Guevara, because his interests were varied, wrote on a good many subjects. Fundamentally, however, what he wrote may be classified in two basic categories: theory and narration. Guevara was a man of action as well as of thought, and his writings reflect this fact. The theoretical works are significant because they embody the thinking of the Number Three man (after the Castro brothers) in the Cuban revolution—and because these writings carried an influence of their own. Guevara's narrative writings constitute the only substantial account by a top commander of the guerrilla campaign that culminated in victory in January of 1959.

The following bibliography is based on a perusal of most of the more important magazines published in Cuba in the period 1959 to early 1968. The magazines studied included military, doctrinal, financial, and general-readership publications of the Castro regime.

Three books bear Guevara's name. These are:

Guerra de guerrillas, a basic textbook on guerrilla warfare published in 1960. (Excerpts were published in the May, 1960, issue of *Trabajo* and the October 29, 1961, issue of *Bohemia*.)

Pasajes de la guerra revolucionaria, a compilation of first-person accounts by Guevara of the campaign in the Sierra Maestra Mountains, published in 1963. (These accounts were originally published in the military magazine *Verde Olivo*.)

Diario del Che en Bolivia, the diary Guevara kept during his Bolivian guerrilla campaign, published in 1968. (The diary was also published in the July 5, 1968, issue of *Bohemia*.)

Guevara wrote one full account of the 1956-1958 guerrilla campaign, and this was published in Brazil (see below). The *Pasajes* were a series of brief accounts, published at irregular intervals in *Verde Olivo*. Guevara evidently intended to put together a history of the 25-month campaign, and other former guerrillas were urged to send in material for inclusion in this work. Each Guevara article was published under the general heading "Pasajes de la Guerra Revolucionaria," but each in addition had its own title. The "Pasajes" were as follows:

"Alegría de Pío," February 26, 1961. (Reprinted in *Bohemia*, December 6, 1963, and in *Verde Olivo*, December 3, 1967.

"El combate de La Plata," March 12, 1961.

"Combate de Arroyo del Infierno," March 26, 1961.

"Ataque aéreo," April 16, 1961.

"Sorpresa en Altos de Espinosa," June 25, 1961.

"Fin de un traidor," July 9, 1961.

"Días amargos," July 23, 1961.

"El Refuerzo," August 13, 1961.

"Adquiriendo el temple," October 1, 1961.

"Una entrevista famosa," October 15, 1961.

"Jornadas de marcha," December 24, 1961.

"Llegan las armas," January 7, 1962.

"El combate de 'El Uvero,' " February 4, 1962. (Reprinted in *Verde Olivo*, May 28, 1967.)

"Cuidando heridos," April 29, 1962.

"De regreso," June 10, 1962.

"Se gesta una traición," August 5, 1962.

"El Patojo," August 19, 1962. (Reprinted in *Pensamiento Crítico*, October, 1967.)

"El ataque a Bueycito," August 26, 1962.

"El combate de 'El Hombrito,' " November 18, 1962.

All of the above were included in Guevara's second book, *Pasajes de la Guerra Revolucionaria*. (Unlike the other accounts, "El Patojo" was not originally published under the heading "Pasajes" in *Verde Olivo*, but Guevara apparently decided to include it in the book. Whereas the other articles were all narrations of events, "El Patojo" was a tribute to one of Guevara's men.)

The nineteen accounts listed above were not the only "Pasajes" (episodes) that Guevara wrote. More followed, and probably the intention was to include them in a later book once the series had been completed. The following additional "Pasajes" were published in *Verde Olivo*:

"Pino del Agua," March 17, 1963. (Reprinted in *Verde Olivo*, September 17, 1967.)

"Un episodio desagradable," April 28, 1963.

"Lucha contra el bandidaje," June 9, 1963.

"El cachorro asesinado," June 23, 1963. (Reprinted in *Verde Olivo*, October 22, 1967.)

"El combate de Mar Verde," September 8, 1963.

" 'Altos de Conrado,' " October 6, 1963.

"A la deriva," December 8, 1963.

"Un año de lucha armada," January 5, 1964. (Reprinted in *Pensamiento Crítico*, October, 1967.)

"Pino del Agua II," January 19, 1964.

"Interludio," August 23, 1964.

"Una reunión decisiva," November 22, 1964.

A few weeks after "Una reunión decisiva" was published, Guevara left on an extended voyage abroad. He returned to Cuba four months later, and then vanished. Thus, as far as is known, he never completed writing this history of the 1956-1958 guerrilla campaign.

Guevara did, however, write a three-part account of the guerrilla war for the Brazilian magazine *O Cruzeiro*. This was published in June and July of 1959 in the international edition of that magazine. Portions of this were reprinted in the November 30, 1962, issue of *Bohemia* under the title "Valía la pena morir por un ideal tan puro . . . ," and in the December 3, 1967, issue of *Verde Olivo* under the title "Una revolución que comienza." Part of the account was also included in the book, *Geografía de Cuba*, written by Antonio Núñez Jiménez (1959).

Not until after Guevara was killed did *Verde Olivo* reveal that it had once published a number of articles by Guevara under a pseudonym. These evidently appeared for a few months only. Brief, sardonic comments on current affairs, they were published as being written by "El francotirador," and had the general heading "Sin bala en el directo." These articles included the following:

"El más peligroso enemigo y otras boberías," April 17, 1960. (Reprinted October 29, 1967.)

"No seas bobo, compadre y otras advertencias," May 1, 1960.

"Los dos grandes peligros, los aviones piratas y otras violaciones," May 22, 1960.

"El salto de rana, los organismos internacionales y otras genuflexiones," May 29, 1960.

"Para muestra basta un botón y otras historias breves," August 7, 1960.

"Había una vez un central azucarero y otras leyendas populares," August 14, 1960.

"La democracia reprentativa sudcoreana y otras mentiras," October 29, 1967. (Reprint of an article published earlier.)

Other articles by Guevara ranged over a wide spectrum of interests. His topics included such varied matters as the Cuban economy, Communist theory, international affairs, and guerrilla warfare. Although he was best noted as a guerrilla warrior, planner, and theoretician, only a few of his works dealt with this subject in a theoretical way. The first work was his aforementioned book, *Guerra de guerrillas*. Then followed his article, "Guerra de guerrillas: un método," considered by some experts to be the single most important work by Guevara. First published in the doctrinal magazine *Cuba Socialista* in September, 1962, the article was reprinted in the September 20, 1963, issue of *Bohemia* and the September 22, 1963, issue of *Verde Olivo*, as well as in the

October, 1967, issue of *Pensamiento Crítico*.

Two other theoretical works on guerrilla warfare were the following:

"Guerra de guerrillas—expresión de la lucha de masas" (prologue to a book by North Vietnamese General Vo Nguyen Giap), *Verde Olivo*, December 27, 1964.

"Crear dos, tres . . . muchos Vietnam, es la consigna" (Guevara's message to *Tricontinental* Magazine), *Bohemia*, April 21, 1967, and *Verde Olivo*, April 23, 1967. (Reprinted in *Pensamiento Crítico*, October, 1967.)

On economic and related subjects Guevara wrote the following articles:

"Tareas industriales de la revolución en los años venideros," *Cuba Socialista*, March, 1962. (Reprinted in *Bohemia*, March 9, 1962.)

"Mínimo técnico" (portion of a directive), *Bohemia*, May 4, 1962.

"Contra el burocratismo," *Cuba Socialista*, February, 1963. (Reprinted in *Verde Olivo*, February 17, 1963, and in *Bohemia*, February 15, 1963.)

"Sobre el sistema presupuestario de financiamiento" (a reprint from *Nuestra Industria Económica*, probably *Nuestra Industria—Revista Económica*), *Trimestre*, July-September, 1963.

On doctrinal and international matters Guevara wrote the following:

"Moral y disciplina de los combatientes revolucionarios," *Verde Olivo*, March 17, 1960.

"Cuba ¿excepción histórica o vanguardia en la lucha anticolonialista?" *Verde Olivo*, April 9, 1960. (Reprinted in *Pensamiento Crítico*, October, 1967.)

"Notas para el estudio de la ideología de la revolución cubana," *Verde Olivo*, October 8, 1960. (Reprinted in *Pensamiento Crítico*, October, 1967.)

"Un pecado de la revolución," *Verde Olivo*, February 12, 1961.

"Discusión colectiva; decisión y responsabilidad únicas," *Trabajo*, second fortnight, July, 1961. (Reprinted in *Verde Olivo*, July 30, 1961.)

"El cuadro, columna vertebral de la revolución," *Cuba Socialista*, September, 1962. (Reprinted in *Bohemia*, September 14, 1962, and in *Pensamiento Crítico*, October, 1967.)

"El partido marxista leninista" (excerpt from prologue to a book of the same name), *Verde Olivo*, January 26, 1964.

"El socialismo y el hombre en Cuba" (originally published in the Montevideo weekly *Marcha* in the form of a "letter"), *Verde Olivo*, December 31, 1967. (Reprinted in *Pensamiento Crítico*, October, 1967.)

The following interviews with Guevara were published:

"No guarda el gobierno para sí el derecho absoluto y exclusivo de la industrialización," *Bohemia*, January 31, 1960.

"El trabajo voluntario en la zafra del '62," *Verde Olivo*, February 4, 1962.

"A cortar la caña de este año" (portion of an interview on television), *Bohemia*, February 4, 1962.

"El Che con las delegaciones fraternales extranjeras," *Bohemia*, May 11, 1962.

Like his writings, Guevara's speeches reflected his thinking. One of his earliest ideological speeches, "Proyecciones sociales del Ejército Rebelde," was included in the documentary *Fidel Castro—La Revolución Cubana*, published in Argentina in 1960. Other speeches by Guevara (those with asterisks were published in excerpt form or do not appear to be complete) include:

"En defensa de la soberanía y la economía nacional," *Verde Olivo*, April 3, 1960.

"Adoctrinamiento,"* *Bohemia*, August 28, 1960.

"Todos los pueblos del mundo deben unirse para conseguir lo más sagrado, que es la libertad," *Verde Olivo*, October 8, 1960.

"La victoria de Cuba está en la unión, en el trabajo y en el espíritu de sacrificio de su pueblo," *Bohemia*, April 9, 1961.

"Listos para la gran batalla,"* *Bohemia*, April 23, 1961.

"Informe del Comandante Guevara sobre la conferencia del CIES" (Punta del Este conference), *Verde Olivo*, September 3, 1961.

"La idea de la defensa de la revolución no puede desligarse de la idea del trabajo,"* *Bohemia*, October 1, 1961.

"En la Universidad Central de Las Villas,"* *Bohemia*, February 11, 1962.

"Premio a los héroes del trabajo,"* *Bohemia*, May 4, 1962.

"Producir, producir, producir cada día más," *Verde Olivo*, May 13, 1962.

"Mientras no sea necesario tomar el fusil el trabajo es el lugar cotidiano de lucha," *Bohemia*, August 31, 1962.

"Dos lecciones para la historia," *Bohemia*, December 14, 1962.

"Hay que crear la leyenda del combatiente del trabajo," *Bohemia*, February 1, 1963.

"Las características de nuestra revolución también son propias,"* *Bohemia*, March 29, 1963.

"Los compañeros del partido tienen la obligación de ser la vanguardia,"* *Verde Olivo*, April 7, 1963.

"Capacitación, normas y salarios,"* *Trabajo*, second fortnight, May, 1963.

"Los pueblos de América ven en nosotros una esperanza nueva de redimirse de sus cadenas," *Bohemia*, May 10, 1963.

"Los ideales del verdadero comunista,"* *Bohemia*, January 17, 1964.

"La producción industrial de Cuba: ascenso sin tregua,"* *Bohemia*, March 6, 1964.

"La única solución correcta a los problemas de la humanidad en el momento actual es la supresión absoluta de la explotación de los países capitalistas desarrollados" (speech in Geneva), *Bohemia*, April 3, 1964.

"¡Cuba no fallará! es la voz que se ha hecho oir en América y en todo el mundo," *Bohemia*, May 8, 1964.

"3 fábricas en 15 días"* (excerpts from three speeches), *Trabajo*, first fortnight, June, 1964.

"Camilo sería una columna firme en la organización del ejército," *Verde Olivo*, October 8, 1964.

"Ya ha sonado la hora postrera del colonialismo en América Latina, Asia y Africa" (speech at United Nations), *Bohemia*, December 18, 1964; *Cuba Socialista*, January, 1965. (Reprinted in *Pensamiento Crítico*, October, 1967.)

"Todo el pueblo de Cuba luchará con su gobierno hasta la muerte si es agredido" (speech at United Nations), *Bohemia*, December 18, 1964; also in *Cuba Socialista*, January, 1965. (Reprinted in *Pensamiento Crítico*, October, 1967.)

"En nuestra marcha hacia el futuro nos une una aspiración común: la derrota del imperialismo" (speech in Algiers), March 5, 1965. (Reprinted in *Pensamiento Crítico*, October, 1967.)

Two smaller items by Guevara are the following:

An eight-stanza poem, "Canto a Fidel," written in Mexico in 1956 and published in a Havana newspaper in 1959, was reprinted in *Unión*, issue of April-June, 1967. Guevara's farewell letter to Castro, first read in a speech delivered by Castro, was printed in various magazines, including:

Bohemia, October 8, 1965.

Nuestra Industria, November, 1965.

Casa de Las Américas, November-December, 1965.

Following Guevara's death in Bolivia in October, 1967, Cuban magazines honored him by extensively reprinting a number of his articles and speeches, as well as publishing reminiscences by persons who had known him. In addition to those already listed in the preceding categories, the following were among the reprints:

"Cuba: la voz de los pueblos de América" (1965 Algiers speech), *Verde Olivo*, November 19, 1967.

"Palabras a los jóvenes" (1961 speech), *Verde Olivo*, November 26, 1967.

"Homenaje a Maceo" (1962 speech), *Verde Olivo*, December 10, 1967.

"Palabras sobre el partido" (excerpts), *Verde Olivo*, January 7, 1968.

Letters and speeches, and portions of speeches, *Pensamiento Crítico*, October, 1967.

INDEX